SO-AAE-924

WYNDHAM LEWIS
AND MODERNISM

PERCY WYNDHAM LEWIS

A self-portrait (1932) by Wyndham Lewis, 1882-1957

WYNDHAM LEWIS
AND MODERNISM

Andrzej Gąsiorek

Northcote House
in association with the
British Council

First published in 2004 by Northcote House Publishers Ltd, Horndon, Tavistock, Devon, PL19 9NQ, United Kingdom.
Tel: +44 (01822) 810066. Fax: +44 (01822) 810034.

British Library Cataloguing-in-Publication Data
A catalogue record for this book is available from the British Library

ISBN 0-7463-1126-5 hb
ISBN 0-7463-0952-X pb

Typeset by TW Typesetting, Plymouth, Devon
Printed and bound in the United Kingdom by Athenaeum Press Ltd., Gateshead

Contents

Acknowledgements

Various friends and colleagues have helped during the writing of this book. I would like to thank Isobel Armstrong for offering me the opportunity to write on Lewis. Thanks are also owed to colleagues and students at the University of Birmingham, especially those involved in the *European Modernisms* postgraduate programme, which has allowed me to develop some of my ideas about Lewis. In this and in other respects, Tony Davies, Deborah Parsons, and Mark Storey have been particularly supportive. I am grateful to David Aers and Sarah Beckwith for inviting me to talk about Lewis at Duke University in April and October 2000; both occasions were extremely helpful in forcing me to clarify my thinking. More recently, dialogue with Alan Munton about Lewis and related topics has been a source of immense pleasure. I owe an enormous debt of thanks to Nick Dent and Paul Edwards for reading the manuscript through in its entirety and for making a number of invaluable suggestions. Conversations with Nick over the years have given me more than I can say here, and Paul has been extremely generous with his knowledge of Lewis.

Biographical Outline

1882 Born Percy Wyndham Lewis on 18 November to Charles Edward Lewis and Anne Lewis. His parents separate in 1893.

1897 Lewis enters Rugby School. Educated at Rugby, without distinction, until December 1898.

1898 Enrols in the Slade, where he stays until expelled in 1901.

1902 Beginning of friendship with Augustus John.

1903 Lewis begins a five-year period in which he travels a good deal in Europe, staying for varying periods of time in Spain, Holland, Paris, and Germany, spending most of his time on studying art, painting, attending lectures, and reading widely.

1904 Beginning of affair with Ida Vendel.

1907 Visits Brittany for the first time.

1908 Brittany and England. His experiences there result in his first published stories (later heavily revised for *The Wild Body*), which appear in the *English Review*, *The New Age*, and *The Tramp* between 1909 and 1911. Lewis writes *Mrs Dukes' Million* (published in 1977).

1911 Beginning of affair with Olive Johnson. Exhibits in the first Camden Town Group exhibition at the Carfax Gallery. Birth of son, Hoel Lewis, to Olive Johnson.

1912 Exhibition of Italian Futurist paintings at the Sackville Gallery. 5th Allied Artists Salon in which Lewis's painting *Kermesse* is exhibited. Lewis contributes decorations to the Cave of the Golden Calf nightclub. Meets Richard Aldington.

1913   *Timon of Athens* portfolio. Joins the Omega Workshops. Row with Roger Fry over the commission for the decoration of a Post-Impressionist Room at the Ideal Home Exhibition. Lewis leaves the Omega Workshops and directs the rival Rebel Arts Centre. Birth of daughter, Betty, to Olive Johnson. Dinner in honour of F. T. Marinetti.

1914   Creation of Vorticism. Publication of the first issue of *Blast*. First exhibition of works by the London Group at the Goupil Gallery. Publication of 'Vital English Art, Futurist Manifesto', signed by F. T. Marinetti and C. R. W. Nevinson. Meets T. E. Hulme.

1915   Second issue of *Blast* – 'The War Number'. Vorticist Exhibition. Meets T. S. Eliot.

1916   Lewis enlists but does not go to France until 1917, as a 2nd Lieutenant. Beginning of serialization of *Tarr* in *The Egoist*.

1917   Lewis sees action at the 3rd Battle of Ypres. *The Ideal Giant*. Lewis commissioned to paint for the Canadian War Memorials Fund, eventually producing several paintings, most notably *A Canadian Gun Pit* and, for the Ministry of Information, *A Battery Shelled*.

1918   Book publication of *Tarr*. Death of Charles Lewis. Meets Gladys Anne Hoskins ('Froanna').

1919   Lewis's one-man show *Guns* held at the Goupil Gallery. *The Caliph's Design: Architects! Where is your Vortex?* Birth of son, Robin, to Iris Barry.

1920   Membership of *Group X*. Visit with Eliot to Paris. Meeting with Joyce. Birth of daughter, Maisie, to Iris Barry. Lewis's mother dies.

1921   Launches *The Tyro*, a journal. Exhibition, *Tyros and Portraits*, at Leicester Galleries. Meets in these years various figures such as the Sitwells, the Schiffs, and Richard Wyndham, all of whom he will later satirize in *The Apes of God*.

1922   Second and last issue of *The Tyro*.

1924   Publication of 'Mr Zagreus and the Split-Man' and 'The Apes of God' in Eliot's *Criterion*.

1925   Delivery of *The Man of the World* manuscript to Chapman & Hall. This huge work eventually divided up, rewritten, and added to when it is turned into the books Lewis publishes over the next five years. 'The Dithyrambic Spectator: An Essay on the Origins and Survivals of Art' published in *The Calendar of Modern Letters*.

1926   *The Art of Being Ruled*. The General Strike.

1927   Launches another journal, *The Enemy*. *The Lion and the Fox*, *Time and Western Man*, and *The Wild Body*.

1928   Part 1 of *The Childermass*, which Lewis renames *The Human Age* when he takes it up again in the 1950s. A rewritten version of *Tarr*.

1929   *Paleface: The Philosophy of the 'Melting Pot'*.

1930   Visits Berlin. *The Apes of God*. Marriage to Gladys Hoskins. Publication of pamphlet on *The Apes of God* furore, *Satire and Fiction*.

1931   Articles on Hitler published in *Time and Tide*. Later published in book form as *Hitler*. *The Diabolical Principle and the Dithyrambic Spectator* published in book form. Travels in Morocco. *The Roaring Queen* written (unpublished until 1973).

1932   Publication of a revised version of *Enemy of the Stars*; *The Doom of Youth*; and *Filibusters in Barbary*. Alec Waugh threatens a libel action over his depiction in *Doom*. Chatto & Windus eventually withdraw the book. *Snooty Baronet*. *Snooty* hit by an embargo from the circulating libraries. Lewis visits Berlin again. *Thirty Personalities* portfolio.

1933   *The Old Gang and the New Gang*. *One-Way Song*. T. C. MacFie charges libel over *Filibusters in Barbary*.

1934   *Men Without Art*. Rupert Grayson accuses Lewis of libel in *Snooty Baronet*.

1936   *Left Wings over Europe: Or, How to Make a War about Nothing*.

1937   *Count your Dead: They Are Alive! Or, A New War in the Making; The Revenge for Love, Blasting and Bombardiering*. Visits to Berlin and Warsaw. Exhibition at the Leicester Galleries: *Paintings and Drawings by Wyndham Lewis*.

1938   *The Mysterious Mr Bull*. Exhibition at the Beaux Arts Gallery. Lewis's portrait of T. S. Eliot rejected by the Royal Academy.

1939   *The Jews: Are they Human?*; *Wyndham Lewis the Artist: From 'Blast' to Burlington House.* Lewis and Froanna sail for Canada. Toronto, Buffalo, and New York. *The Hitler Cult.*

1940   *America, I Presume.*

1941   *Anglosaxony: A League that Works*; *The Vulgar Streak.* Montreal. Lewis visits Halifax, Nova Scotia. Starts to experience problems with his eyes.

1943   Lewis teaches in the United States, principally at Assumption College. The Tudor Hotel, where the Lewises lived, burns down. Lewis meets Marshall McLuhan.

1945   The Lewises return to England. Death of Hoel Lewis.

1946   Lewis made art critic for the *Listener.* He holds this post until 1951, when he is forced to give it up because of his failing eyesight.

1948   *America and Cosmic Man.*

1949   Exhibition at the Redfern Gallery. Paints second portrait of Eliot. Visits Paris.

1950   *Rude Assignment: An Intellectual Autobiography.* Various visits to hospitals and specialists to find out what is wrong with his eyes.

1951   Lewis virtually blind. Writes a farewell piece for the *Listener*, 'Sea Mists of the Winter'. *Rotting Hill*, a collection of short stories.

1952   Lewis awarded a Civil List Pension. *The Writer and the Absolute.* Awarded an honorary doctorate by Leeds University.

1954   *Self Condemned*; *The Demon of Progress in the Arts.*

1955   *Monstre Gai* and *Malign Fiesta*, the second and third volumes of *The Human Age. The Human Age* broadcast on BBC radio.

1956   Tate exhibition: 'Wyndham Lewis and Vorticism'. Publication of *The Red Priest.* BBC broadcast of *Tarr.* A slightly revised *Childermass* reprinted as the first volume of *The Human Age.* Controversy with William Roberts over Vorticism.

1957   Lewis dies in Westminster Hospital.

Abbreviations

ABR   *The Art of Being Ruled*, ed. Reed Way Dasenbrock (Santa Rosa, Calif.: Black Sparrow Press, 1989)

AG   *The Apes of God* (Harmondsworth: Penguin, 1965)

B1   *Blast 1*, ed. Wyndham Lewis (Santa Barbara, Calif.: Black Sparrow Press, 1981)

B2   *Blast 2*, ed. Wyndham Lewis (Santa Barbara, Calif.: Black Sparrow Press, 1981)

BB   *Blasting and Bombardiering: An Autobiography (1914–1926)* (London: John Calder, 1982)

CD   *Count your Dead: They Are Alive! Or, A New War in the Making* (London: Lovat Dickson, 1937)

CHC   *Creatures of Habit and Creatures of Change: Essays on Art, Literature and Society, 1914–1956*, ed. Paul Edwards (Santa Barbara, Calif.: Black Sparrow Press, 1989)

CPP   *Collected Poems and Plays*, ed. Alan Munton (Manchester: Carcanet, 1979)

DPA   *The Demon of Progress in the Arts* (London: Methuen, 1954)

E1   *The Enemy 1* (1927), ed. Wyndham Lewis (Santa Rosa, Calif.: Black Sparrow Press, 1994)

E2   *The Enemy 2* (1927), ed. Wyndham Lewis (Santa Rosa, Calif.: Black Sparrow Press, 1994)

E3   *The Enemy 3* (1929), ed. Wyndham Lewis (Santa Rosa, Calif.: Black Sparrow Press, 1994)

H.   *Hitler* (London: Chatto & Windus, 1931)

HC   *The Hitler Cult* (London: Dent, 1939)

L.   *The Letters of Wyndham Lewis*, ed. W. K. Rose (London: Methuen, 1963)

LF   *The Lion and the Fox: The Role of the Hero in the Plays of Shakespeare* (London: Grant Richards, 1927)

LWE   *Left Wings over Europe: Or, How to Make a War About Nothing* (London: Jonathan Cape, 1936)

MMB   *The Mysterious Mr Bull* (London: Robert Hale, 1938)

MWA   *Men Without Art*, ed. Seamus Cooney (Santa Rosa, Calif.: Black Sparrow Press, 1987)

OG   *The Old Gang and the New Gang* (London: Desmond Harmsworth, 1933)

P.   *Paleface: The Philosophy of the 'Melting-Pot'* (London: Chatto & Windus, 1929)

RA   *Rude Assignment: An Intellectual Autobiography*, ed. Toby Foshay (Santa Barbara, Calif.: Black Sparrow Press, 1984)

RL   *The Revenge For Love*, ed. Reed Way Dasenbrock (Santa Rosa, Calif.: Black Sparrow Press, 1991)

SB   *Snooty Baronet*, ed. Bernard Lafourcade (Santa Barbara, Calif.: Black Sparrow Press, 1984)

SC   *Self Condemned* (Santa Barbara, Calif.: Black Sparrow Press, 1983)

T.   *Tarr*, rev. edn, 1928 (Harmondsworth: Penguin, 1982)

TWM   *Time and Western Man*, ed. Paul Edwards (Santa Rosa, Calif.: Black Sparrow Press, 1993)

VS   *The Vulgar Streak*, ed. Paul Edwards (Santa Barbara, Calif.: Black Sparrow Press, 1985)

WA   *The Writer and the Absolute* (London: Methuen, 1952)

WB   *The Wild Body* (London: Chatto & Windus, 1927)

WLA   *Wyndham Lewis on Art: Collected Writings, 1913–1956*, ed., Walter Michel and C. J. Fox (London: Thames & Hudson, 1969)

I will war, at least in words (and – should
My chance so happen – deeds), with all who war
With Thought . . .

(Byron, *Don Juan*, IX. 24, 1823)

1

Introduction: 'The Politics of Style'

Wyndham Lewis's reputation has until recently been uncertain. It may long have been recognized that he was an original writer and a major literary presence, but the image of him as a maverick, misanthrope, and outsider dies hard. Lewis's tendency to play up to this image, though usually with an irony lost on his detractors, meant that he was subjected to *ad hominem* attacks during his life and after it. Add to this his political convictions of the early 1930s, his apparent misogyny and homophobia, and his anti-empathic style of writing, and it is easy to see why his work might have fallen into neglect. The writer seen as 'a more scandalous and explosive Waugh' appalled many who read him on account of the content of his texts and the nature of his aesthetic.[1] His preference for an external aesthetic that favoured 'the shield of the tortoise, or the rigid stylistic articulations of the grasshopper' (*MWA* 99) over inward-looking depictions of the 'stream of consciousness', and his willingness to lambaste his contemporaries for what he saw as their capitulation to a destructive *Zeitgeist*, won Lewis little support. He became the forgotten figure of 'the men of 1914' (Eliot, Joyce, Lewis, and Pound) and his contribution to English modernism slid from view.

Serious scholarship on Lewis has rectified this situation. He is now rightly seen as both a key player in the formation of English modernism and its major internal critic. Yet it is still important that we do not reduce Lewis's multifaceted work either to his 'difficult' personality or to his image of outsider. Such accounts obscure the nature of his *œuvre*, because they

1

position him as an aberrant figure, thereby simplifying our understanding of the complex, interleaved trajectories within modernism. They also occlude the nature of his involvement with other groups and individuals, the significance of the alliances he struck up, and the reasons for the polemics in which he engaged. Lewis certainly refused to compromise his views, and it is arguable that he paid a heavy price for this, but he made the refusal because there were real intellectual issues at stake, and there is evidence to suggest he did not relish his isolation, grasping that it diminished the seriousness with which his views were taken.[2]

What kind of modernism was Lewis's? What was the nature of his contribution to the wider movement in relation to which his modernism emerged? How did it differ from the work of his contemporaries? Why did he embark in the 1920s and 1930s on a critique of avant-gardism? What was the relationship between this critique, his politics, and his writing? Such questions lie at the heart of this book, which aims to introduce Lewis's work to readers who may be unfamiliar with it and to clarify the nature of his participation in the period's cultural and aesthetic upheavals. Lewis's importance in this respect cannot be denied. He was the driving force behind the Vorticist movement prior to the First World War; he edited and wrote many of the contributions for the journal *Blast*, the vehicle for the avant-gardism he promoted in opposition to competitor movements; he organized various groups of painters before and after the war; he wrote key critical works that explored the presuppositions and ramifications of influential intellectual and artistic currents; and he produced a corpus of powerfully imagined paintings and novels that stand alongside the best work of his contemporaries. Even if his hubristic claim that 'Vorticism, in fact, was what I, personally, did and said, at a certain period' (*WLA* 451) is on a par with some of Ford Madox Ford's more exaggerated pronouncements, Lewis was of decisive importance to the emergence and development of modernism and it is in this context that his work is most profitably seen.[3]

Lewis is important to us today for several reasons, and it is hoped that a book such as this will encourage readers either to turn to him for the first time or to return to him with renewed

interest. As I have suggested, his cultural and literary significance cannot be questioned. Critics may disagree with the
illiberal social and political views he advocated (though these
have in the past all too often been simplified so that Lewis can
be treated as a convenient whipping boy) or may deplore his
seemingly inhuman aesthetic, but if we seek to practise
responsible literary history then we cannot ignore his contribution to the debates of the day or his major works of fiction and
criticism. I would suggest that Lewis remains important for
three key reasons. First, because his work helps us better to
understand the whole phenomenon of modernism, since he
was not only involved in it from the outset but also became one
of its severest internal critics, so that to read Lewis is to see
how certain modernist trajectories developed and to grasp how
and why other possible paths were deemed problematic or
unviable by one of modernism's key protagonists. Second,
because Lewis practises a powerful and extremely wide-
ranging brand of cultural criticism, a way of thinking that has
been developed in a number of directions since the 1960s but
that in Lewis's hands dismantled the very terms in which
existing political positions were articulated in order to try to
break out of the realm of ideology altogether; a dialogical
thinker and writer, he becomes a symbol of the Vortex, a
(critical) nodal point for the cultural practices of his day, a
figure through whom ideas (his own and those of his contemporaries) are constantly rushing, ideas that he tries to sift for
what is of value and what is to be discarded.[4] Third, there is
the *œuvre* itself. Lewis produced a good deal of occasional
writing that is of mixed quality, but his most innovative, most
considered works are extraordinary prose artefacts that continue to dazzle, entice, bewilder, and infuriate his readers.
Ultimately, we read Lewis in order to try to get to grips with
these carefully honed works, which are so rich and strange,
and which can still give the engaged critical reader much
pleasure of the text.

Born in 1882, Lewis was educated at Rugby and the Slade.
He travelled and lived in Europe for several years after leaving
the Slade in 1901, returning to England in 1908 and gradually
establishing himself as a painter and a writer. He exhibited in
the first Camden Town Group exhibition in 1911 and was

3

involved in other artistic initiatives such as the London Group, the Omega Workshops, and the Rebel Art Centre, before going on to launch Vorticism, the movement that urged 'the creation of a language absolutely distinct from what was handed us by nature' (*WLA* 455).[5] Lewis edited two issues of *Blast* before enlisting in 1916, seeing action in 1917, and then gaining a commission as a war artist. His novel *Tarr*, which he was desperate to complete in case he was killed at the front, was published in 1918. After the war, Lewis concentrated on the critical works, novels, and satires that he published at a tremendous rate from the mid-1920s to the end of the 1930s, although he continued to paint throughout the period. In these books he gradually distanced himself from his pre-war avant-garde positions, offered sharp criticisms of most of the major modernists of his time, and turned increasingly to satire. He also devoted a great deal of attention to political issues, concerning himself with the conflicts brewing in Europe and with the effects on the arts of ideological pressures. During this period he argued in favour of some form of intellectual autocracy and produced his disastrous book on Hitler, which read in places like a defence of German fascism. Lewis spent the years of the Second World War in Canada, returning to London in 1945, working as art critic for the *Listener* between 1946 and 1951 while continuing to write and paint, and in this last burst of creativity he produced some of his finest work. He gradually lost his sight in the early 1950s, and he died in 1957.

Lewis returned throughout his writing career to a number of related preoccupations. He was primarily interested in articulating a new vision for the arts and in working out what forms they could take in an age dominated by industry, science, and technology. For Lewis, art was indispensable to civilization – arguing that it must in key respects be organic with its epoch, he saw it as a valuation that interpreted, criticized, renewed, and transformed. How it was to survive, and how make the kinds of intervention through which it asserted its creative power, were crucial concerns, as was the further problem (which the avant-gardes put into such sharp focus) of identifying the limits it should not try to exceed. The question of human identity, a prevalent modernist concern, was linked to these issues, since any account of art is inseparable from a view of the self and its needs. Lewis's view of this question differed from that of most modernists, leading him to defend an aesthetic focused on the externals of life, 'the *shell*, the *pelt*, the physical behaviour of people', and to denigrate other writers' concern to display the often haphazard workings of the mind as 'only appropriate to the depiction of children, morons, and the extremely infirm' (L. 191). He conceived the subject in structural terms, arguing that purposive agency depended on a view of the self that could at once acknowledge its multiple facets and assert the necessity of at least a measure of cohesiveness, integrity, and stability. The individual self was the *fons et origo* of the autonomous creative art and the independent critical thought needed by a modernity seemingly hell-bent on crushing it out. So Lewis attempted not just to defend a version of the subject in which the role of reason played a decisive role but to analyse the threats posed to it by social and economic change, which, he argued, was disintegrating shared cultural norms, eroding the public sphere, and undermining individual freedom. Always susceptible to dualistic ways of thinking, he saw the individual's inner conflicts in terms of a struggle between reason and desire, and its outer conflicts in terms of a dialectic between self and other.

Lewis explored these issues across a wide range of works, critical and fictional. It is an irony that a writer so committed to a purist view of the arts devoted so much time to writing about these external pressures rather than getting on with the creative work he valued.[6] Yet there is an element of self-deception in Lewis's repeated claims that he was 'not interested in politics' (L. 483) and that he was forced into the political arena by the circumstances of the time. He was passionately interested in political thought and deeply knowledgeable about it. The division he sought to establish between politics and art, on the grounds that the *'politicisation* of art is a human catastrophe' (E3 68), led him to urge the writer to 'take no notice at all of politics, since you cannot be a politician and an artist too' (E3 76), but he himself took no notice at all of this advice. Lewis believed in the freedom of art from political interference as strongly as he believed in anything, but his inability simply to state this conviction and then move on tells us a great deal about the period in which he was living and

5

working, for 'art' and 'politics' proved to be as closely connected in it as two sides of a sheet of paper. The significance of his brand of modernism lies in the interplay in his work between art and philosophy, literature and politics, the 'creative' and the 'critical'.

Lewis was a dialogical writer: he engages in a systematic assessment and critique of his contemporaries, defining his own positions in relation to those adopted by them; his critical texts always have an 'implied reader' in mind, often interpellating such readers by entering into imaginary debate with them; he stages parodic dialogues with his opponents in the course of his polemics against them; he refers to his own work, frequently quoting from or alluding to it; and he is an inveterate reviser who rethinks and rewrites his earlier texts. His writing orientates itself to the present 'moment', and he addresses his time through his works of cultural critique and through his fiction. In this book I deal in detail with Lewis's critical writing, treating it not as background 'context' to the novels but as an integral part of his creative achievement.[7]

The book is divided into seven chapters. Necessarily selective, it does not attempt to provide an overview of Lewis's entire career, nor does it have the space to discuss his paintings, but it tries to come to terms with the issues I have suggested should be seen as central to his work. Chapter 1 focuses on the 'moment' of *Blast* and Vorticism, paying especial attention to this avant-garde's attempts to define itself against other avant-gardes, principally Italian Futurism, before going on to consider *Tarr*, which I read as an aporetic auto-critique of Lewis's own aesthetic convictions. Chapter 2 concentrates on Lewis's critique of the post-war avant-gardes (especially his polemic with *transition*) and other modernists (principally Eliot, Joyce, and Pound), concluding with an analysis of his account of behaviourism and his satiric novel *Snooty Baronet*. The third chapter explores the attractions of the return to a so-called classicism; suggests that, despite his sympathy for it, Lewis cannot be aligned with any classical revival; situates his theory of satire in relation to the impossibility of classicism; and reads *The Apes of God* in terms of his metaphysical concern with the nature of human identity in an absurdist world. My greatest regret here is that I have not had the space to consider *The Childermass*, a key Lewisian text of the 1920s, an omission I hope to remedy elsewhere.[8] Chapter 4 analyses Lewis's political views, considers the changes in these views from the time of the First World War to the 1950s, and assesses the novel most obviously relevant to these concerns – *The Revenge for Love*. Chapter 5 returns to Lewis's artistic convictions, asking how far his views had changed during the course of his life, and looking at his novel *Self Condemned*, arguing that it is in dialogue with *Tarr*. In my concluding chapter I reconsider Lewis's highly original contribution to modernism, suggesting that it invites us to rethink the ways in which we construe modernism.

Before turning to these issues, I want to consider the question of Lewis's style, for no account of his modernism can succeed if it does not confront the strange power of his highly charged prose. Lewis was obsessed with finding ways to articulate a view of how the arts could transfigure the present. In the first period of his activity as a writer and painter he focused his attention on the stultified nature of salon art, seeking to overthrow academicism and replace it with a new Vorticist vision of the world. But, in the second phase, which may be said to have begun in the mid-1920s, he embarked on a broader sociocultural analysis, and this led him to a version of what we now think of as ideology critique. According to his diagnosis, the revolution within the field of art had by and large been successful, but society, in the wake of the war and far-reaching economic and technological change, was disintegrating. The task in this situation was to link any vision of the form the arts could take with a wider social critique.

It is in *this* context that Lewis's self-descriptions as 'outlaw' and 'enemy' should be seen. For Lewis, there was no longer any overarching tradition or recognizable *milieu* within which to work; he saw himself, not as an exotic descendent of a *poète maudit* like Rimbaud, but as part of an elite who were disenfranchised because 'there is no law to which we can appeal, upon which we can rely, or that it is worth our while any longer to interpret, even if we could' (*P.* 81–2). Worse still, he argued that very few people had even a rudimentary understanding of the extent to which social change was taking place. The combined impact of economic globalization and the proliferation of new media meant that a new era had begun, since designated as the postmodern society of spectacle (Debord) or simulacrum (Baudrillard).[9] Hence Lewis's claim that accepted ways of thinking and writing were artificial, since 'it is the end of history, and the beginning of historical pageant and play' (*MWA* 165). Language was at the heart of the problem, for it was failing to keep pace with the radical alteration to twentieth-century life. Outworn, belated, and reified, language itself was in need of renewal.

This demand is, of course, a key aspect of all modernisms. But it was Lewis, above all other modernists, who mounted a full-scale assault on the reification of language, which, he argued, embalmed the dead husks of obsolete norms and thus blocked the emergence of new valuations. Referring to the 'conservatism peculiar to language', he noted that language 'has to be destroyed before you transform ideas at all radically' (*TWM* 4–5). His own style embodies this twin goal of destruction and transformation. Certainly, it varies in important respects from text to text, so strictly speaking it is more accurate to talk of styles in the plural. But, at its most distinctive, Lewis's surcharged, disjointed prose defamiliarizes the discourses by which reality is habitually 'known' in an attempt to break up and reconstitute language so that writer and reader can go beyond ossified categories of thought.

In order to illustrate this point, a couple of examples are in order. Consider the following speech from *Tarr*:

> 'Fiancée! – observe how we ape the forms of conventional life in our emancipated Bohemia: it does not mean anything so one lets it stop. It's the same with the Café fools I have for friends – there's a greek fool, a german fool, a russian fool – an english fool! There are no "friends" in this life any more than there are authentic "fiancees": so it's of no importance what we choose to call each other: one drifts along side by side with this live stock – friends, fiancees, "colleagues" and what not in our unreal gimcrack artist-society.' (*T*. 23)

Conventional language and reality have cracked apart here; words are ridiculed as second-hand counters that bear no relation to the world they claim to describe. Yet there is no attempt to bridge the gap; instead, the writer locates it as the

8

source of his pungent satire. It is in the ambiguous space that opens up when the stale language of cliché and stereotype is seen through but is still in force that Lewis finds his material.

Consider next a longer scene from *Snooty Baronet*, the prelude to an amorous encounter:

> 'Happy days' I said and carried the glass to my lips.
>
> Old Val stood a pace or two off from where I was. She drank a little Three Star. Then she put down the glass, pushing it on to the table, and stood with downcast eyes – she was white-collared, stiff, shut up in a 'mutinous silence,' parading the archaic reserve of the Children's Nursery. My old imitation-Society-'piece' – modelled on the best Late Mayfair (Peter Pan Model) was out to perform before me (a Command Performance, I don't think!) the chidden aproned Miss. She was a damask-cheeked Miss of fourteen or fifteen Springs (say in a mid-victorian Boarding Establishment). Sullenly she awaited the executioner's pleasure, with neck-bent, and a well-whipped sanctimonious 'poke' thrust of the pentathletic head. She was in the presence of *The Principal*: he (with all his rods in pickle) was about – so old Val would interpret it – to up with her dimity frock and administer a well-deserved *fessée*. But (overcome by the luscious contacts) destined to follow this up with extremely improper advances.
>
> 'Lonely nights!' she gave the correct Music hall response, piling on the demureness in chrismatic clots, outcloying Devon (her lips succeeding in becoming the ripest of prime hothouse strawberries) but with as much of the sly as became a wronged woman – or a victorian flapper-minx-in-the-wrong, her B.T.M already smarting in anticipation. So we stood, face to face.   (*SB* 47–8)

Filtered through the impoverished imagination of an obtuse first-person narrator, this scene teems with images taken from popular culture, specifically that of the music hall. The point here is not to denigrate music halls but to suggest the farcical nature of the imminent sexual union by showing that behaviour is modelled on a self-mocking comedy routine. Alienation lies just beneath the surface here, discernible in the narrator's covert derision at Val's 'performance', the concealment engaged in by both characters, and the conflict between them suggested by the violent imagery.[10] Yet if Val can only mimic roles that are themselves already parodies, then the narrator can only interpret this masquerade in terms of a music hall fantasy that stirs his own lubricity. They play out a scripted scene that makes puppets of them both. It is *Lewis* who transforms their derivativeness into comedy through his iterative style, his use of comic inversion, and his grotesque elaboration of the initial music hall conceit.[11]

The style of this passage verges on the excess so often found in Lewis's prose and which he knew sometimes threatened to distract readers from his seriousness of purpose.[12] One of his favourite satiric strategies was to ridicule his targets by reducing their behaviour to some senseless motive force and then grossly to exaggerate it, making them appear far more inane than they ever could be in reality. Heaping image upon image, insult upon insult, and clause upon clause, he overwhelmed his victims in a cascading prose that swept away everything in its path. When he unleashes himself on Hemingway, for example, his grotesque imagery proliferates with such energy that it gradually transfers itself from Hemingway's fictional characters to the author himself, before burying the whole lot of them in an avalanche of adjectives.[13] The hybrid entity generated by Lewis's wicked prose fuses Hemingway with his simple-minded protagonists, and in this way his literary 'ability' is placed on a par with their linguistic retardation.[14]

Lewis attacks Hemingway for his participation in the exaltation of a *naive* outlook, which was for him hostile to the values of 'the civilised intelligence' (*RA* 154). Lewis held that this outlook produced an impoverished prose and undermined the power of thought, disclosing a hatred of word and intellect. Modernism's inward turn, its desire to represent the actual working of the mind as a more or less inchoate 'flow', was a prime example of this tendency, since it vitiated artistic form and eschewed clarity of perspective. Lewis differentiated his own practice from that of competitor modernists by focusing on what he saw as their fundamentally different approaches to language and, by extension, artistic form. He saw his own language use as 'critical'; it was concerned to uncover the complex workings of ideology. Other modernists, he claimed, all too often fell victim to the blandishments of positions they scarcely understood.[15] The writer or painter had to be able to withdraw from life, observe from a distance and then isolate, objectify, and crystallize that which was selected for artistic treatment. Only thus could order be impressed onto the welter of inchoate experience. This view of art led Lewis to a spatializing aesthetic that sought to escape the temporal flux by breaking it up into concrete 'moments'.[16]

The one crucial thing I have not yet remarked upon is the self-reflexive performativity of Lewis's writing. This style is *productive*: it imposes form on the world, yes, but it also proclaims its own creation of meaning, figuring the writer as an Aristotelian maker engaged in transformative *poiesis*.[17] And this takes us to the heart of what Lewis called 'the *politics of style*', of which he wrote:

> In literature it should always be recalled that what we read is the speech of some person or other, explicit or otherwise. There is a *style* and *tone* in any statement, in any collection of sentences. We can formulate this in the following way: There *is an organic norm to which every form of speech is related. A human individual, living a certain kind of life, to whom the words and style would be appropriate, is implied in all utterance.* (*TWM* 113)

Animadverting against those styles that capitulate to the child-cult, Lewis held up lucidity as the most desirable alternative, for when 'the mind is most active it is least personal, least mannered' (*TWM* 114). Yet this hardly described his own writing, which is characterized by an extraordinary *will to style* that points to the tenuous hold language has over recalcitrant reality.[18] This tension between sign and referent marks Lewis's work, which persistently draws attention to the constructed nature of discourses and to the cultural meanings they uphold.[19] At the same time, this performativity protests against literary and cultural belatedness – a personal signature, it testifies to the writer's originality and warns of his inimitability, thus deflecting worries about the burden of the past and warding off the anxiety of influence. A darker reading might suggest that it provides the writer with a way of holding an absurd reality at bay through the sheer *force* of style even as it recognizes this for the voluntarist strategy it is. This suggests, in turn, that Lewis's rejection of other versions of modernism is linked to his refusal to identify with 'life' and to his conventionalism. If style supersedes reality, then it emerges in

11

Lewis's aesthetic as pure originary act: style overcomes the futility and anarchy of contemporary history.[20]

And yet. The flip side of this strategy is linguistic scepticism, and some of Lewis's texts seem to take us into a self-referential realm of signification in which language is all and the possibility of any kind of epistemological or metaphysical grounding in 'the real' disappears.[21] It might be said that Lewis's work continually reverts to this problematic and that his *œuvre* is built up out of his different responses to it. The inorganic external aesthetic represents an extreme attempt to control the arbitrariness and mutability of life through an art that risks being completely cut off from life, which it is nonetheless called upon to interpret. This dilemma is clearly expressed in relation to the problem of subjectivity, since the turn away from life may originate in a self-disgust that is simultaneously projected onto the other, as Arghol in *Enemy of the Stars* seems to suggest:

> Men have a loathsome deformity called Self; affliction got through indiscriminate rubbing against their fellows: Social excrescence.
>
> Their being is regulated by exigencies of this affliction. Only one operation can cure it: the suicide's knife.
>
> Or an immense snuffling or taciturn parasite, become necessary to victim, like abortive poodle, all nerves, vice and dissatisfaction.
>
> I have smashed it against me, but it still writhes, turbulent mess.
>
> I have shrunk it in frosty climates, but it has filtered filth inward through me, dispersed till my deepest solitude is impure.   (B1 71)

In Lewis's work, I would argue, the sliding apart of the symbolic from the material results in an existential dread and a sense of the absurd expressed through a self-deconstructing textuality. The question that haunts his writing and to which we will return more than once in this book is: what are the limits of an art that goes so fiercely *against* life?

2

Blast, Vorticism, and *Tarr*

Between 1910 and 1915 Lewis was involved in several artistic ventures, which ranged from the Camden Town Group, the London Group, the Omega Workshops, Italian Futurism, the Rebel Art Centre, and Vorticism, the movement christened by Pound but in which Lewis was the key figure. The break with Roger Fry's Omega has been discussed in detail elsewhere, and this ground does not need to be raked over again, but F. T. Marinetti's Italian Futurism was hugely important to the development of Vorticism and I shall discuss the relationship between the two movements in some detail.[1] Futurism was the first avant-garde to have a wide public impact in England, courtesy of several visits by Marinetti, whose spectacular public performances garnered much press coverage. Futurism attacked all previous artistic traditions, which it sought to destroy; saw art as an explosive cultural and political force; celebrated technological dynamism (especially the car and the aeroplane), a cult of youth, and militarism; promoted Italian nationalism; and exalted the present in all its kaleidoscopic chaos.[2] Vorticism was to draw on Futurism even as it distanced itself from many of that movement's principle tenets.

The painter C. R. W. Nevinson described Lewis as 'the most brilliant theorist [he] had ever met', and Lewis and Pound were a powerful combination.[3] When Nevinson and Marinetti published a Futurist manifesto in June 1914, writing on Rebel Art Centre paper, Lewis saw the opportunity to assert the independence and uniqueness of his own movement. A week later, a letter of protest from the Rebel Art Centre was published in which a number of disaffected avant-gardists repudiated the Futurist tag. The spat was not without its amusing aspects, which bring to light the hothouse atmosphere in which avant-garde politicking was played out: David Bomberg's keenness to clarify that he was not a member of the Rebel Art Centre but an 'independent', the Rebel Art Centre's plaintive insistence that Marinetti's use of its address was 'unauthorised', the refusal of most reviewers to distinguish between Futurism and Vorticism (*L.* 62–3). The cultural situation was in fact remarkably fluid, and, as Judith Collins has pointed out, temporary tactical alliances were often forged so that a common front against philistinism might be presented.[4]

The first issue of *Blast* was published in June–July 1914. An overdetermined production, it asserted a strong group identity as a way of differentiating Vorticism from competitor groups, emphasized the metropolitan nature of modernity, presented England as a potential source for the regeneration of European culture, and defended a particular version of what Richard Cork has termed 'the first machine age'.[5] *Blast* was dialogic in conception. Lewis was the organizing influence, and he wrote most of the polemical material, but the manifestos had several signatories and were presented as the outcome of a group ethos. Vorticism was defined in opposition to competitor tendencies and in relation to movements that were viewed sympathetically, such as Cubism. Despite its bold pink cover, explosive title, typographical explorations of the spatiality of the page, and warlike pronouncements, *Blast* was also a 'review', and it considered the artistic context of the period.[6] The title page signalled its cultural ambitions through its language and through other markers, such as its association with John Lane's The Bodley Head and its listing of London, New York, and Toronto as places of publication. Just as these cultural markers welcomed a certain kind of 'sophisticated' reader, so *Blast* distanced itself from the philistine it imagined would deplore its aesthetics. *Blast 1* aimed a curse at 'those who will hang over this Manifesto with SILLY CANINES exposed' (*B1* 17), and in *Blast 2* Pound castigated the *homo canis* who 'snarls violently at the thought of there being ideas which he doesn't know' (*B2* 85).[7] By these means *Blast* sought to establish a brand name for itself as a particular *kind* of avant-garde within the cultural economy of an emergent modernism.[8]

Dialogism extended to the periodical's figuration of England. Blasted for its climate, geographical isolation, reliance on sport and humour, Victorian heritage, and provincialism, England was displayed in all its phlegmatic torpor. Paradoxically, however, this stagnation was represented as the larval state from which the winged creature of a renewed culture could take flight; it was 'why a movement towards art and imagination could burst up here, from this lump of compressed life, with more force than anywhere else' (*B1* 32). The adversity of the conditions obtaining in England could give rise to an efflorescence of creativity. The 'Siberia of the mind' that was philistine England 'should be the most likely place for great Art to spring up' (*B1* 146), and this kind of rhetoric informs Hugh Kenner's claim that Vorticism proposed 'a distinctively English art, to comport with London's distinction as a world capital and England's status as a maritime nation'.[9] The present was the moment in which this regenerative possibility existed. Opposed equally to sentimental accounts of the past and evasive projections of the future, Vorticism claimed to plunge 'to the heart of the Present' so as to produce 'a New Living Abstraction' (*B1* 147) and to create 'the Poetry which is the as yet unexpressed spirit of the present time, and of new conditions and possibilities of life' (*B2* 5).

Blast identified the potential of modern English life in the machine. Its mission of national regeneration centred on the country's industrial might.[10] If England was blasted for its thralldom to a decayed Victorianism, then it was blessed for its position as an 'Industrial Island machine, pyramidal workshop, its apex at Scotland, discharging itself on the sea' (*B1* 24). But it did not extol technological dynamism; on the contrary, machines of swift movement and boundless energy were compromized by their association with Futurist modernolatry. The machines used as touchstones in *Blast* were industrial megaliths such as factories, buildings, bridges, dredgers, and cranes, the graceful colossi whose power was titanic but stately. They embodied the control required by the Vorticist aesthetic, which, in John Rothenstein's words, claimed that Futurism's 'insistence on movement sacrificed clarity'.[11] They functioned as a spur to creativity and as a model of aesthetic form.[12] Vorticism, Lewis was later to claim, actively 'sought out machine-forms', setting out to make pictures that 'were a sort of *machines*' (*WLA* 340). The artist, a kind of architect or engineer, was to produce artefacts that were justified as 'MACHINES OF LIFE, a sort of LIVING plastic geometry' (*B1* 140). The resultant dehumanization was said to correspond with 'the plastic, architectural quality, of art itself', for 'all the grandest and most majestic art in the world . . . has rather divested man of his vital plastic qualities and changed him into a more durable, imposing and in every way harder machine' (*B2* 43).[13] This emphasis on a static machine aesthetic indicates that Vorticism defined itself against the Futurism that had preceded it.

Laurence Rainey has suggested that Pound's and Eliot's denial of F. T. Marinetti's influence on Vorticism and *Blast* falsifies literary history. Marinetti's exploits were reported in the press and enabled him to reach a wider audience than Pound could by lecturing to a coterie audience. Marinetti presented an interventionist art of spectacle, drama, and provocation; he revealed the power of 'theatricality and publicity' and taught Pound to reconceive 'art as public practice'. Rainey argues that *Blast* was an imitative and belated attempt to upstage Marinetti's first mover advantage.[14] There is truth in these arguments and, although Lewis scholars have acknowledged the influence of Futurism on Vorticism, Eliot, Pound, and Lewis underplayed it.[15] Yet the differences between the two movements are crucial, and Rainey's filiative narrative, with its emphasis on origins, tends to elide them. In *Blast* Lewis and Pound articulated an aesthetic that is at odds with Marinetti's dynamism and voluntarism. Furthermore, as Lewis's career unfolds, it will emerge that Vorticism's alternative aesthetic is inseparable from a version of the self and the role that reason plays in the constitution of that self, which opposes the Futurist cult of force and action.

Marinetti's opening manifesto begins with a baptismal fable in which the impassioned advance guard of a society yet to be born embraces technology – symbolized by the automobile – and plunges into the 'nourishing sludge' of an industrial 'factory drain' to emerge with 'the white-hot iron of joy' in their hearts and aesthetic pronouncements on their lips. The bullet points of the rapid-fire manifesto that follows speak of danger, revolt, speed, primordiality, and violence. Invoking a cult of youth and strength, Marinetti urges his followers to 'set fire to the library shelves' and 'flood the museums', to 'take up [their] pickaxes ... and wreck, wreck the venerable cities, pitilessly'.[16] The last word is key; the absence of an ethical discourse encourages an aesthetic predicated on the assertion of self; artistic renewal comes through the expression of a desire based on the destruction of the other.

There are parallels between this rhetoric and the *agon* between Arghol and Hanp in *Enemy of the Stars*, the expressionist 'drama' written by Lewis for *Blast 1* and described by Paul Edwards as 'a founding text of Modernism' on account of its exploration and critique of transcendental aspirations as well as its stylistic experimentalism.[17] Jeffrey Meyers pointed out as long ago as 1980 that the play drew on Marinetti's *Conquête des étoiles*, and Edwards considers this link by looking at Lewis's use of gnostic dualism, which played an important role in Futurist thought.[18] *Enemy of the Stars*, the boldest piece of writing to appear in either of the two issues of *Blast*, displays a primordial energy: darkly expressionist, violent in syntax, imagery, and theme, elliptical in its transitions, and philosophically forbidding, it articulated in prose a vision that approached the abstraction of Vorticist painting. The search for a kind of 'radical purism' (*L.* 491) in words, to match the 'stark radicalism of the *visuals*' (*L.* 491) found in Vorticist art, resulted in a 'play' that minimized the use of connectives, articles, pronouns, and prepositions, making it edgy and charging it with a visceral power, which gave it the feel of some *ur*-text of the doomed search for an untrammelled self, a search called into question from the outset by the dialogic conception of the drama, said to be 'VERY WELL ACTED BY YOU AND ME' (*B1* 55). The rebarbative *style* of *Enemy of the Stars* immediately comes to the fore; it is acted by author and reader in that the former has created a textuality that requires the reader to participate self-reflexively in the production of its meaning. The play is as much about the performance of its language as it is about the conflict between Arghol and Hanp, for a dislocating violence traverses both 'form' and 'content', marking their inseparability. Consider, for example, the following:

First they hit each other, both with blows about equal in force – on face and head.

Soul perched like aviator in basin of skull, more alert and smaller than on any other occasion. Mask stoic with energy: thought cleaned off slick – pure and clean with action. Bodies grown brain, black octopi.

Flushes on silk epiderm and fierce card-play of fists between: emptying of 'hand' on soft flesh-table.

Arms of grey windmills, grinding anger on stone of the new heart.

Messages from one to another, dropped down anywhere when nobody is looking, reaching brain by telegraph: most desolating and alarming messages possible.

The attacker rushed in drunk with blows. They rolled, swift jagged rut, into one corner of shed : large insect scuttling roughly to hiding.

Stopped astonished. (*B1* 75)

No less than the protagonists locked in mortal combat, the style engages in a 'fierce card-play' of its own as the text struggles to break through the accretions of language in order to hit the bedrock below. Arghol's attempt to regain purity of identity by obliterating 'accumulations of Self' (*B1* 78) through a destruction of his surroundings or of his parasitic other is the counterpart to the text's wider search for an originary language.

Enemy of the Stars enacts the conflict between the lone artist-figure seeking to maintain an unsullied identity by conceiving it in unitary terms as self-grounding; the idea that it may emerge out of and depend on intersubjective relations is rejected in favour of a myth of self-creation or a desire to return to a Platonic transcendent origin. Contact with others is depicted as degrading, since it places the the self in jeopardy by allowing these others to destroy its isolated 'purity' or to batten on it parasitically. Hence the desperate search for a way to free the supposedly pure, original self both from entrapment in false social norms and from the other's importunities, a search the text suggests must fail: 'Between Personality and Mankind it is always a question of dog and cat; they are diametrically opposed species. Self is the ancient race, the rest are the new one. Self is the race that lost' (*B1* 66).[19] Yet this binary is overturned, when Arghol, in a fleeting moment of self-recognition, acknowledges that the other cannot be dismissed:

> I am amazed to find that you are like me.
> I talk to you for an hour and get more disgusted with myself.
> I find I wanted to make a naif yapping Poodle-parasite of you.
> – I shall always be a prostitute.
> I wanted to make you my self; you understand?
> Every man who wants to make another HIMSELF, is seeking a companion for his detached ailment of a self.
> You are an unclean little beast, crept gloomily out of my ego.
> You are the world, brother, with its family objections to me.
> Go back to our Mother and spit in her face for me! (*B1* 73)

Arghol is horrified to realize that Hanp is not as different from his own supposedly unique identity as he had thought, but this leads only to greater self-disgust, since the despised other is revealed as a presence within. Figured as 'the world' that lies outside the self and threatens it, Hanp is nonetheless recognized as the externalization of an 'impure' part of the self that may have been disjected but that shares a line of descent with it. Thus, when Arghol tries to purge himself of Hanp, the attempt proves an impossible dream: 'He had ventured in his solitude and failed. Arghol he had imagined left in the city. – Suddenly he had discovered Arghol who had followed him, in Hanp. Always a deux!' (*B1* 80). The inseparability of Arghol from Hanp is connected with the inseparability of Arghol from the universe whose enemy he is, since, as Edwards notes, he can be seen as 'part of the same system that is symbolized by the stars', which suggests in turn the 'ultimate identity of Arghol with the principle he opposes'.[20] The text never avows this identity in any clear way, but if Arghol claims that to 'leave violently slow monotonous life is to take header into the boiling starry cold' – a fate so awful that you 'cling to any object, dig your nails in earth, not to drop into it' (*B1* 67) – then he also admits that the energy of the stars that might 'some day reach Earth like violent civilisation' (*B1* 64) appears to have 'been fixed on [him] from nowhere' (*B1* 68). And this suggests that it is not just isolation from the other that is unviable but equally any view of the world that sees it as a threat, a theme to which *Tarr* returns in its exploration of an anti-vitalist aesthetic.

19

Enemy of the Stars indicates that *Blast* was influenced by Futurism's *energeia*, but it also opposed this aspect of Futurism, and this opposition led Lewis to deny the important role played by Marinetti in helping him to clarify his own ideas. Quite simply, Lewis in 1914 identified Marinetti as the intellectual precursor and avant-garde competitor from whom he needed to sever himself, a point noted by Jeffrey Meyers.[21] This was not a matter of aesthetic differences alone; it was a matter of cultural politics, with Lewis and Pound finding themselves in danger of being outmanoeuvred in the avant-garde arena by a more experienced campaigner. So Lewis made the shrewd tactical move of portraying Marinetti as naive and sentimental; he was presented as the purveyor of an ideology of sensational romance that celebrated the machine age uncritically and thus constructed an aesthetic in which speed and movement were presented as intrinsically good. Lewis praised Futurism's anti-academicism, agreeing that its critique of salon art was needed, but he shared neither its contempt for *all* earlier art nor its desire to replace that art with an iconoclasm that exalted the willing self.[22] Futurist vitalism, he argued, offered a picturesque account of modernity as melodrama.[23] Linked to this charge was the distinction *Blast* made between northern and southern art and culture, which Lewis deployed to heap scorn on the excesses of emotion and volubility that he associated with Marinetti. Invoking geographical boundaries and national characteristics, he argued that what was valid in one environment was unworkable in another and insisted that 'the art for these climates . . . must be a northern flower' (*B1* 36). Northern art conjoined comedy and tragedy: it yoked together controlling form with torrential power and, out of the resulting tension, produced the vortex, Pound's 'point of maximum energy' (*B1* 153). The rigour imposed by form and structure was to distinguish 'northern' austerity from 'southern' expansiveness, and this is why Lewis favoured clearness and restraint (*B1* 144). Whether *Enemy of the Stars* could be said to embody these theoretical tenets remains a moot point.

Vorticism instantiated a drama of tensionality in its art, opposing controlled energy to a rhetoric of agitated motion. Lewis contrasted Futurist paintings, which he described as 'swarming, exploding or burgeoning with life' with Vorticist art, which was 'electric with a more mastered, vivid vitality' (*B2* 38). Vorticism impelled intensity into stabilizing forms; Futurism extolled force in a celebration of chaotic momentum. In T. E. Hulme's influential terms, the hard angularity of Vorticism was 'geometrical', whereas the fluid naturalism of Futurism was 'vital'. Hulme, favouring an inorganic art, noted that Futurism was 'the exact opposite of the art I am describing, being the deification of the flux, the last efflorescence of impressionism'.[24] Lewis's view was Hulme's; Futurism was 'largely Impressionism up-to-date' (*B1* 143). Impressionism suggests a degree of passivity on the part of the perceiving subject. Vorticism sought to inhabit 'a purer region of art' (*B1* 144), which looked for creative power through an Apollonian harnessing of energy, not through a Dionysian *Rausch*. So, although *Blast* was obsessed with energy, it sought to control it, not to abandon the self to its force – the Vorticist was at 'his maximum point of energy when stillest' (*B1* 148).

Vorticism was also metamorphic – the artist was to transmute the raw material of life into form. In Pound's words, 'Futurism is the disgorging spray of a vortex with no drive behind it, DISPERSAL', but Vorticism is seen 'as DIRECTING a certain fluid force against circumstance, as CONCEIVING instead of merely observing and reflecting' (*B1* 153). This aspect of Vorticism underpinned its commitment to a geometrization of art, which signalled its distance from naturalistic values by subordinating the demands of life to the exigencies of aesthetics. Naturalism, Lewis argued, was escapism, an avoidance of the challenge of *poiesis*; in 'the revolt against Formula, revolutionaries in art sell themselves to Nature', never realizing 'that Nature is just as sterile a Tyrant' (*B1* 129). Vorticism distanced itself from nature, defending rigid demarcations, sharp outlines, and spare forms; it endeavoured to capture the essence of reality not through *immersion* in experience but through *observation* of it.[25]

This emphasis on the need to *synthesize* modern life in order to distil its inner meaning was central to Vorticism's opposition to Futurism. Lewis argued that the 'essence of an object is beyond and often in contradiction to, its simple truth: and literal rendering in the fundamental matter of arrangement and logic will never hit the emotion intended by unintelligent imitation' (*B2* 45). Futurism was for him a form of 'unintelligent imitation'; presenting modernity *tout court* as possessing value, it produced an art lacking the power to analyse and discriminate. Futurism's euphoric plunge into the modern maelstrom was also seen as atavistic. Its desire to blur the boundaries between self and world by engulfing modernity with arms spread wide was opposed by Vorticism's stark alternative – an aesthetic purged of human sentiment and based on a *cordon sanitaire* between the realms of life and art.[26] Tarr articulates the position as follows: 'Deadness is the first condition for art: the second is absence of soul, in the human and sentimental sense. With the statue its lines and masses are its soul, no restless inflammable ego is imagined for its interior: it has *no inside*: good art must have no inside: that is capital' (*T* 311–12). Deadness in this context does not just favour form over content, it gives priority to a cold, impersonal mode that rejects empathic identification in favour of plastic values – line, proportion, mass. Ortega y Gasset has this aspect of modern art in mind when he observes that it discloses a 'will to style', pointing out that 'to stylize means to deform reality, to derealize; style involves dehumanization'.[27]

Blast identified a utopian 'moment' in 1914 when the chance for a national transformation of art was seen to be briefly possible. That this hope was predicated on the need to displace competitor groups in a struggle over cultural hegemony is clear. But it is risky to take *Blast*'s utopianism straight, for it ironized the politics of nascent avant-gardism, positioning itself as a playful, self-reflexive, tongue-in-cheek production, which was all too aware of its place in the world of putsch and counter-putsch.[28] It utilized a dyadic structure in which it asserted one view before averring its opposite – this was especially true of its 'blasts' and 'blesses' – with the result that both were destabilized. The second manifesto asserted that 'we . . . set up violent structure of adolescent clearness between two extremes', before going on to announce that 'we discharge ourselves on both sides' (*B1* 30). The polarities set up (north/south, England/Europe, Futurism/Vorticism) were parodied as instances of youthful immaturity, and the description of Vorticists as mercenaries who fight on both sides hinted at a kind of role playing at odds with the notion of commitment to a cause. *Blast* exploited the avant-garde ritual of manifestos and counter-manifestos even as it dismantled the ritual's conventions, displaying its inner workings to the public with a nod and a wink. Its humorous side was in evidence when Lewis informed Pound that he would not publish Eliot's 'Bullshit' and 'Ballad for Big Louise' because he planned to 'stick to [his] naif determination to have no "words ending in – Uck, – Unt, and – Ugger" ' (*L.* 67). And the social ferment around the early avant-gardes, especially the involvement of fashionable society in its antics, suggests that the proponents of 'radical' artistic reform were willing to play along with the public view of avant-gardism as jokey spectacle.[29] Looked at from this perspective, we do well not to take *Blast*'s pronouncements at face value; while its opposition to key Futurist tenets was genuine, its own national utopianism may have been a gesture, a thumbed nose aimed at an upstart Milanese and his fervent cohorts.

Vorticism calls into question Peter Burger's account of the avant-garde.[30] It did not attack the institution of art *per se* but assaulted the specific hegemony of the salon art promoted by the Royal Academy, and it defended an autonomous view of art on the grounds that creativity would be weakened by any overt preoccupation with political or ethical ends. Vorticism pinned its colours to the mast of aesthetic 'purism'; it did not seek to overthrow the institution of art as such nor to unify life and art through social praxis, although it certainly did have utopian social aspirations.[31] As Lewis put it in an early manifesto: 'The Vorticist does not suck up to Life. He lets Life know its place in a Vorticist Universe!' (*B1* 148). Life exacted a sharp revenge for such temerity, and Vorticism, which flared so briefly before the war snuffed it out, proved to be a dead end. Looking back, Lewis zeroed in on its failed utopianism: 'We are not only "the last men of an epoch" . . . *We are the first men of a Future that has not materialized.* We belong to a "great age" that has not "come off" ' (*BB* 256). His political pessimism originated in this moment of failure. There was a connection between politics and art in *Blast*, of course, though its terminology tended to be taken from the aesthetic realm.[32] The First World War was the apocalypse that put paid to Vorticist millenarianism, but it is hard not to see the threat of war prior

23

to 1914 as a spur to its dream of national revival through the purity of art. Hulme, following Worringer, had emphasized that a geometric aesthetic offered escape from contingency, and he had looked to it for a repudiation of post-renaissance humanism. Translated into the language of Vorticism, this line of thought produced an artistic practice that envisaged rebuilding society in accordance with the logical structure of a smoothly purring machine.

Tarr, the novel Lewis was keen to complete as a testament to his skill as a writer, in case he was killed at the front, calls the Vorticist aesthetic into question. The novel is easily summarized: it satirizes the life led by bohemian artists in pre-war Paris, focusing on an artist (Tarr) who puts forward various theories about the need for art to be severed from life, even as he is himself caught up in irksome entanglements with lovers and rivals. A parallel plot concerns the figure of Kreisler, a German student and would-be painter, who gradually descends into psychotic despair, before eventually committing suicide. At the end of the novel, Tarr is unable to choose between his two lovers – Bertha and Anastasya – and a pattern is thereby established for his future life. *Tarr* is an uneasy text. It probes the flaws in its protagonist's aesthetic, suggesting that it is based on horror at the materiality of existence and fear of the human other. It is structured, I shall argue, around a series of ambivalences: it articulates a modernist aesthetic through its main character but eschews this aesthetic in its own narrative procedure; it opposes the values of life and art through Kreisler and Tarr but ironizes both figures; it dramatizes the painter's self-creation but leaves him caught in a sexual dialectic from which he cannot escape; and it vociferates a misogyny that it reveals is the product of existential dread.

Tarr is a paradoxical text in which the artist-figure puts forward a theory of art that is at odds with the novel's own controlling mode.[33] Why, if Lewis is committed to the ascetic severity defended by Tarr, is the novel a character study? What is the relation between its exploration of psychology, reflections on aesthetics, and stylized form? *Tarr* is simultaneously a novel of ideas in which characters exist to voice contrasting viewpoints *and* a psychological study of desire, conflict, and

24

psychosis. The text posits a world characterized by the struggle for prestige and power, with violence lurking just below the surface of social relations, but it suggests that identity must be formed within this world. In *Tarr*, identity is neither monadic nor stable; it is in process, forming and reforming itself through interaction with others. The novel's view of the self is intersubjective, but its view of intersubjectivity is Hobbesian. Tarr's aesthetic is based on an anthropology in which the self is conceived in terms of a mind/body dualism and is seen to be under threat from all other selves. This view of the subject is then mapped onto a theory of the aesthetic in which art and life are divided into two realms and onto a view of politics in which the gifted individual is to be demarcated from the mediocre herd.

The retreat from life into the deadness of art offers a solution to the perils of intersubjectivity. Yet the detachment Tarr preaches is a negative response to anxieties about the body's uncontrollable materiality as much as a positive account of an aesthetic project, and it is in the tension between fear and creativity that the novel's preoccupation with abjection and *ressentiment* is to be found. Kreisler and Tarr are both traversed by the abject: Kreisler is caught up in a repetition compulsion in which the need for self-humiliation before others vies with the urge to destroy them; Tarr is trapped in a dynamic that casts the other from the self, suggesting alienation not just from corporeality but from human existence as a whole. The Tarr–Kreisler dyad is the hinge around which the novel pivots, because it makes the issue of recognition – around which abjection and *ressentiment* always mobilize – a structural principle in the formation of identity.[34] Whereas Kreisler's fight for self-recognition plunges him into the abject, Tarr's struggle for self-preservation holds the abject at bay by refusing to grant recognition to the potentially threatening other.[35] *Tarr* stages various oppositions (art/life, mind/body, individual/group, male/female) without resolving them, and this is a consequence of its multiple perspectives and its refusal of closure.[36] For Tarr, art offers escape from the tragicomic spectacle of a sordid, violent, and ersatz life, but it does so at the price of renunciation. Reflection on this renunciation is the novel's subject.

Nietzsche identified *ressentiment* as the negation of an affirmative stance vis-à-vis external reality.[37] Accounts of abjection reveal what is implicit in *ressentiment*, that the turn outward is also a turn inward.[38] In Melanie Klein's terms, introjection and projection reinforce each other, since introjected external objects give rise to the negative projections that are then attributed to the malevolence of the world or of other people, and a self-perpetuating cycle is born.[39] The resulting fragmentation of the ego, in which aspects of the self are projected onto objects and then taken back, involves a form of intrapsychic abuse, giving rise to what Max Scheler describes as 'a self-poisoning of the mind'.[40] Klein, of course, was primarily concerned with the child–mother dyad, but her observations are suggestive for the relationship between father and son that is crucial to the formation of Kreisler's reactive character.

Kreisler is from the outset associated with the death instinct – his room is 'a funerary chamber' while he is a recluse quartered in a 'rock-hewn death-house' (*T*. 75) – and with the patriarchal power that is its emblem:

> And how about his father, what was that letter going to contain? Mr. Kreisler senior had got a certain amount of pleasure out of him: the little Otto had satisfied in him in turn the desire of possession (that objects such as your watch, your house, which could equally well belong to anybody, do not satisfy), of authority (that servants do not satisfy), of self-complacency (that self does not) – he had been to him, later, a kind of living cinematograph and *Reisebuch* combined; and, finally, he had inadvertently lured with his youth a handsome young woman into the paternal net. There was no further satisfaction that he now could ever be expected to procure to this satiated parent. Henceforth he must be a source only of irritation and expense. (*T*. 124)

Point of view is unstable here, for the free indirect discourse with which the passage begins modulates into perceptions that cannot be attributed to Kreisler, while the last sentences could be Kreisler's or the narrator's. But, whether the passage reflects Kreisler's paranoid perception of his childhood or a more detached account, the instrumental and dominative nature of the relationship between father and son is clear. When his father supplants him – in a reversal of the oedipal scenario –

Kreisler's place in the family economy is rendered nugatory. But Kreisler is not free from oppressive paternal power; having staged a minor rebellion by refusing to work, he chooses (first sign of the paradoxes of abjection) to remain dependent on his father for subsistence. The letter for which he waits is the symbol of paternal authority. When the father's sanction is finally withdrawn (and the money is refused), Kreisler's suicide is a foregone conclusion, but in a deeper sense his physical death is simply a distant echo of the annihilation of his ego in childhood.

Kreisler's *ressentiment* manifests itself in passivity and inertia, in a need for others to fill the emptiness within. But the persecutory delusions that haunt him are bound up with the desire to re-experience the original pain. Nietzsche's view that in *ressentiment* one 'cannot get rid of anything, one cannot get over anything, one cannot repel anything – everything hurts' is taken a step further, for Kreisler seeks catharsis not by repulsing the suffering but by plunging into it.[41] Self-abasement offers the paradoxical route by which revenge against a malign world may be taken. His memory of a childhood scene in which a schoolboy, jabbed in the hand with a penknife, invited his assailant to repeat the action, seeming 'to wish to see his hand a mass of wounds and to delect himself with the awful feeling of his own black passion', suggests how far his 'self-humiliation was wedded with the notion of retaliation' (*T*. 125). The collocation of retaliation with self-humiliation points to Kreisler's doom, for the aggression he aims at the social formation is also directed at himself, with the result that the talionic impulse destroys him as surely as it does his symbolic scapegoat – Soltyk. The originary scene of self-mutilation (by proxy) discloses the bond between abjection and *ressentiment*, since the desire for self-humiliation is put in motion by an insult, which is then to be perversely avenged by being redoubled – 'Do it again! Do it again' (*T*. 125). This repetition compulsion (to wreak vengeance through a return to the suffering that first caused the pain) is disclosed by Kreisler's need to abase himself before Anastasya in the extraordinary desire to transform himself into her dog.[42] The ironies are bitter here, for the 'self-possession' of which Kreisler dreams rests on the abject denial of his own humanity. The 'self' is what cannot be 'possessed' in a state of abjection: it is disjected, dispersed, leaving the 'void' that Kreisler projects on to the other.

The aetiology of Kreisler's *ressentiment* may be traced to the relationship with the father, but it has wider ramifications, for Kreisler's dread of the world is linked to what the father symbolizes: the social realm of privilege and position from which the son is excluded. Thus his desire for revenge must be played out on this public terrain: 'Kreisler did not know how he should wipe out his score, but he wanted it bigger, more crushing. The bitter fascination of suffering drew him on, to substitute real wounds for imaginary. But Society at the same time must be taught to suffer, he had paid for that' (*T.* 125). Desire is the ruse by which Kreisler covers his tracks for it is in fact the *absence* in his psyche, an absence he seeks to fill through a plea for recognition (*T.* 314). There are lives, Kristeva writes, 'not sustained by *desire*, as desire is always for objects. Such lives are based on *exclusion*.'[43] So it is the bitterest irony of all that the recognition Kreisler seeks is what he cannot grant others, as disclosed by the devastating rape scene, which portrays a psychosis in which the reality of the other is negated (see *T.* 190–5).

There is an inexorable logic to Kreisler's scapegoating. Soltyk is described as Kreisler's 'efficient and more accomplished counterpart' (*T.* 89). His grace and polish are the social signs of Kreisler's lack. And Kreisler's obsession with Soltyk is inseparable from his feelings of inferiority: 'As to the Poles, a gentle flame of social security and ease danced in their eyes and gestures: he was out in the dark, they were in a lighted room!' (*T.* 272). Kreisler is the outcast who is described by the novel's characters in a dehumanizing language that excludes him from the symbolic order – brute, dog, cow, idiot, trash, joke, ape, are some of the epithets by which they 'name' him – and this refusal of recognition exacerbates his sense of weakness: 'the outcast feeling returned in the presence of these toffs – class-inferiority-feeling beset him' (*T.* 159). His reaction to this strategy of exclusion reaches its conclusion in the abortive duel scene. The duel, a rigorously codified ritual for the management of conflict, exists to resolve disputes of honour between *equals*. Kreisler chooses this method of engaging with Soltyk as a protest against exclusion.[44] Before the duel collapses into farce, his fantasy of omnipotence is expressed through the abject:

> he occupied himself with the notion that that man yonder might in a few minutes be wiped out – he would become a disintegrating mess, more repulsive than vitriol or syphilis could make him: all that organism he, Kreisler, would be turning into dung, as though by magic. He, Kreisler, is insulted: he is denied equality of existence . . . he, Kreisler, lifts his hand, presses a little bar of steel and the other is swept away into the earth. (*T*. 277–8)

In this fantasy of omnipotence, a potent expression of damaged narcissism, the excluded self wreaks vengeance by turning the hated other back into the formless matter (dust to dust) from whence he came.[45]

The abject is the permeable membrane through which Kreisler moves as he wavers between vengeance against the world and mutilation of the self. Two figures symbolize the split between abjection and *ressentiment*: 'Anastasya-Soltyk: Soltyk-Anastasya: that was a bad coupling!' (*T*. 121). The defeat of the attempt to gain salvation through retaliation against Soltyk, when self-humiliation through Anastasya has failed, is prefigured earlier in the text. Imagining the two of them ridiculing him behind his back, only to discover that they have long left the room, Kreisler sights 'a more terrible, abstract, antagonist'; instead of a climax, there is '*nothing*' (*T*. 160). This 'nothing' refers to an absence in the constitution of the self. When the attempt at self-healing through purgative violence ends in disaster, self-murder is the only path left: 'His throttling by Soltyk had been Kreisler's last milestone: he had changed, he now knew he was beaten, and that there was nothing to do but die. His body ran to the german frontier as a chicken's does down a yard, headless, from the block' (*T*. 289).

If Kreisler is traversed by the abject, then Tarr is his opposite – the cold aesthetic purist who polices the boundary between life and art. His coding of this division in terms of gender; his disgust with corporeality and the processes of generation; and his defence of an aesthetic in which the perspective of the eye tropes art as fixity mark the line between these two realms. Tarr's fastidiousness manifests itself in a variety of ways: he resists any merging with crowds; he resents his bodily (especially sexual) urges; he sees love as a contagion in which the self is put at risk; and he protects his inner being through irony, aggression, and camouflage. A natural solipsist, Tarr deploys a declamatory mode of address that replaces dialogue with the monologism of the self-obsessed mind:

> When he solicited advice, as now he was doing of Butcher, it was transparently a matter of form. No serious reply was expected from anyone except himself: but he appeared to need his own advice to come from himself in public. . . . He was the kind of person who, if he ever should wish to influence the world, would do it so that he might touch himself more plastically through others. (T. 30–1)[46]

Tarr's contempt for life signals his alienation from corporeality and from intersubjective relations. Social life in the novel is portrayed as a black farce in which cardboard cut-outs posture clumsily in a masquerade of life. Lewis's essay 'Inferior Religions' plays with the idea of inert matter, in the form of physical husks from which purposiveness has been removed, mimicking human life. This conceit foregrounds the materiality that human existence cannot escape. One response to this all-devouring materiality is to reify the achievements of the mind, a strategy that may alienate the subject from its own bodily existence, a self-alienation that characterizes Tarr's perennial battle with his senses. It is a self-alienation that can recoil from the body as unreactive tissue: 'the dressing-gown was open and one large thigh, with ugly whiteness, slid half out of it. It looked dead, and connected with her like a ventriloquist's dummy with its master' (T. 50). Or it can recoil from generation, seeing sex as 'a monstrosity' (T. 17) and abjuring the 'slop and spawn of children and the bawling machinery of the inside of life' (T. 23). But it cannot evade the self's own implication in the *souillure* of existence, a fact occasionally recognized by Tarr.[47]

The body is the *locus* of abjection, since it is the sign of the materiality and mutability that threaten structuration and symbolization. Corporeality, Elizabeth Grosz has argued, is what the symbolic must conceal because it discloses 'the precariousness of the subject's grasp of its own identity' and warns that the subject 'may slide back into the chaos from which it is formed'.[48] Tarr's disgust with human life is expressed in terms of the familiar oppositions that keep the abject at bay. Nor can we ignore the gendered nature of the oppositions he invokes, for his misogyny upholds a specific social hierarchy: 'God was man: the woman was a lower form of life. Everything started female and most so continued: a jellyish diffuseness spread itself and gaped upon all the beds and bas-fonds of everything: above a certain level sex disappeared, just as in highly-organized sensualism sex vanishes. On the other hand, *everything* beneath that line was female' (*T*. 327–8). In a familiar move, the abject is associated with women so that the male self can remain inviolate.

But the language of sexual difference is in this text deployed to ward off a more general anxiety (*T*. 203).[49] Existential dread is the real object of horror. Burgeoning rooms and buildings, inanimate objects, bustling crowds, involuntary physical contacts, the strangeness of the body and its appurtenances, procreation, and the uncontrollable flux of life all threaten to disintegrate the subject. Tarr's aesthetic is based on a distinction between life and art, which is in turn figured as a split between male and female. Yet these binaries are the products of the 'indigestion of Reality, from which this fastidious soul suffered acutely, without ever recognizing the cause' (*T*. 203). Tarr grasps that 'his contempt for everybody else in the end must degrade him' (*T*. 246), but he is not permitted to move beyond a subject position in which body and mind are seen to be at war and in which women are conceived as threats to stability of self.

In *Dr Jekyll and Mr Hyde*, one of *Tarr's* more obvious intertexts, Jekyll's repressive strategy is hopelessly ineffective, but at least Jekyll can see Hyde as an integral part of his psyche: 'when I looked upon that ugly idol in the glass, I was conscious of no repugnance, rather of a leap of welcome. This, too, was myself.'[50] In contrast, Tarr splits the senses from the mind in cartesian fashion.[51] But he can no more escape the consequences of the dualism he sets up than Jekyll can evade the clutches of Hyde. Tarr's reason has 'conspired to the effect that his senses never should be wakened' (*T*. 213), but when they finally are they proclaim the triumphant return of the repressed: ' "Ha ha! Ha ha! Kreisleriana" he shouted without his voice. The indignant plebs of his glorious organism rioted around his mind. "Ah-ha! Ah-ha! Dirty practical joker, dirty intellect, where are you leading us now?" They were vociferous' (T. 326). Tarr does not really give 'life' (in the form of Anastasya) a chance, since he rejects the possibility of reciprocity out of hand: 'such successful people as Anastasya and himself were by themselves: it was as impossible to combine or *wed* them as to compound the genius of two great artists' (T. 327). Thus there is no *structural* difference between Anastasya and Bertha; depicted in terms of a contrast between slatternly domesticity and intellectual chic, they are caught up in an instrumental dynamic where sexual relations are conceived in terms of the satisfaction of desire. Hence his functionalist language and his reduction of male–female relations to the dictates of biology: 'One solitary thing is left facing any woman with whom [the artist] has commerce, that is his sex, a lonely phallus' (T. 20). At the end of the novel Tarr remains stuck in this dynamic, and the swing of the pendulum with which the novel closes points to the extremes – swagger sex and bovine domesticity – to which an anti-vitalist aesthetic may lead.

Fredric Jameson has claimed that it is 'disingenuous to read Lewis's work ... as the *critique* of violence rather than as its expression'.[52] But the obvious retort is that there is no either/or choice here, because *Tarr* turns ambivalence into a structural principle. The positions Tarr adopts are disassembled before our eyes. He admits early on that he does not have 'the knack of handling the various personalities gathered beneath [his] roof' (T. 23), and, when the plebs of his organism riot in his mind at the end of the novel, he has still not mastered the trick. Lewis wrote in *Time and Western Man* that a 'matching of opposites' within the individual may save him 'from dogmatism and conceit' by placing him 'at the centre of the balance' (TWM 133), but Tarr is the dogmatist *par excellence*, aggressively championing a philosophy in which art and life are '*de puntos* for ever and ever' (T. 311). Lewis himself held this view, and I am not suggesting that he repudiates it here, rather, that in texts such as *Tarr* he submitted this conviction to searching scrutiny. What, finally, are the consequences of this scrutiny in *Tarr*?

Hulme suggested that when geometric art reproduced natural objects it sought 'to purify them of their characteristically living qualities in order to make them necessary and immovable'; this art, though the reverse of optimistic, was marked by a 'religious intensity'.[53] In *Tarr*, the resolutely secular framework seems to push abstraction into ontological pessimism. The drive to stabilize reality, to freeze it in spatiality, represents a desire to escape the flux so as to evade mutability and to impose form on a reality that appears to be irredeemably contingent. Yet this rage for order seems to require the cauterization of affect and the negation of the other, giving rise to an inorganic aesthetic, and producing an account of the self as a solitary entity striving forever to resist relations with others, since these are seen as threatening incorporation of the self in a communal miasma. The price to pay for this strategy is clear: self-alienation, loss of affect, an instrumental view of human relations. If the artist's 'first creation is *the Artist* himself' (*T*. 20), and if the first condition of art is 'deadness' (*T*. 312), then he must, it seems, purge himself of the emotions and desires that are a part of life. It was not until texts such as *The Revenge for Love* that Lewis was able to go beyond this renunciative conception of self and art, perfectly caught in this text by Anastasya's blank look at Tarr, 'as though he contained cheerless stretches where no living thing could grow' (*T*. 332). But the novel's refusal to blink this impasse is revealing: it rejects those modernisms that embrace psychological inwardness in an attempt to represent life more fully, but it shows uncompromisingly that another modernism – Lewis's own – may entomb reality in a mausoleum. On this reading, Kreisler is a 'wild body' run amok, and Tarr is a frozen *ratio* masquerading as a human being. Death is their shared obsession: the flight from abjection leads either to self-murder or to the immolation of life to art.

3

Avant-Garde and Modernist Polemics

After the war Lewis tried to come to terms with his experiences and embarked on his analysis of contemporary culture and society. He was later to view the years 1918–26 as the post-war period proper, in that the war's impact was then at its greatest, and the period beginning with the General Strike of 1926 as marking the end of this interregnum. He claimed in *Blasting and Bombardiering* (1937) that he chose to go underground after 1918 before emerging again in 1926 as a philosopher and critic, but he was not as invisible as this account suggests. He wrote essays on art; he held a one-man show (*Guns*) in 1919; he helped organize Group X, a phalanx of painters committed to pursuing artistic innovation; he started another review (*The Tyro*) and painted a series of grotesque figures, also called Tyros, which he exhibited in 1921; and he worked on the massive *Man of the World*, the ambitious project that was eventually chopped up into separate books.[1]

Lewis initially saw the First World War as a watershed marking the end of a decayed culture and the possible birth of a new society.[2] There was for Lewis no possible return to the values or conditions of pre-war social life, and he directed his artistic and critical effort in the 1920s to exploring the possibilities of this new landscape.[3] But his initial post-war optimism was soon dispelled, and his work gradually assumed a darker complexion. Lewis's writing in the inter-war years was wide-ranging, covering politics, painting, literature, philosophy, sociology, and cultural criticism. He was pre-eminently concerned to forge a new aesthetic, which could deepen the advances made in the pre-war years. This entailed analyses of the artistic context and the sociocultural situation, since Lewis argued that, although art was an autonomous sphere of activity, it 'must be organic with its time' (*B1* 34). Simplifying greatly, it may be said that in the field of the arts he was concerned to establish the terms on which creativity could be conceived, and that this led him to clarify the differences between himself and modernists such as Eliot, Joyce, and Pound, as well as to explain his opposition to the avant-gardism of Dada, Surrealism, and the 'revolution of the word' trumpeted by the 'little magazine' *transition*.

For Lewis, the success of pre-war innovations meant that earlier rhetorics of publicity and polemic were no longer appropriate; the danger now was that experiment would be fetishized as a sufficient goal, the *new* being conflated with the *good* (see *WLA* 97, 114, 116). Lewis was distancing himself from the view that avant-gardism was required in all contexts and that its artefacts were of intrinsic value. Pre-war battles had centred on the need to destroy the influence of academic art and to evolve a new painterly language; he considered that a breakthrough had been made and that artists should not mimic pre-war strategies. As he later put it: '*Avantgardism* in itself, at any time, is not a merit or a demerit' (*RA* 132).

Two related concerns came to the fore: fashion and the art market. These issues were linked because Lewis grasped that in a society in which patronage was in decline the economics of art were determined by dealers who stimulated demand by marketing up-to-dateness. Lewis was hardly naive about such issues, believing that art was a product commanding a price. But he distinguished art that followed the dictates of fashion from art that represented an attempt at transfiguration. He wrote, for example: '*No* serious artist thinks or propagates the notion for his own use that anything *better* can be done than such works as hang above Rembrandt's name in Amsterdam or the Hermitage' (*WLA* 115). This sort of attitude had nothing to do with the search for a form and a vision pertinent to the day, since 'slavery to fashion is a different thing from the acceptance of the data and atmosphere of a time' (*WLA* 162). Art, he declared in *Time and Western Man*, 'is as much a "timeless" thing as technical invention is a creature of time. Its values are more static, as physically it is more static; in its greatest or most universal expression it is in another world from that of fashion' (*TWM* 36).

By the early 1920s, then, Lewis was defining his position in relation to several issues. He sought to avoid the trap of a formalist view of experimentation that construed innovation as a guarantor of artistic quality; he argued that art was being reduced to a fashionable commodity for the securing of profit and symbolic capital; and he suggested that much of the art passed off as ground-breaking was recycling older styles (see *WLA* 127, 132). Lewis set himself the task of forging an aesthetic through which art and society could be transformed. *Time and Western Man* aimed to provide a 'rigorous restatement . . . of the whole "revolutionary" position', especially in the two provinces of 'art and literature' (*TWM* 22). This restatement led Lewis to rethink his own positions in relation to post-war artistic and intellectual currents, especially the influence on cultural life of philosophers such as Henri Bergson and William James. The analysis was partisan; oriented towards the needs of a writer and painter committed to 'the exactly-defined' and 'the physical or the concrete' (*TWM* 109), it asked 'not whether the great *time-philosophy* . . . is viable as a system of abstract truth, but if in its application it helps or destroys our human arts' (*TWM* 110).[4]

Lewis argued in *Time and Western Man* that the greater part of post-war avant-garde art and writing was derivative and in thrall to philosophies of flux, which dissolved a shared public world into subjective sensation. No longer committed to the distillation of meaning by the search for conceptual clarity, such art immersed itself in the flux (for example in Futurist celebrations of movement, modernist evocations of the stream of consciousness, Surrealist defences of aleatory writing) and succumbed to its contingent, formless, and arbitrary temporal flow. Lewis followed Schopenhauer in believing that art should concentrate on particular objects, remove them from temporality, and, by so isolating them, reveal their essential qualities (*WLA* 208). Bergson argued the opposite, claiming that the act of conceptualization falsifies human experience of reality since it obscures temporality and cuts out discrete 'moments' from an interrelated whole. For Lewis, this neoheracliteanism condemned human beings to a life where public criteria were dissolved into a self-asserting solipsism in which individuals were 'thrown back wholesale from the external, the public world' and driven into their 'primitive private mental caves' (*P*. 103). The result was a loss of agency, for individuals needed to be able to grasp the nature of the external world if they were 'to be capable of behaving in any way but as mirror-images of alien realities, or as the most helpless and lowest organisms, as worms or sponges' (*TWM* 132). So *Time and Western Man* was written as a defence of common-sense reality on Berkeleyan lines, because for Lewis this was the reality required by the visual and plastic intelligence (*TWM* 392).[5]

The politicization of art was another pressing issue. Lewis maintained a 'purist' view in which art was conceived as an autonomous practice that functioned at its best when free from all extraneous pressures, ideological or otherwise. In the post-war context this issue became urgent, for he saw the new avant-gardes turning what for him had been an *aesthetic* revolution into a *political* one. Thus *The Art of Being Ruled* was partly written to save the creative force of artistic radicalism from political imperatives, and *Time and Western Man*, asserting that 'art is a truer guide than "politics" ' (*TWM* 116), continued the fight. It is important to note, however, that Lewis did not oppose the politicization of art because he wished to preserve existing social structures but because he believed this would compromise art's visionary power.[6] Lewis saw his attack on post-war avant-gardism as the preliminary to a more radical practice in the realms of art and politics.[7] Global politics had become the dominant issue of the period: 'the central problem of this intensely political time is *the political artist*, or, better, the *politician as artist*' (*E3* 68). His position was that writers and painters were at their most challenging when they viewed their time without any *parti pris*. Hence his praise for a Molière, who 'would have done you a *bolshevik* with as much relish as a *bourgeois*, for his *Précieuses* were equally *ridiculous*' (*E* 28), or for a Shakespeare, described as 'the *ideal spectator*' (*LF* 149) with the necessary '*sang froid*' (*LF* 14) to be impartial.

Lewis was particularly bothered by the fact that the art he assailed seemed to propagandize for a sham politics, which, under the guise of radicalism, gave a bohemian elite cultural kudos. He wrote:

> my revaluation of the european world, were I given carte blanche to build it in conformity with my view of perfection, would be very much more fundamental than that contemplated by *Transition*. And that is even one of my main objections to these particular transitionist radicals. They are, for me, false revolutionaries, and they wish for a *transition* into a New Philistinism ... and not a *transition* of a more truly revolutionary order, into an order of things radically different from the 'capitalist state'. (*E3* 25)

But he believed by the late 1920s that this revaluation could not take place. He argued that science, industry, and capitalism had given rise to an administered world in which vast corporations and entrenched institutions controlled all significant aspects of social life. One consequence of this process was the loss of a meaningful public sphere, for the individual had become a pawn whose subject positions were mapped out in advance: 'The *person* is a thing of the past, in public life ... no single individual can ... effectively, *be* anything, politically, at all, except quite simply a "capitalist" or a "communist" ... there is no margin in which the individual can exist, *effectively*, outside these gigantic organisations' (*E3* 78–80).

The loss of a public sphere has serious consequences for a politically motivated art, which may be rendered ineffectual irrespective of the content of its protests. But also, if avant-garde art is welcomed as an amusing diversion by a knowing elite, then its alleged radicalism is further compromised, since it becomes a form of radical chic, a fashionable badge worn by a cultural aristocracy to show how sophisticated they are. And this was Lewis's contention. He argued that in advanced cultural circles so-called revolutionary thought had become a new orthodoxy.[8] A hegemonic but ersatz revolutionary art is a boon to capitalism, of course, for it siphons protest away from dangerous waters; but it is also a *product* of capitalism, institutionalizing the demand for newness on which the latter depends. When critics like Suzy Gablik and Gerald Graff argue that the avant-garde search for the new slots into capitalism's need for repetitive consumption, giving rise to a situation in which 'the idea of *tradition* gives way to the idea of *fashion*, and revolt against tradition becomes profitable', they are walking in Lewis's steps.[9] For Graff, making a critique first offered by Marx and Engels in *The Communist Manifesto*, 'the real "avant-garde" is advanced capitalism, with its built-in need to destroy all vestiges of tradition, all orthodox ideologies, all continuous and stable forms of reality in order to stimulate higher levels of consumption'.[10] On this analysis, to fetishize constant change is to succumb to the imperatives of the capitalist economy and so to strip the word 'revolution' of content.[11] For Lewis, politically motivated avant-gardism was problematic both because it undermined art's autonomy and because it was blind to its own place in the cultural economy it ostensibly wanted to overthrow.

The arguments canvassed thus far concentrate on the socio-economic context within which avant-garde art made its interventions. Lewis also offered a *substantive* critique of specific movements – principally those, like Dada and Surrealism, that were linked to the 'little magazine' *transition*, edited by Eugène Jolas between 1927 and 1938. During these years *transition* set out to disseminate the most challenging experimental writing being produced in Europe, giving space to writers such as Arp, Beckett, Breton, Doblin, Joyce, Kafka, and Stein. The main influences on Jolas were German Romanticism, Expressionism, Dada, and Surrealism. Although Jolas argued that *transition* was simply a forum for experimental writing, it had close links with the Dadaists and Surrealists, especially in its early days. In a phrase that discloses *transition*'s affinities with Surrealism, Jolas noted that he conceived his work 'as primarily a research into the modern spirit.[12] *Transition*'s editorials and much of the writing it published could almost have been calculated to aggravate Lewis. Jolas's desire to overcome humanity's alienation from the world led him at different moments in his life to primitivism, occultism, and mysticism. Each phase was characterized by the search for a new mythos that could transform modern life.

Lewis's critique of *transition* focused on what he saw as its propagandist conception of art (which he associated mainly with Surrealism) and its nihilist irrationalism. With respect to the first charge, he was wrong, although *transition*'s early association with Surrealism made the mistake an easy one to make. He conflated Surrealism's various strands, ignoring their key disagreements over aesthetics and politics, then he conflated Surrealism with *transition*, presenting it as the mouthpiece for Surrealist doctrine. On this basis, he argued that *transition* sought to bring about revolutionary change and was committed to the idea that art should serve as a conduit for political propaganda. This argument was misleading.[13] In fact, although Jolas admitted that *transition* and the surrealists had been fellow-travellers, his early editorials show that he consistently opposed all notions of *engagement*, and in this respect, his position was close to Lewis's.

But this similarity should not obscure the differences between Jolas and Lewis. Jolas's commitment to a metamorphic art was inseparable from his search for a new conception of the self, a figure who would not just overcome old antinomies but, following Nietzsche, would shatter the prosaic world by immersing itself in the primitivist realm of the pre-logical and the unconscious. The revolution of the word was central to this quest; it disintegrated language and then recast it into new forms, acting as an analogue for the desired recreation of the self. Lewis offered an anti-promethean view of the self as an antidote to this apotheosis of the self:

> My standpoint is that we are creatures of a certain kind, with no indication that a radical change is imminent; and that the most pretentious of our present prophets is unable to do more than promise 'an eternity of intoxication' to those who follow him into less physical, more 'cosmic' regions; proposals made with at least equal eloquence by the contemporaries of Plato. (*TWM* 110)

He was exercised above all by the connection between sensationism and irrationalism in 1920s avant-gardism, arguing that it led to a nihilism that was equally the logical terminus for the vitalism of thinkers such as Nietzsche, Bergson, and James. This charge had a good deal of truth in it. Bergson, for example, tried to short-circuit reason by way of voluntarism ('You must take things by storm: you must thrust intelligence outside itself by an act of will') and James saw reality as 'if not irrational then at least non-rational in its constitution', claiming that it was incommensurable with logic.[14] It is a short step from such sentiments to Aragon's assertion that: 'Nothing can assure me of reality. Nothing, neither the exactness of logic nor the strength of sensation, can assure me that I do not base it on delirium of interpretation.'[15]

Lewis rightly saw a dissolution of cognition in avant-gardes such as Futurism, Dada, and Surrealism, and he saw a link, which he asserted rather than argued, between these movements and philosophers such as Nietzsche and Bergson.[16] For him, no art that urged psychic disequilibrium – a continuation of Rimbaud's *dérèglement de tous les sens* – could offer the emancipation it promised. There is a real disagreement here, which pinpoints the reason for the split of avant-gardism into two broad, and mutually opposed, trajectories. Lewis desired the overthrow of capitalism no less than other avant-gardists but questioned the subordination of art to political imperatives; this questioning arose from his conviction that art was 'a constant stronghold ... of the purest human consciousness' (*TWM* 23) and from his belief that avant-garde art was part of capitalism's cultural economy. But his critique of irrationalism was of a different order; the argument here focused not on the function of *art* but on what version of *reality* was articulated by different kinds of art. For Lewis, art that depicted reality as a chaos valorized instinct and desire. Art that ratified this move seemed to him to abandon its *raison d'être*, to extract from life that which elevated humans to as high a plane as their material nature allowed. His was an active, transfiguring aesthetic, based on the belief that value did not lie in life *qua* life ('life' being a meaningless abstraction, for Lewis) but had to be drawn out from its latent possibilities. So Lewis argued that art should articulate valuations as to what *kind* of life was desirable. He was convinced that art (itself a form of *techne*, of course) should substitute the hard-won achievements of civilization for the blind pulsions of instinct:

> The art impulse reposes upon a conviction that the state of limitation of the human being is more desirable than the state of the automaton; or a feeling of the gain and significance residing in this human fallibility for us. To feel that our consciousness is bound up with this non-mechanical phenomenon of life; that, although helpless in face of the material world, we are in some way superior to and independent of it; and that our mechanical imperfection is the symbol of that. (*WLA* 204)[17]

Instinct is here aligned with mechanism, so that to be a full human being is to refuse the comfort of an existence lived in obedience to the dictates of drives.

How fair was Lewis's critique of the avant-gardes associated with *transition*? It was impaired, I think, by his unwillingness to admit that his hostility to *transition* was at least in part motivated by political considerations. His claim that the conflict was about opposing views of reason, language, and the self was misleading, for his attack was political as much as aesthetic. The socio-political transformation Lewis desired was of a different kind from that sought by the *transitionists*. It responded to a perceived erosion of the public sphere and the consequent threat to the status of the intellectual by arguing for the need of a cultural elite.[18] Rather like the conception of a natural aristocracy outlined at the turn of the century by French intellectuals, whose work Lewis knew well, such an elite was to be created out of all social groups, in this way overcoming the stifling influence of heredity and class.[19] Lewis disbelieved in the natural equality of all individuals, argued that political systems based on this principle vitiated society, and defended the need of cultural hierarchies. His alternative to capitalism envisaged a kind of political despotism, which was operated not by intellectuals but rather by Lenin-like figures under whose aegis intellectuals would be free to engage in creative thought and the production of art.[20]

But Lewis knew that, despite his predilection for the impartial perspective, art and politics were not easily separable, since 'all art must be a political expression to some extent' (*ABR* 351). The truth of this admission emerges in his critique of *transition*, where it becomes clear that it is not just competing accounts of aesthetics that are at stake. Equally important was Lewis's hostility to the communist politics urged, as he saw it, by *transition* and the Surrealists because these politics ran counter to his own. Communism was 'a gospel of the Average' (*E3* 81), and, since most people were inartistic and mediocre, any art that tried to crown them betrayed its function, which was to appeal to and to refine the 'best' elements in society.[21] Lewis was not, I shall argue in Chapter 4, absolutely opposed to communism, but he did want to ensure that it be led by an enlightened minority and not by a philistine mass (see *E3* 80).[22]

42

So the analysis of *transition*, as well as containing a critique of its irrationalism and nihilism, was motivated by political imperatives too: leftist art, it claimed, brings about the hegemony of the herd and topples intellectuals from their position of cultural pre-eminence.

Lewis's assault on the figures associated with *transition* has affinities with his critique of another writer in search of a new mythos: D. H. Lawrence. The latter's animist primitivism (most clearly expressed through his invocations of 'blood consciousness') seemed to Lewis to be just another manifestation of sensationist philosophies. Lawrence, he argued, not only emphasized subjective experience at the expense of public norms but also sought to destroy them by opposing a primitivist consciousness to the rationally conceived values defended by Lewis himself. Lewis read this as the direct outcome of the loss of faith in the idea of 'Europe' after the First World War, arguing that, instead of offering a careful critique of his own culture, Lawrence was simply jettisoning the entire enterprise. Lewis had similarly radical tendencies, as I have argued, but he saw Lawrence's sensationist primitivism as a capitulation 'to the mystical communistic Pan' (*P*. 194). It was little more than a sentimental response to the appeal of the exotic, an appeal that was in itself explicable in terms of European cultural decay.[23] No less than T. S. Eliot (on whom more below), Lawrence was the victim of a romantic agony, and his depreciation of the achievements of the mind belonged to those flux-driven philosophies that were for Lewis emblematic of a 'disintegrating metaphysic' (*RA* 58): 'There is here a principle of decay, a *suicide club* effect: with all the animal pleasures of life, and borrowing from the intellect a destructive intensity, and dragging the intellect with them down into their frantic maelstrom – "In the destructive element immerse"!' (*MWA* 149).

Former collaborators, like Eliot, Joyce, and Pound, posed a different kind of threat. The relations between these writers have been extensively studied.[24] Whether they were a coherent 'group', as Dennis Brown has argued, or a loosely knit collection of individuals who occasionally joined forces, by the mid-1920s their paths had diverged.[25] Lewis made their differences public in uncompromising fashion: he criticized all three writers in print; Eliot and Pound would not be drawn, but Joyce responded in *Work in Progress* (*Finnegans Wake*).[26] Lewis and Pound had collaborated during the *Blast* period, and the letters they exchanged in the years 1914–19 suggest a broad unity of purpose. But their differences, which had hovered in the background, emerged in the 1920s. Lewis saw Pound as obsessed with the past, and he contrasted Pound's romantic predilection for history with his own desire to transform the present. Pound, he argued, was a pasticheur whose fondness for archaism compromised his avant-gardist rhetoric, since he seemed concerned to reanimate what was culturally dead. The novelty of his poetry at the time of *Blast* 'consisted largely in the distance it went *back*, not forward; in archaism, not in new creation' (*TWM* 38). In as far as Lewis *did* recognize Pound's efforts at cultural renovation, he presented them as lacking seriousness. He portrayed Pound as 'a revolutionary simpleton', a naif whose energies were directed to anything that sounded 'radical', and this propensity for stir and disturbance, Lewis suggested, aligned him with Marinetti's cult of action. Pound, furthermore, had failed to see that the cultural situation had changed and that the 'purely "revolutionary" value' (*TWM* 39) of the visual and plastic arts was after the war exhausted. For Lewis, as we have seen, the original avant-garde impulse had entered the cultural mainstream. It was a common coin, casually spent by anyone wishing to clothe themselves in the garb of radical chic, and Pound's refusal to divest himself of such false trappings meant that the history of *Blast* was repeating itself, but this time as farce (see *TWM* 39). The clincher, for Lewis, was Pound's involvement with the composer George Antheil, because it signalled Pound's turn away from the communicative power of language to the emotional register of sound and suggested that he was in thrall to philosophies of time as much as Joyce or Stein (see *TWM* 39, 111–12). This charge enabled Lewis to 'blast' Pound by associating him not only with figures such as Marinetti, Stein, and Valéry but also with an aesthete like Pater, thereby compromising him still further by implying that his real affinities lay with the detested late Victorians.

As so often with Lewis, what was presented as a purely intellectual matter had other dimensions. Lewis and Pound had in 1925 exchanged tetchy letters concerning Pound's involvement in Lewis's affairs, and Lewis seemed increasingly frustrated by what he perceived as Pound's lack of discrimination; Lewis had also quarrelled with Robert McAlmon, who had introduced him to the editors of a new Paris-based journal, *This Quarter*, which never ultimately published his work and which he attacked in *Time and Western Man* as an example of cod avant-gardism; and Lewis was exercised by the fact that inferior writers were being lauded in ostensibly cutting-edge journals. Despite Pound's urgings, Lewis had chosen to remain in London, and his attack on his former ally seems in part to have been motivated by his sense that the artistic community in Paris was exercising too strong a control over post-war European literary culture, a control that threatened him professionally and economically. Lewis's tactic was to insist on the purity of revolutionary art and to accuse his opponents of diluting its creative potency, but it is clear that the differences between him and Pound went beyond aesthetics.[27] Their respective readings of the contemporary cultural situation diverged widely. Lewis saw most post-war avant-gardes as compromised and adopted the persona of the outsider who is sceptical of all groups and ideologies. Pound saw avant-gardism as the best means of promoting artistic radicalism, was active in new movements, and maintained that propaganda was effective: 'DAMN it all manifestos work; count; there are traces of intelligence and disgust, all of which need focus.'[28]

Time and Western Man also contained Lewis's pugnacious dissection of Joyce's work. Lewis and Joyce were often seen by their contemporaries as the most important prose-writers of their generation, and they clearly saw themselves as rivals, referring to and parodying each other's work in their fiction.[29] Lewis's reading of Joyce went to the heart of the differences between their aesthetics. It is significant that it was at the outset of his chapter on Joyce that Lewis made the programmatic statement, almost as though he were clarifying something for himself, that there 'is nothing for it today, if you have an appetite for the beautiful, but *to create new beauty*. You can no longer nourish yourself upon the Past' (*TWM* 81). *Ulysses*, he charged, was 'scraped together into a big variegated heap', and its scrapings were 'the material of the Past' (*TWM* 81).

Joyce, then, was aligned with Pound; he, too, was a man in love with the past whose work embellished the literature of a bygone age through a series of stylistic arabesques. For Lewis, Joyce's achievement was first and foremost of a *technical* order. This line of argument enabled him to claim that Joyce was a conduit, an impressionist who was at the mercy of whatever ideology was dominant at the time.[30] This ideology was, of course, that of the various time philosophies, so Joyce was portrayed as a writer whose work was vitiated by their disintegrative tendencies, in contrast to the concretion and conceptual clarity of the spatial forms favoured by Lewis.

This argument ignored *Ulysses*'s own spatializing tendencies, especially in its use of the city, but, in focusing on Joyce's use of interior monologue, Lewis pointed to the naturalism of the stream-of-consciousness technique, which in his view did not just drive narrative into the *cul-de-sac* of an updated impressionism but threatened to destroy artistic form. For Lewis, it robbed Joyce's writing 'of all linear properties whatever, considered as a plastic thing – of all contour and definition in fact' (*MWA* 99). The emphasis here on plasticity reminds us how strongly Lewis's aesthetic canons depended on the perspective of visual art and specifically on an anti-humanist view of art in which the inorganic took precedence over the living. There was a direct link, he argued, between hellenic artistic canons and the modernist exploration of interiority; the latter simply extended the premisses of the former, since its psychological realism took the Greek concern with depictions of the body *inwards* in an attempt to represent the workings of the mind. He contrasted this kind of writing with the achieved stability and graceful power of eastern hieratic art, which revealed the aesthetic control so precisely described by Eliot in *Four Quartets*: 'The stillness, as a Chinese jar still | Moves perpetually in its stillness.'[31] When he proselytized on behalf of his own aesthetic, the terms he used – coldness, polish, resistance, stiffening, rigidity – revealed his indebtedness to these alternative traditions. Such an aesthetic was always going to devalue the psychologism of writers like Joyce or Woolf, and it goes some way to explaining why Lewis found satire so congenial a mode and why, in a text like *The Apes of God*, parody was his chosen weapon.[32]

Lewis prosecuted his case against Eliot with care. He regarded Eliot, for all the weaknesses he sought to expose, as a genuine thinker. The three linked issues around which his critique of Eliot revolved were his conception of the personality, his account of the writer's relation to history, and his theory of poetry. Lewis's opposition to Eliot on these questions is inseparable from his critique of the cult of scientific impersonality, his attack on behaviourism as a reductive account of human agency, and his commitment to a transformative art. Eliot's views about the dissociation of the poet who creates from the man who experiences are too well known to require much repetition. 'Tradition and the Individual Talent' (1919) saw the artist's work as 'a continual self-sacrifice, a continual extinction of personality'.[33] The self was to be subordinated to something of greater value, and Eliot described the resulting process of depersonalization in scientific terms. The self becomes a 'medium' and what it produces is work that expresses not a personality but another 'medium', that of poetry itself.[34] This anti-Romantic account of creativity drives against the perceived danger of subjectivism, resulting finally in the claim that poetry offers an escape from the self, that it is to be valued in isolation from the poet, and that at its best its emotional charge is impersonal. Eliot's anxieties about an unchecked subjectivism mark much of his critical writing. He was concerned to discover a systematic means of curbing the unruly individual and of ordering a fragmented society. The individual could not be a self-willing source of value (*à la* Nietzsche), and this was why the poet's surrender of himself to a tradition that transcended his contingent existence led to a self-effacement that properly allowed the tradition to assert its claims.[35]

Eliot's insistence on the need for teaching the individual his place in a greater scheme of things paralleled his concern with the poet's grasp of historicity: the individual marked by an exaggerated view of his own importance was in a similar case to the poet lacking a proper sense of the past. In both cases the claims of the individual were rejected not just because they were destabilizing but because they contradicted a canon of religious beliefs. In 1919 this was hardly explicit, but after his conversion to Christianity the connection between Eliot's aesthetics and his religion became apparent, and the earlier desire to escape from the self could be seen as the nascent articulation of a theological view of human wretchedness.[36] In his critique of Eliot in *Men Without Art* (1934) Lewis homed in on this link in Eliot's thought between his Christian view of humanity's fallenness and his theory of poetic impersonality. Lewis dismissed naive claims about human perfectibility, like Eliot finding Hulme congenial in this respect, but his anthropology was not doctrinaire; men and women were in the main not depraved creatures but 'peacable, humane and well-behaved' (*MWA* 74). Nonetheless, though not an impressive species, they occasionally threw up genuinely creative individuals. Eliot's depersonalization argument threatened this creativity by depriving artists of the very power – to transform, to create values, to analyse – that Lewis saw as their *raison d'être*. For Lewis, Eliot's theory led to a dissociation of the poet's beliefs from his works, with the twin result that the subject becomes split and his art collapses into an aestheticism that capitulates to the decadent values of the day.

Lewis did not uphold individualism as an intrinsic good. He was as hostile to cults of the self as Eliot.[37] Rather he defended a structural conception of the self in which subjectivity was associated with cohesiveness, integrity, and stability.[38] Reason was of decisive importance to this conception of the self, since reason alone, he argued, could harmonize the otherwise discordant elements of the psyche and in so doing sustain purposive agency.[39] The self was for Lewis not just a bastion of stability in a fragmenting world but the only place from which he could conceive a philosophical, political, or artistic critique of modernity to emerge. And, for this to be possible, the artist had to be 'identified with his beliefs' (*MWA* 74) and to articulate them with as much vigour as possible, not retreat behind a mask of impersonality. If anything, the artist 'should exaggerate, a little artificially perhaps, his beliefs – rather than leave a meaningless shell behind him, and go to hide in a volatilized hypostasization of his personal feelings' (*MWA* 75).

When Lewis insisted on the active presence of the artist's individuality in the creative process, he was also objecting to Eliot's and Pound's overvaluation of the past, which he saw as mere exoticism (see *L*. 214–15).This orientation to the past was for him the dying breath of a romantic agony at odds with their professed admiration for classicism. In this respect, the contrast between Eliot and Lewis is at its clearest in 'Tradition and the Individual Talent' and *The Caliph's Design*, both published in 1919. Whereas Eliot looked to the civilization of the past for a sustaining vision, Lewis focused on the present. The parable of the caliph who demands that a new city be built overnight is an originary modernist moment in the post-war period but of a kind that is completely opposed to the path chosen by Eliot and Pound. It is a fantasy of creativity *ex nihilo*, a utopian belief in the immediate possibility of a transformative art that, taken out of the studio and into the streets, would be capable of bringing beauty, order, and consciousness to urban life.[40] But it is predicated on the artist's *active* intervention in the historical process (understood as *this* moment, *this* present) and not on a *passive* surrender to the values of the past. As Lewis put it: 'What I am proposing is activity, more deliberate and more intense, upon the material we know and upon our present very fallible stock' (*WLA* 156). In terms of Paul de Man's still useful distinction between our age's two impulses – either to 'modernity' or to 'history' – Lewis at this period threw all his energies behind the former, since, as de Man has it, the anti-historical modernist displays 'a desire to wipe out whatever came earlier, in the hope of reaching at last a point that could be called a true present, a point of origin that marks a new departure'.[41]

Lewis's emphasis on the importance to the artist of articulable beliefs can hardly be stressed too much. It is the connecting thread that runs through his criticisms of Eliot, Joyce, and Pound, his dismissal of claims about the impersonality of science, and his contempt for behaviourist explanations of human life. Lewis's position was that agency of some kind always lay behind human affairs and that concealment of this fact was a ruse of power that made it difficult to grasp the social forces at work and destroyed any notion of accountability. So the artist who adopted a theory of impersonality was undermining the very idea of agency that his creativity required as well as succumbing to a view of the self that he should be combating. For Lewis, artistic creation 'is always a shut-off – and that is to say a *personal* – creation' (*LF* 286).

If Eliot's view of the poet's function was in thrall to a scientism that emphasized impersonality, then behaviourism was its *reductio ad absurdum*: 'The delusion of impersonality could be best defined as that mistake by virtue of which persons are enabled to masquerade as *things*' (*ABR* 34). This view portrayed the self as 'non-human, feelingless, and thoughtless' (*ABR* 35) and could only pull people back into the life of mechanism they should be trying to transcend. This is why a favourite Lewisian contrast was between humans and insects. Communal insect life embodied order but lacked the consciousness that could make it anything else; its perfect organization and beautiful structures were monuments to an evolutionary logic from which the possibility of thought had been expunged. Behaviourism was the theory *par excellence* that translated human existence into mechanistic terms, extinguishing mental life along the way. It focused on action at the expense of consciousness; reduced language use to the formation of word habits on a par with physical movements; and saw all action as the product of stimulus response.[42] If individuals were reducible to their behavioural patterns and if these were just involuntary responses to external stimuli, then the 'self' was nothing more than a machine to be programmed as its rulers saw fit. Redundant in such a model is the concept of a deliberative, willing *mind*. Pointing out that in behaviourism 'there is no metaphysical or non-metaphysical element of personality', Lewis argued that it shattered the possibility of agency by conceiving the human entity as 'an unwieldy and breathless mechanism' in which the mind 'is gradually crushed out' (*ABR* 339–40).[43]

Snooty Baronet (1932) provides a wonderful parody of behaviourism and a revealing commentary on the issues I have been discussing. The novel focuses on the attempt of a behaviourist of sorts – Sir Michael Kell-Imrie, the Snooty Baronet of the title – to free himself from entanglement in a plot (or plots) not of his own making. Kell-Imrie is a naturalist who models himself on the entomologist Fabre, observing people in action and treating them 'upon exactly the same footing as ape or insect' (*SB* 64). Having had some success as an author of popular books on the subject, he is perturbed to find that public perception of him differs from his own self-image as a serious scientist; first, his work is compared to the paintings of the Douanier Rousseau, and he is treated as a picturesque primitivist fascinated by the naive outlook on contemporary life, but then the Douanier is displaced by the image of the baronet, when the reviewers discover his background. Kell-Imrie suspects that his literary agent Humph has leaked this information to the press, and he embarks on a campaign to destroy the persona of the baronet (thus foiling Humph's attempted narrativization of his life), while at the same time escaping the attentions of another character, Val, an aspiring popular novelist who seeks to trap him in a different kind of plot, that of marriage. Kell-Imrie's plan is to bring these two figures together, thereby avoiding their clutches. This plan fails when it turns out that Humph already knows Val and regards her as an aggravating obstacle to his plans for Kell-Imrie. Humph wants to send the baronet to Persia (in a spurious quest for the cult of Mithras), where it has been arranged that he will be kidnapped by bandits in order to generate publicity for his work. The plan ends disastrously when Kell-Imrie, during a skirmish with the bandits, inexplicably turns his gun on Humph and fires at him twice, claiming that the first shot was a pure reflex but insisting that the second shot, which kills Humph, was not only deliberate but also intensely pleasurable. The novel then concludes with a brief coda, an SOS from Kell-Imrie in which he protests against Val's version of events (which seeks to exonerate him) and, describing his actions as systematically those of a behaviourist, demands that he must be judged according to behaviourist principles.

From the outset *Snooty Baronet* signals the parodic nature of its textuality. It parodies the novel as a genre, the behaviourist account of human subjectivity, and the language of cliché through which its characters construct their paper-thin identities. Because the novel has an obtuse first-person narrator, its language is overtly palimpsestic: just behind the narrator's dumb 'perspective' may be discerned the implied viewpoint of the puppet-master who plies the strings. And in its opening paragraphs it announces its metafictional concern with the status of fictional narrative and its implications for the representation of subjectivity:

The face drew back. The door opened. Grasping the forward jamb, a large man thrust out one leg, which was straight and stiff. Pointing the rigid leg downwards, implacably on to the sidewalk, the big man swung outward, until the leg hit terra-firma. The whole bag-of tricks thus stood a second crouched in the door of the vehicle. Then stealthily there issued from its door, erect and with a certain brag in his carriage, a black-suited six-footer, a dollar-bill between his teeth, drawing off large driving gauntlets.

The face was mine. I must apologize for arriving as it were incognito upon the scene. No murder has been committed at No. 1040 Livingston Avenue – I can not help it if this has opened as if it were a gunman bestseller. – The fact is I am a writer: and the writer has so much the habit of the anonymous, that he is apt to experience the same compunction about opening a book in the First Person Singular (caps. for the First Person Singular) as an educated man must feel about commencing a letter with an 'I.' (*SB* 15)

It is precisely the meaning and status of the 'I' that is at issue in *Snooty Baronet*. There is an abrupt shift here from a third-person depiction of the protagonist, which gives a *mechanical* description of the body in motion, to a first-person discussion of the difficulties involved in making certain narrative choices. This shift signals the novel's interest in the vital difference between conceptions of the human as a kind of machine or as a conscious, thinking entity. Despite his confused forays into the realm of thought, Kell-Imrie (like his *doppelganger* Humph) is a grotesque 'wild body', a cousin to the tyro whose keynote is 'vacuity' since 'he is an animated, but artificial puppet, a "novice" to real life'.[44] He is a parody of automatism (the artificial leg functioning as a metonym for the defectiveness both of his mechanistic theories and his own bodily mechanism), just as he himself, reducing people to their actions, parodies human identity in his 'scientific' theories. But the twist in the tale is that the text's characters are themselves all parodies of meaningful human subjectivity, so, in a wonderful paradox, it turns out that behaviourism is all too depressingly (but also amusingly) *true* as an account of how most people are in fact '*things* . . . behaving as *persons*' (*WB* 246), from the baronet himself, who pretends to inhabit a persona modelled on the satirist Samuel Butler whenever he is puzzled or wishes to dissimulate, to Val, with her 'stage-impersonation' of 'the shattering gaiety of the mayfairish highlife drama, as arranged for the suburbs' (*SB* 24), and on to the fantastically prognathous Humph, the 'big carnival doll' (*SB* 59) who allows Lewis to indulge his taste for grotesque excess.

In keeping with its metafictional mode, *Snooty Baronet* turns on the double meaning of the word 'plot', oscillating between the intrigues against others engaged in by the novel's various characters and Kell-Imrie's attempt to write the narrative of his life in terms of his own self-understanding as a scientist, so as to evade the plotting of Humph and Val (*SB* 65, 134). It emerges that the text we are reading is an apologia written by Kell-Imrie to vindicate his actions as a behaviourist and his name as a scientist. This requires him to take responsibility for the murder of Humph in Persia and, in order to explain how this act occurred, to narrate the events that led to it. In a master stroke, Lewis places his puppet in the invidious position of having to provide a psychological account of his actions when his own behaviourist theory denies the plausibility of any such interpretation. *Snooty Baronet* is thus a slippery and paradoxi-cal text, which keeps turning itself inside out; double-voiced throughout, it lets the first-person narrator expose himself in a way that contradicts his own self-perception. Kell-Imrie, for example, seeks a rehabilitation that could be conferred only by his scientific peers, since he claims at all times to have acted in accordance with the precepts of behaviourism, arguing that he should therefore be judged in its terms. But the novel in which he parades his simplistic views discloses the inane nature of behaviourism not just by showing that it cannot account for his actions at all but also by having him write a kind of fictionalized autobiography in which the very issues that behaviourism ignores must assume centre stage: motives, intentions, feelings, thoughts, language.

One of the reasons *Snooty Baronet*'s palimpsestic narrative mode is confusing is that some of Kell-Imrie's indictments sound as though they might be Lewis's own pronouncements, the author choosing to speak through his dummy like a ventriloquist. I think here of his identification with the whale against Ahab, on the grounds that Ahab is 'the spearhead of the Herd', whereas the whale represents 'the private soul' (*SB*

63). This reading of *Moby-Dick* leads Kell-Imrie to assail 'members of those ape-like congeries – gangs, sets, ant-armies, forces of Lilliput, number-brave coteries, militant sheep-clans – fraternities, rotaries and crews' (*SB* 63). For Kell-Imrie, this herd life suggests that humanity is 'compacting with the insects!' with the intention of destroying 'all the noble values' of those seeking 'a higher perfection of living' (*SB* 64). Lewis, of course, had been advancing similar sorts of arguments against *homo stultus* from the early days of *Blast*, so here Kell-Imrie sounds as though he is speaking for his author. There is a crucial difference, however. Kell-Imrie's contempt for mankind leads him to make a compact with nature (against man), which he conceives as a dionysian *energeia* that draws in about equal measure on Lawrence and the Italian Futurists:

> I was ever upon the side of any wild force. I had thrown in my lot for better or for worse with Mother Nature ... (I would sooner repose upon the hundred-mile-per-hour bosom of a destructive wind, or lay me down for a slight siesta upon the tail of a whirlwind, than confide my destiny to the tepid hands of a brother or sister mountebank of the same flesh, spirit, speech, genus and biology as myself.   (*SB* 83)[45]

It is to the life of *sensation* – always Lewis's *bête noire* – that Kell-Imrie is devoted: 'To *feel*, I take it, is to *live* ... What I feel to-day, I think tomorrow' (*SB* 99). It turns out, then, that, when the baronet articulates views held by his author, he does so (fittingly in a novel built round the notion of unthinking behaviour as parodic mimicry) for all the wrong reasons.

Kell-Imrie's behaviourism mechanizes the realm of nature that he extols, and in this way he evacuates human existence of conscious intentionality. Lewis's opposition of 'art' to 'life' rested on the conviction that, even if human beings are merely creatures idiosyncratically endowed with consciousness, then this still posed the question whether we should use 'this verbal machinery, this dialectic, to *humanize* ourselves, or to *dehumanize* ourselves', whether reason, in short, should be seen as nothing more than a refinement 'of the mechanical animal condition ... a "word-habit," which we certainly should have been better without', or 'as a *gift*' (*MWA* 232–3). Kell-Imrie's perception of himself and others as machines marks him as a behaviourist enemy of thought. He is ridiculed as a bluff nonentity, a Tyronic imbecile whose limited intelligence leaves him barely able to cope with ideas. He is, by his own admission,

> preternaturally obtuse . . . a kind of inspired moron' (*SB* 65). In a belated self-examination he concludes: 'In all but purely mechanical things, of an external order (that is my strong suit) I am a profoundly dense person, I cannot help it. Mine is anything but a quick mind. – This may be why I am a *behaviourist*. If there is such a thing as a 'soul', I at all events have never been able to catch it on the hop. (*SB* 134)

Kell-Imrie, in short, is cut from the same cloth as those he contemns. His behaviourist theory, moreover, provides him with no basis for making the kinds of discriminations between people (the 'noble' versus the 'herd') that he claims are so important. Kell-Imrie is, in fact, a mirror image of Humph, is no less a machine than his grotesque double, a point brought home to him during the episode of the hatter's automaton just after he has realized that in his battle for power with Humph and Val it is unclear who is the monster and who the Frankenstein.[46] The scene with the hatter's automaton leads Kell-Imrie to question, first, whether he is any more real than the mechanical puppet in the shop window and, second, with a nod to Berkeley, whether people have a continuous existence when there is nobody to observe them. The one speculation follows on from the other, since a clockwork toy like the hatter's automaton is inert (lifeless, dead) when its mechanism is not causing it to jerk its limbs about; its *raison d'être*, one might say, is to *act*, is to be impelled into motion by a feat of concealed engineering that fixes the pattern for the movements that follow. This is uncomfortably close both to the behaviourist account of *human* action and, of course, to the third-person description of Kell-Imrie with which the novel began.[47]

If human beings are machines biologically programmed to respond to stimuli, with word-habits just a sophisticated gimmick that has evolved to help facilitate the requisite responses, then they can be reduced to the sum total of their actions. On this view, there is little difference indeed between an automaton and a person; the suggestion that puppet-like creatures like Humph or Kell-Imrie might have no existence outside their actions is simply the *ne plus ultra* of behaviourist doctrine. So it is that Lewis, with real acuity, grants his cipher insight into the 'inner meaning of "Behaviour," as a notion' (*SB* 138) only when he himself begins to *think* in a conscious way:

> As the man at my side observed me putting on my hat, I was for the first time placed in the position *of the dummy!* I saw all round Behaviour as it were – for the first time. I knew that *I* was not always existing, either: in fact that I was a fitful appearance. That I was apt to *go out* at any moment, and turn up again, in some other place – like a light turned on by accident, or a figure upon a cinematographic screen. (*SB* 138)

In his closing SOS Kell-Imrie describes the episode with the hatter's automaton as a turning point in his life, but if this is so it is unclear why he asserts that he will 'continue *to behave* as you have seen me behaving throughout these pages, and as all true Behaviourists *must* behave' (*SB* 252). If he has seen all-round behaviour and grasped that it makes a dummy of him, why does he stick to what he himself describes as an 'implacable doctrine' (*SB* 251)? Lewis, I think, makes sure he has the last laugh on his caricatural victim by granting him a glimmer of insight and no more: behaviourism has exacted its price, and its marionette is not permitted to escape the mechanisms that work it. This is the very essence of caricature. In J. A. Symonds's terms, it 'renders its victim ludicrous or vile by exaggerating what is defective, mean, ignoble in his person, indicating at the same time that some corresponding flaws in his spiritual nature are revealed by them'.[48] If we substitute 'psychological' for 'spiritual' here, we have a fine description of Lewis's procedure in *Snooty Baronet*, and in a work of this kind one does not let one's ludicrous victim off lightly. By pushing behaviourism to an absurd extreme, the text reveals what Kell-Imrie can only haltingly speculate about – namely, that it is 'mad to be a *Behaviourist*' and that he is in fact 'as mad as a hatter, as mad as a Hatter's Automaton' (*SB* 251).

What, then, of the second shot he fires at Humph, the shot that gives him such intense aesthetic pleasure? He is explicit about this: 'I do not believe that any shot ever gave me so much pleasure as that second one, at old Humph's shammyleathered, gussetted stern, before he rolled off his pony and bit the dust. (The first was not great fun – it was almost automatic. I scarcely knew I was doing it. But I knew all about the second)' (*SB* 235). The gap between the two shots points to the absolute distinction between a reflex action and one undertaken as a result of conscious deliberation. This is why Kell-Imrie can reflect with glee that the 'second one was *a beauty!*' (*SB* 240). Humph's death is significant because he has been portrayed as a more obtuse version of Kell-Imrie himself; he is a 'well-drilled' and 'lousy little automaton' who is 'not real' (*SB* 60) and whose existence warns the baronet of his own lack of reality. In consciously choosing to do away with this mechanical *Doppelgänger*, Kell-Imrie proclaims his revolt against the puppet-like existence to which behaviourism has condemned them both. The second shot, I would suggest, is the outward sign of an interior life that is just beginning to show its face. Admittedly, the aesthetic sense disclosed by this act is of a rudimentary Tyronic kind, but in a satiric portrait Lewis would never have allowed a grotesque elemental just emerging from his swaddling clothes more insight than this. Like all tyros, Kell-Imrie is simply left to bask 'in the sunshine of [his] own abominable nature' (*WLA* 188).

4

From Classicism to Satire

Lewis's criticisms of modernists and avant-gardists have in the past led critics to focus on his links with the post-war revival of classicism.[1] There is warrant for this view. Although Lewis did not in the early 1920s abandon his belief in the continuing validity and viability of artistic experimentation, he did contend against the irrationalism that he saw as a dominant feature of the post-war scene, and this viewpoint inclined him towards classicism. But one needs to be careful when invoking this term, which means so many different things. There was certainly a return to classicism in France and England after the First World War, but, though its general lineaments may easily be identified, it took a range of forms. Principally associated with a call to order, a defence of intellectual elites, a distaste for democracy, and an anxiety about the growth of mass society, it took in the Catholic royalism of *Action Française*; the turn to antiquity by painters like Picasso, Severini, and de Chirico; the attempt to temper avant-gardism by combining it with classicism in journals such as Pierre Reverdy's *Nord-Sud* (1917–19); Julien Benda's defence of disinterested speculative thought in opposition to politicized intellectuals; Pound's search for inspiration in the classical models of the past; and Eliot's elaboration of a theory of tradition.[2]

Lewis has been portrayed as a defender of classicism, and his work has been aligned with some of the tendencies outlined above. But this view misapprehends the extent of his alleged commitment to classicism. Lewis could claim that 'any little organization that Europe has ever had has been centred in France, and symbolized by her classicist culture' (*ABR* 313), but he could also write that 'the best West European art has never been able to be "classic", in the sense of achieving a great formal perfection. The nature of our semi-barbaric cultures has precluded that. So in that connection the "romantic" is the real thing' (*TWM* 9). *Blast* had defended northern barbarity, seeing in its vigour a corrective to southern excess (Marinetti) and to salon tastefulness (the Royal Academy and Roger Fry). To recent critics it seems that the goal of post-war classicism was 'to evacuate the picture of any specific reference to the modern world and to invoke instead that side of art connected with tradition and continuity'.[3] For Lewis, it was compromised by this nostalgia for the past.

Most discussions of post-war classicisms conceive them in terms of a reactionary counter-modernism, a retreat from avant-gardism to the conservative values of order, authority, and tradition. Lewis complicates this picture because his politics in the 1920s were illiberal while his aesthetics were avant-garde, even if his view of what constituted avant-gardism put him at odds with almost everybody else. His pre-war Vorticism had been at the forefront of English abstraction, but, as I argued in the previous chapter, Lewis believed new initiatives were required after the war and that experimentation should not be fetishized. This meant that the impulse to new creativity had to be encouraged while uncritical exaltation of it had to be resisted. Perhaps even more importantly, the equation of artistic vanguardism with left-wing political beliefs was for Lewis a false equation. Political radicalism had to be separated from artistic radicalism not just because in his view politics corrupted the autonomy of the aesthetic but because it was possible to hold anti-left-wing views and yet still be committed to reform of the arts. Lewis's task in *Time and Western Man* was to differentiate art that 'has attempted something definitely new' from art that passed itself off as such but was in reality either traditional but lightly spiced with the new or looked novel because it was reverting 'to standards or forms that are very ancient, and hence strange to the European' (*TWM* 24).[4]

Lewis was an anomaly in 1920s debates over romanticism and classicism, for he refused the easy terms of the binary it instantiated. Certainly he sided on intellectual grounds with the basic tenets of classicism: the flawed nature of the human creature, seen as a finite and limited being; the defence of reason; the view that art creates order, harmony, and proportion. Romanticism, in contrast, he associated with solipsism. Romanticism has, of course, long been indicted for its promethean hubris, *Frankenstein* offering the great internal critique of its fantasies of perfectibility and omnipotence. Classicism is characteristically a response to the disorder it fears such idealism will foment, urging in its stead the value of moderation and insisting that the dream of self-overcoming will always be tragic in its consequences. Lewis's aesthetic can be aligned with these sentiments. He did, after all, defend an art 'of the most extreme and logically exacting definition' (*TWM* 109) that aspired to 'the noble exactitude and harmonious proportion of the european, scientific ideal' (*TWM* 110), arguing that the alternative was chaos:

> All compact of common sense, built squarely upon Aristotelian premises that make for permanence – something of such a public nature that all eyes may see it equally – something of such a universal nature, that to all times it would appear equal and the same – such is what the word *classic* conjures up. But at *romantic* all that falls to pieces. There is nothing but a drifting dust, a kaleidoscope of undirected particles, which no logical pattern holds together, or only a very feeble one. (*MWA* 153)

And this view of classicism was bound up with Lewis's advocacy of the external aesthetic that informed his account of satire. Claiming that the *'external* approach to things belongs to the "classical" manner of apprehending' (*MWA* 103), he argued that it is 'the shell of the animal that the plastically-minded artist will prefer' (*MWA* 99) because in satire 'the eye is supreme' (*MWA* 103).

To take all this at face value is to see Lewis as an ardent classicist. But I have already pointed out that he acknowledged the genuineness of at least some romantic art. As early as the Vorticist phase, moreover, he was championing Shakespeare as his emblem of an aesthetic that conjoined comedy and tragedy, arguing that in future northern art would 'partake of this insidious and volcanic chaos' (*B1* 38). Lewis had always argued that the impetus to create was 'primitive' and that the products of art's transmuting impulse combined energy with stability. A key passage from *The Caliph's Design* asserted: 'The artist's function is to create – to make something; *not to make something pretty*, as dowagers, dreamers, and art-dealers here suppose. In any synthesis of the universe, the harsh, the hirsute, the enemies of the rose, must be built in for the purposes as much of a fine aesthetic, as of a fine logical structure' (*WLA* 153).[5] Lewis, then, is not consistent in his views about classicism and romanticism, and there are, I think, two reasons for this, one historical, the other metaphysical. The historical dimension to Lewis's scepticism about classicism is inseparable from his analysis of the post-war world, which in his view had entered a transitional phase in which shared norms were disintegrating. He argued that the arts attendant on this crisis were capitulating to it, were avatars of the chaos they described. But classicism, he argued, was strictly unviable in a fragmenting society, since it could only operate meaningfully in stable, homogeneous societies where artistic criteria and cultural standards were broadly held in common. The conditions required for such art were absent in a post-war period shattered by the collapse of pre-war certainties and sceptical about the alternatives.[6] Classical values might be intact in some abstract Platonic sense but had been compromized by history. Yet it is clear that there is more than a whiff of scepticism about the plausibility of these values in Lewis's writing, an anxiety that order does not inhere in reality at all but is *imagined* there, and this points to the metaphysical aspect of his doubts about classicism. The spectre menacing his thinking is that of a disenchanted world in which human valuations are arbitrary, bearing no necessary relation to the reality they ostensibly describe. From this perspective, classicism is redundant not only because it has no purchase on contemporary history but also, and more damagingly, because its fundamental tenets are philosophically unsustainable.[7]

The practical impossibility of classicism, combined with a deep-rooted scepticism, led Lewis to transmute his external aesthetic into a theory of satire. He had always been a satirist, of course, but it was not till the late 1920s that satire emerged as a dominant mode in his writing, as attested by works such as *The Apes of God*, *Snooty Baronet*, *The Doom of Youth*, and *The Roaring Queen*. Satire enabled him to combine metaphysics with history: his pessimism about human life melded with his reading of modernity to produce a writing that portrayed Western society in its death throes and that set out to bring 'human life more into contempt each day' by demonstrating its 'futility and absurdity' (*MWA* 183). He provided the clearest account of his view of satire in *Men Without Art* (1934). The book argued that contemporary society had degenerated so far that art *had* to be satiric. But, whereas satire tended to be conceived as a tool of reproof and instruction, his view of it was non-ethical and non-political. Aligned with 'the "truth" of the intellect' (*MWA* 100), satire was associated with an objectivism that took no sides and ignored emotional sentiment: 'Satire is *cold*, and that is good! It is easier to achieve those polished and resistant surfaces of a great *externalist* art in Satire . . . There is a stiffening of Satire in everything good . . . the non-human outlook must be there . . . to correct our soft conceit' (*MWA* 99).

This view of satire was continuous with the stylization and dehumanization defended by Lewis in the days of *Blast*. It allowed him to present externalist satire as the logical corollary of classicism and to oppose both to the romanticism inherent in contemporary modernism. But Lewis's version of satire had deeper roots. It took as its target the conditions of the present, but it also articulated a general sense of life's meaninglessness. Thanks to the ambiguous gift of consciousness, human beings were capable of self-reflection, but this only brought them awareness of their entrapment in a corporeality they could never transcend. He had argued in *The Wild Body* that our animality renders us absurd because the root of comedy lies 'in the sensations resulting from the observations of a *thing* behaving like a person', and people 'are all *things*, or physical bodies, behaving as *persons*' (*WB* 246). Satire extends this insight, generalizing it to embrace human existence as a whole. It describes

an 'expressionist' universe which is reeling a little, a little drunken with an overdose of the 'ridiculous' – where everything is not only tipped but *steeped* in a philosophic solution of the material, not of mirth, but of the intense and even painful sense of the absurd . . . by stretching a point, no more, we can without exaggeration write *satire* for *art* – not the moralist satire directed at a given society, but a metaphysical satire occupied with mankind. (*MWA* 232)

Lewis's metaphysical satire was primarily concerned with subjectivity. Pessimistic about most people's capacity to fulfil their potential, Lewis was haunted by visions of their entrapment in blind mechanism. The real nightmare was not that individuals were slothful, since this might change, but that they were determined, for this was unalterable. In his various satiric portraits of subjectivity he deployed his marionettes to suggest that in some cases there may be no cartesian ghost in the machine at all: to be human was to be wound up like a clockwork device and propelled into motion until the mechanism stopped. The essay 'Inferior Religions' paraded before us Lewis's 'wild bodies', which unthinkingly latch onto some fetish or other and are described as 'shadows of energy, not living beings', for their 'mechanism is a logical structure and they are nothing but that' (*WB* 234–5). Lewis tended to portray those he wanted to satirize as lifeless puppets of this sort, but he was capable of extending this line of thinking beyond obvious targets of ridicule. His discussion of admired writers such as Flaubert and Gautier, for example, makes them sound as much victims of mechanism as any of the Breton 'primitives' discussed in 'Inferior Religions'.[8]

In *The Apes of God* the two forms of satire described above – metaphysical and historical – came together, the writer pouring scorn on contemporary decadence, yes, but revealing at the same time the existential horror at the whole *comédie humaine* that lurks beneath the surface of his prose. The circumstances surrounding the publication of *The Apes of God* shed a good deal of light on its concerns. Lewis had throughout the 1920s embraced for polemical purposes the stance of the outsider who assaults the allegedly dominant tendencies of the day. This was in part a rhetorical matter; he was constructing a 'persona' that would enable him to write effectively as critic and satirist.[9] But in many respects he felt himself to be a cultural outsider. He was convinced that the loose network of friends and acquaintances labelled 'Bloomsbury' had too much influence. He believed that in the aftermath of the war literary culture was dominated by nostalgia for the past, a tendency

63

that gave rise to painting and writing of the salon scale, which was, in turn, hostile to the vigour of his own favoured aesthetic. At the same time, the reputation of a writer such as Joyce was gaining ground while Lewis was mainly known as a critic and controversialist.[10] Furthermore, his approach to public polemic made him enemies: he had uneasy relationships with publishers, could not always find outlets for his writing, found himself isolated, and came to believe that various factions were conspiring either to prevent his work from entering the public domain or to deny it the oxygen it needed (in the form of articles and reviews) to survive.

These backgrounds are important because they show how difficult was Lewis's cultural and economic position at this time, how much was riding on the publication of *The Apes*, and also the extent to which its satire was bound up with personal grievances as well as public issues. When the editor of the *New Statesman* suppressed a positive review of the privately printed *Apes* by Roy Campbell, it seemed to him that everything he had claimed about the inward-looking world of literary London (the subject of his satire) was being amply demonstrated. In his energetic response, the pamphlet *Satire and Fiction*, Lewis defended his satiric approach, but the controversy really highlighted the degree to which he felt himself to be a martyr to a dying out class that still exercised a good deal of cultural power, and this aspect of the furore occasioned by the publication of *The Apes* points to the institutional context in which the book needs to be placed.[11] Lewis, of all the major modernists writing at the time, was in the most precarious institutional position. Compared with Eliot, Joyce, and Woolf, say, who had loyal patrons and strong relationships with particular presses, he was a man adrift.[12] *The Apes*, a self-confessedly partisan text, is as much a testament to its author's professional and personal frustrations as it is a general indictment of a class and its cultural values.[13] The *ressentiment* that Lewis identified as the source of his apes' spurious creativity – their envy of the superior talent of those they mimicked and travestied – played an inverted role in the writing of this massive bonfire of the vanities: Lewis's anger at the success of those who in his view did not deserve it burns through the text.

The Apes of God is a belated war novel, which focuses not on the war itself but on its after-effects as seen in 1920s society. In his introduction to the twenty-fifth anniversary edition of *The Apes* (1955) Lewis emphasized the significance of the war to it, describing the 1920s as a 'shell-shaken society' dominated by a 'carnivalesque' atmosphere.[14] Looking back on the period, he claimed that it was marked by three broad responses to the 'shattering events' of the war: an excessive liberalism, in which social bonds and cultural values were loosened; a critical spirit, which aimed to expose earlier pretensions; and sexual inversion. These shifts threatened to dislocate society altogether; they inaugurated a time of misrule during which the world had been turned upside down. Lewis, as we have seen, was concerned throughout the 1920s to defend a hierarchy of values that he saw being destroyed by the combined effect of subjectivist time philosophies, the globalization of a standardized culture, and processes of democratization, all of which were in his view destroying the public realm and diminishing the potency of the autonomous individual, factors that pointed to 'the desirability of a new, and if necessary shattering criticism of "modernity," as it stands at present' (*P.* 106).[15] *The Apes* was intended as just such a shattering criticism, taking as its main focus the artistic world with which Lewis was most familiar. It was a bleaker, harsher update on the satire of the pre-war bourgeois-bohemians earlier cauterized in *Tarr*.

The text's indictment of this aspect of post-war society is both familiar and easily summarized. *The Apes* portrays an artistic milieu dominated by minor figures who lack talent and who are thus forced to imitate those who have it while they seek to deny their own derivativeness. The poetasters lampooned in its pages are effete and enervated; their work and their lives parody the energy and power that should lie behind serious creativity. Thus they are fitting symbols of a wider social decadence, that 'moronic inferno of insipidity and decay' that for Lewis marked 'the trough between the two world-wars' (*RA* 183). *The Apes*, then, does not just attack individuals, but sees them as part of a wider social malaise, which it identifies as a desire to regress to the comforting pleasures of infancy (troped in the novel as a return to the nursery); a voluntary self-enslavement to group fashions and herd instincts; a refusal to acknowledge the far-reaching nature of social change, which manifests itself in the upholding of sham-antique values that have no purchase on post-war realities but exist as pure façade; and, finally, a defensive and incestuous reliance on the coterie, which functions to protect those who are inside and to repel those who wish to criticize from the outside.[16] The book was driven by two linked charges: that real writers and artists were being displaced by shambolic amateurs, with the result that cultural standards were collapsing; that this process was being aided and abetted by a decadent ruling class whose economic and social supremacy was on the wane. *The Apes* was thus an explicitly political text, as Lewis was later to assert: 'All social satire is political satire. And in the case of my solitary book of Satire, that is the answer too. If anyone smarted because of it . . . they smarted for a political reason. As a class, they had outstayed their usefulness and had grown to be preposterous parasites' (*RA* 57).

The political aspect of the novel is clear from its opening with a grotesque parody of the seeming immortality of a Victorian matriarch and its concluding with the dashed hopes of the General Strike of 1926. *The Apes* begins with a funereal description of the Lady Fredigonde, whose life spans the Victorian era and beyond, and whose existence symbolizes that period's refusal to die out while her decrepitude signals its obsolescence. The bulk of the novel, aptly described by one critic as 'a picaro romance', is concerned with the exposure of the artistic world of bohemian London as seen through the eyes of a bewildered neophyte, Daniel Boleyn, who has usually been taken to be modelled on Stephen Spender but who resembles a mentally stillborn Stephen Dedalus even more.[17] Under the tutelage of a mocking trickster-figure (Horace Zagreus), himself merely the spokesman for the off-stage popish figure of Pierpoint, Boleyn embarks on a fool's progress through this dumbed-down underworld, comprehending nothing. Parodying the *Divine Comedy*, *The Apes* has Zagreus play Virgil to Boleyn's Dante, leading him neither to wisdom nor to beatitude but rather to baffled dismay. Zagreus's Pierpointian analysis of the cultural scene is essentially Lewis's: the proper hierarchy of artistic values has been inverted, so that subjective and private norms have displaced objective and public ones; the cultural milieu has been overrun by moneyed individuals and self-seeking coteries who distract the public from the work of real artists; these groups of dilettantes lack the talent, discipline, and originality to create art, thus they borrow from others, unwittingly parodying and debasing genuine creativity. Art is reduced to the tasteful gentility of the salon, the voyeuristic pleasures of the gossip sheet, and the mind-numbing needs of public opinion. Having prosecuted this case at great length, the novel despatches Boleyn and concludes with a brief coda: during the General Strike of 1926 society is temporarily paralysed and there is the suggestion that the old order may be swept away, but this tantalizing possibility is negated by the opportunistic alliance forged between the ageless Zagreus and the doughty Fredigonde, whose long overdue death appears to occur immediately afterwards.

A summary of this kind cannot begin to do justice to a work of this scale and complexity, nor does it say anything about *The Apes'* extraordinary style and its chiasmic narrative mode. These two facets of the novel take it far beyond straight satire. Certainly it lambastes a culture for its self-abasement before 'decadent' values, but its assault on the London art world is in the end less interesting (as cultural diagnosis) than its concern with the problem of writing and the nature of subjectivity in a profane world. Almost entirely structured around the principle of regress, it reveals all 'realities' to be the simulacra of some prior entity or truth that can never be discovered. This of course raises questions about the text's own point of view, and, in exploring the basis on which satire may be predicated, it is arguably more pessimistic about these questions than about the objects of its satire, since it appears to conclude that genuine individuality and artistry are always beyond reach: all, as the book's title has it, are God's apes, thus the text reverses itself. It is revealing, for example, that it offers no alternatives to the debased values it excoriates. No one is upheld as an exemplar of the kind of art that might count as genuine. The author, ironized as 'our solitary high-brow pur-sang Lewis', makes a fleeting appearance, but his writings are described by Zagreus as *'teiloperationen'* (*AG* 419). Lewis himself, it seems, though able to see this artistic milieu as a shadow dance, is unable to provide it with substance. Yet this implication of the author in the farce he derides – the satirist satirized – is part and parcel of the text's recursive structure: eventually, the puppet-master must himself be exposed. So *The Apes* stands revealed as an ambivalent, Janus-faced work, which looks two ways at once: at the objects of its campaign of ridicule and at the marshall conducting the campaign – Wyndham Lewis, 'personal appearance artist' (*MWA* 95).[18]

Lewis 'appears' in this text in more ways than one, however. In keeping with the time-honoured strategies of satire, *The Apes* glories in excess and exaggeration, above all that of its own language, and by this means it proclaims its author's vibrant presence on every page. Condemned as pale shadows of real creative individuals, the victims of his satire are made to look ridiculous by the *contrast* between Lewis's surcharged style and their bland mimicry. *The Apes* proliferates tropes so as to juxtapose unusual images and ideas, stretches unexpected metaphors to snapping point in its desire to push absurdity as far as language will allow, and punctures its victims' pretensions through rhetorical overkill. The result is a self-advertising, performative style that overwhelms its objects of ridicule even as it trumpets the gulf between their *lack* of ability and the writer's over-abundant possession of it. In a book claiming that the artistic culture of the day is dominated by second-rate imitators and pasticheurs, this style flaunts its own inimitability.

One could give any number of examples to illustrate this point, but I shall limit myself to the text's depictions of character because of the link between its caricature of the buffoons it ridicules and its exploration of the wider implications for subjectivity of its satiric approach. Clarifying this approach in *Rude Assignment*, Lewis described *The Apes* as a 'gargantuan puppet-show' (*RA* 215), aligning his writing with the pictorial satire of the cartoonist David Low.[19] In some instances, Lewis chose to portray his puppets as overgrown babies whose brains, such as they were, had not even begun to catch up to their outsized bodies (Boleyn and Whittingdon being the most obvious examples); in other cases, he concentrated on their lack of identity (Kein, Ratner) or their inveterate role-playing (the Finnian-Shaws). Consider this description of the dilettante artist Dick Whittingdon:

The floor shook slightly: a confused disturbance occurred immediately without. Then the door rocked, there was a sound of blows, and then one loud distinct rap cut them short . . . For a moment there was a cessation of these sounds of a disquieting irregularity. But the door slowly came ajar, it seemed to hesitate: a further fumbling occurred outside: next it flew briskly open and an enormous bronzed and flannelled figure burst in, exclaiming in deafening point-blank discharge:

'Hallo Aunt! May I come in?'

A lush vociferating optimism, hearty as it was dutiful, was brutally exploded in her direction: a six-foot two, thirty-six-summered, army-and-public-school, Winchester and Sandhurst, firework – marked 'boyish high spirits' – simply went off; but only as a preliminary demonstration, as a benefaction by-the-way to the world-at-large.

This huge ray of sunshine hung fulgurously in the doorway. All towering bright-eyed juvenility, Dick was respectfully backward in coming too rapidly forward. But at last . . . he started himself off. Flinging forward tremendous feet to left and to right, he got well into the place, piecemeal, in jolly sprawling fragments, and looked round with the near-sighted surprise of a rogue elephant who had perhaps burst into a parish church.   (*AG* 33–4)

This 'pelting' style is classic Lewis.[20] In the first paragraph, agency is displaced from the human subject onto the inanimate objects he clumsily, violently negotiates; the shaking floor and the hesitating door appear to be alive here, whereas the body that finally effects entry is just an exploding mechanical contrivance. This pathetic toy has no control over its own actions; introduced by a passive construction ('was . . . exploded'), its release of energy is involuntary ('simply went off'). Whittingdon's 'reality' is further undermined by Lewis's use of parodic cliché to depict him, his proliferation of hyphenated adjectival phrases, and his characteristic tactic of delaying the introduction of the subject of the sentence, which thus subordinates the protagonist even more. Whittingdon's immaturity is signalled by his inability to control his body, which, in satiric reversal of the expected relation, seems to have his mind well in hand. Jerking spasmodically across domestic interiors like a jack-in-the-box wrenched from its casing, his body appears to dismember him even as it propels him forward.

A different kind of linguistic excess is at work in the following description of Julius Ratner, the 'split-man' whose 'automatic writing' is derided as nothing more than the excretions of another self, the 'spook' he faces 'in the looking-glass' (*AG* 169):

> This highbrow-sub-sheik of the slum had been the triste-est Tristan tricked out in the dirtiest second-hand operatic wardrobe – the shoddiest Don Giovanni – the most ludicrous Young Lochinvar – the most squalid Sorel, he had been the most unprepossessing sham Ratnerskolnikoff without the glamour of poverty of the Russian (because of his healthy business sense) – he had been the Judas without the kiss (for no fairly intelligent Christ would ever trust him) with a grim apocryphal lech for a Magdalen – he was the Childe Harold without the Byron collar, and worse, sans genius – the Childe Roland without the Dark Tower, or corpse-like Adolphe, a Manfred or a Zara, risen again, but who could only half-live – the eternal imitation-person in a word, whose ambition led him to burgle all the books of Western romance to steal their heroes' expensive outfits for his musty shop – the split-man of another tale. (*AG* 153–4)

In a passage such as this, Lewis achieves his satiric effect by relentlessly piling up images of potency, comparing Ratner with a wide range of dark but vigorous forebears, and then undercutting the comparisons by presenting his gull as *lacking* the very qualities that marked these already ambiguous figures. Ratner is not just metaphorically buried by this cascading prose, he is paradoxically defined, such as he is, as its negative; an intertextual cipher whose subjectivity is pure mimicry and whose art is a parody of what he does not understand, he is the pseudo-artist *par excellence*. A typically dry observation of Eliot's seems relevant here: 'I have no good word to say for the cultivation of automatic writing as the model of literary composition; I doubt whether these moments *can* be cultivated by the writer; but he to whom this happens assuredly has the sensation of being a vehicle rather than a maker.'[21] Lewis's language draws on the cultural legacy he invokes in descriptions like this in order to display his ability to reinvigorate it, to 'make it new', and this act of self-assertion belittles the hapless Ratner still further.

This is not a matter of style alone, however; it goes to the metaphysical core of *The Apes of God*, with its pessimistic view of human identity. Ratner offers a particularly clear example of ersatz subjectivity, but this is no less true of the novel's other protagonists. Behind Boleyn stands Zagreus, and behind him hovers the always absent Pierpoint. Boleyn is Zagreus's ape just as the latter is Pierpoint's (himself a pale shadow of a possible deity), and both characters represent the progressive vitiation of an original truth; Zagreus misapprehends Pierpoint's teachings, but Boleyn, who is a further step from the source, is the moron who cannot begin to understand them. And this principle of regress applies to almost all the figures satirized in the book. The artists Zagreus presents to Boleyn are latecomers who batten parasitically on the work of strong precursors; the Finnian-Shaws are arrivistes who clothe themselves in cod eighteenth-century trappings; and the world of artistic bohemia is emblematic of a desire to return to the primitive satisfactions of the nursery. So it is fitting that, when Zagreus dismisses Ratner, he replaces him with a more extreme caricature of apehood:

> All his instincts are topsy-turvy – where Ratner was merely *split*, this one is inverted and introverted – he does not know what truth means – he has no standards *whatever!* . . . Ratner . . . was a minor Satan perverted by his little literary vanity, and so really a sort of Ape of God rather than a minor Satan. But this one is a perfect minor Satan of the first water (no pretences whatever of intellect). (*AG* 635–6).

The Apes' characters are grotesque caricatures animated by Lewis's effervescent prose. Yet the disjunction between the lifelessness of its subjects and the energy with which they are depicted points to the novel's ambivalence about the issues it raises. Horace Zagreus is the embodiment of this ambivalence; his forename recalls the satirist and the writer of the *Ars Poetica*, while his surname aligns him with the shape-shifting god of transformations, who is linked in Greek myth with the playful Dionysius.[22] Zagreus is contradictory because he aims to restore order to the carnivalesque realm, in this sense posing as a lawgiver, but deploys many of the methods that belong to it.[23] Trickster and fool combined, he is a sower of discord – a prankster, mimic, and ironist – and a messenger from another world who lays down the law in a series of hectoring 'encyclicals' and 'broadcasts'. The trickster is always a crosser of thresholds and a disturber of conventions, of course, in this sense acting as a destabilizing agent, but he can also create new boundaries, structures, and forms, thereby functioning as the 'divine culture hero' identified by Paul Radin.[24] Zagreus, a representative of the limen, straddles the world of the apes and the ideal realm for which Pierpoint is the spokesman, presenting himself half-jokingly as Plato to the latter's Socrates.[25]

But Zagreus is himself just a shadow of Pierpoint, a figure mocked as much as mocking, whose pretensions are in turn traduced: 'All this taking you about to show you *The Apes!* Well of course they *are* Apes. What however in Jesus' name are you but an Ape and Horace Zagreus himself he is the worst Ape of the lot! Does he not take all his ideas from Pierpoint?' (*AG* 502).[26] Pierpoint's absence, like that of Beckett's Godot, is significant here, because, aside from his opening letter to Zagreus, he is known only through the ministry of his disciples, who travesty his message. The role in which he appears, he claims, is 'a caricature of some constant figure in the audience, rather than what I am (in any sense) myself. Or, to make myself clearer, it is my opposite' (*AG* 134). As in the *via negativa* of the apophatic tradition to which this text is indebted, he can be known only by what he is not. Yet Pierpoint is himself no plenipotentiary – and certainly not a deity – but rather the conduit for a viewpoint that seems to have little purchase on contemporary reality, hence the impossibility of his ever appearing on stage. The opening words of his first 'encyclical' are in this respect of great importance:

> In my review of this society, especially with regard to its reaction upon art, I rather insist upon than seek to slur over the fact that I am a party. But it is from amongst the parties that the acting judge is ultimately chosen. Where else should you get him from? The supreme judge is constantly absent. What we call a judge is a successful partizan [*sic*]. It is on account of the superior percentage of truth in the composition of your glosses that your statement is erected into a standard'. (*AG* 125–6).

Pierpoint disavows the authority that others attribute to him, making it clear not only that he is an interested participant in the conflicts he describes but also that they take place in a post-lapsarian world from which God has absconded.[27] And in as much as Pierpoint is an absent presence then God is still less reachable, a fact noted by the former when he claims that there 'is no universal consent upon the subjects of which I am treating' and asserts that the 'finding of the supreme judge would automatically dissolve us all into limbo' (*AG* 126). So Pierpoint's diagnosis, which Zagreus reproduces in his own interventions, is *interested*, not *disinterested*, and its partiality is foregrounded from the very outset. The text reverts to the question of this partiality when it draws attention to its own use of satire as a critical mode by way of a dialogue between Zagreus and Ratner. Zagreus admits that satire is of limited scope because in order to judge people it must rely on social conventions, must remain, in short, 'upon the surface of existence' wherein people may be regarded 'as "good," or as "bad" ' (*AG* 470), and he argues that this necessarily makes satire superficial. From this argument, it emerges that the satirist condemns because he cannot understand, and that this lack of understanding makes satire a cyclopean art:

'Morality is of the surface. But also the values that decide whether a person is ridiculous or free from absurdity are pure conventions of a society, they exist only in a surface-world, of two dimensions.'

'Well.'

'You agree?'

'Please go on.'

'Underneath, if one pricks far enough, in the eyes of a Shake-speare we are *all* ridiculous – we all play those tricks that make the angels weep.'

'Some more than others Horace,' Ratner humbly corrected the rationalizing megaphone at his side bringing order into chaos with broadsides of reason.

'That *more* and that *less* – such fractions are invisible to eyes that are sufficiently unsealed.'

'I suppose so, to eyes that are – as you say.'

'Such a man is no satirist. God could not be a satirist.'

Ratner grinned at God in the glass – the God of Horace.

'So satirists have to be half-blind, there is no other way.' (*AG* 471)

Earlier in the novel it has been suggested that the characters lampooned in its pages are so unregenerate that no satire can puncture their ludicrous self-esteem, a view that calls into question the text's own *modus operandus*.[28] But in this passage satire is exposed as a self-defeating genre not because its victims are too shameless to recognize themselves in its depictions, but because these depictions are themselves pale simulacra of a truth that cannot be grasped by human beings.

With this move, the text reverses itself once more. It turns its satiric eye back onto the literary genre it is itself deploying, inviting its readers to reflect again on the implications of its title. In the patristic tradition the first *simia dei* was, of course, Satan. For Tertullian, to whom this image of the rebel-angel can be traced, the devil was 'the rival and ape (*aemulus*) of God and the corrupter and perverter (*interpolator*) of God's world'.[29] Envy of God's primacy and an abject desire to rival his creative power figure prominently in this account of the fall, and Lewis clearly had these features in mind when he identified *ressentiment* as the motive force behind the posturing of his rather more minor apes, '*those prosperous mountebanks who alternately imitate and mock at and traduce those figures they at once admire and hate*' (*AG* 131). For Tertullian, Satan was God's shadow, the faint but dark semblance of an originary and eternal substance. This image plays an important role in *The Apes*, which deploys it both to suggest the threatening, dwarfing presence of the absent deity who *over-*shadows human beings and to signal their lack of genuine reality. Boleyn, for example, experiences this power in the course of his education by Zagreus when he grasps that the latter is not a source of value and meaning: 'words of his master, that his master had got from *his* master. Always the shadow of the mystery-man – the god-like Pierpoint, whom he hated!' (*AG* 253).

This line of thinking about human belatedness is connected in turn to questions about the security of identity. It is asked, for example, whether Boleyn has 'been manufactured like the – Hoffman doll?' (*AG* 215), a question that he answers in the negative, before starting to wonder and even enjoy its possibilities: 'Am I somebody's doll? Is that why I sit? The doll of Zagreus! He blushed with pleasure at the novel thought. Horace Zagreus's plaything – really!' (*AG* 215–16). And those figures who are of larger stature than this manikin seem in turn to be mere vestiges of original exemplars. Lewis exploits the image of the shadow to great effect:

> Mr Zagreus stared at his imposing shadow moving slightly upon Kein's door . . . Dan's shadow, as well, waited upon him, not upon its original. Dan was there like a shadow too, on and before the door. Were they inside the door as well, in further projections of still less substance – their stationary presences multiplied till they stretched out like a theatre queue? Was there anything after the shadow (as was there anything behind the man)? (*AG* 249)

When the theatre queue appears to come to life, Zagreus is implicated in its endless and recursive process of simulation and mirroring in which the very notion of some identifiable original slides away: 'He had imagined a queue. But here it must be – less and less resembling the original – shadows upon the walls of Pompeii, of Paris, the hot andean plains – a horrible family of shadows. An ape-herd, all projections of himself, or he of them, or another – gathered from everywhere, swarming in after him, or collected to await him' (*AG* 310).[30]

In *The Apes* the presence behind the shadow is always hidden, and, as in *Waiting For Godot*, the yawning gap between profane life and an idealized realm that can be glimpsed but never reached is the source of its dark laughter. If 'even the most virtuous and well-proportioned of men is only a shadow, after all, of some perfection', then '*everyone* should be laughed at or else *no one* should be laughed at' (*MWA* 89). But, if this is so, then the satirist is implicated in the tragicomic spectacle he portrays, and I have suggested that *The Apes* does not shy away from this conclusion. Consider the following peroration from Zagreus:

> 'There in front of us, they sit in two rows (we are in one) – *the people who have never been able to become Fiction*. How portentously they suffer for the want of a great artist to effect that immortal translation – how they suffer! So they cannot exactly be blamed for their attempts at self-creation. – One of these fine days a *real* creator will come along. What a sigh of utter relief there will be – when the Ape can cease from Aping, and the sham-artist lay down his pen and brush and be at rest!' (*AG* 308)

This is not just a clever conceit; the pathos here is genuine. Zagreus's words communicate a sense of loss and longing that haunts this burlesque work, since, in the absence of a *prima causa*, all the characters in the novel are condemned to exist in a spectral limbo. Lewis had addressed this issue in philosophical terms in *Time and Western Man*. In that text he had suggested that the subject cannot truly exist in the absence of a deity – writing favourably of those religions that 'posit a Perfection already existing, eternally there, of which we are humble shadows' (*TWM* 427) – and had invoked the doctrine of anamnesis (which plays a key role in Augustine's thought) to explore the possibility that human beings may have access to the transcendent realm that sustains their existence:

> The sense of personality, of being a person, is, according to us, the most vivid and fundamental sense that we possess: sharper and more complete than sight, built up like sight with reminiscence, though belonging to an infinite rather than a finite memory, so much so indeed that some philosophers have thought that this sense was memory only: and it is also essentially one of *separation*. In our approaches to God, in consequence, we do not need to 'magnify' a human body, but only to intensify that consciousness of a separated and transcendent life. So God becomes the supreme symbol of our separation and of our limited transcendence. He is also our memory, as it were, and when we refer to God it is as though we were bringing memory to life. It is, then, because the sense of personality is posited as our greatest 'real', that we require a 'God', a something that is nothing but a *person*, secure in its absolute egoism, to be the rationale of this sense. (*TWM* 434–5).[31]

Yet *The Apes* describes a fallen world from which God has departed, and it hardly suggests that the kind of personhood imagined here is a real possibility. Zagreus's 'immortal translation' remains a fantasy. A more fitting symbol of the novel's recursive structure and self-consuming textuality is Boleyn's concluding act of literary vandalism: 'His fingers did their sad last work well, and strangled the log and letters. They divided everything – everything in the world – into smaller and smaller pieces – till no sentence at all was intact in all that mass of flattering precept and objurgation. Alas!' (*AG* 631). The novel is, despite its wit, a tragic work steeped in the absurd because it can see no way of endowing human life with meaning. So *Men Without Art* may be taken to suggest that the regress we have seen as such a key part of *The Apes* leads inexorably to 'the conclusion that in some form or other th[e] original "ape" was man!' (*MWA* 101).

5

Literature and Politics

Lewis's politics are a complex affair.[1] As good a place as any to start is the early fragment 'The Code of a Herdsman' (1917), which contains in *nuce* many of the views that informed Lewis's political thinking during the 1920s and 1930s. 'The Code' must be treated with care, since it is not a piece in which Lewis speaks in *propria persona* but a provocative (and thus tinged with irony) document sent by one character to another in a fiction that was later revised and incorporated into *The Crowdmaster*. With these caveats in mind, it is nonetheless worth considering the sentiments of 'The Code' because it pushes to one extreme a viewpoint that tempted Lewis. 'The Code' favoured individualism ('Yourself must be your Caste'); treated women and the processes of generation with suspicion (as 'the arch conjuring trick'); deprecated groups, depicting them as unthinking masses; and defended a hierarchical view of society in which a minority, characterized by intellectual power and the constitutional vigour required to breathe Nietzsche's cold mountain air, differentiated itself from those marked by unconscious animality, policing the boundary between herdsman and herd.[2] 'The Code' announced Lewis's hostility to social groups and his conviction that the gifted few must set themselves apart lest their autonomy be compromized. His language in this text was that of a distaste bordering on dread: herdsmen must protect themselves with masks and thick clothes from the danger of 'stagnant gasses from these Yahooesque and rotten herds'.[3]

Such imagery has always been grist to the mill of Lewis's critics. But we need also to acknowledge his lifelong desire to transform society and to shatter the classist snobbery that prevented so many people from developing their aptitudes (*ABR* 44–5, 324–5). Even as he asserted the patrician claims of the 'Code' against the ruminant insipidity of the 'herd', Lewis directed his efforts to altering the society in which such exclusive functioning was the prerogative of a minority.[4] From Vorticism onwards, he urged an interventionist art based on *poeisis* rather than passive imitation. The Vorticist was to stand in a *productive* relation to the world, even though his activity took place in a realm removed from life and competing with it. Yet this creativity was connected with a form of social engineering too, for *Blast* spoke of its desire 'to make individuals, wherever found'.[5] Although he was no utilitarian, Lewis rejected aestheticism's cult of indifferentism. In 'The Caliph's Design', for example, he insisted that the artist's duty was 'to desire equity, mansuetude, in human relations, to fight against violence, to work for formal beauty, for more intelligent significance in the ordering of our lives' (*WLA* 136). The failure of this imperative to bring about social change, coupled with the impact on Lewis of the First World War, go some way to explaining the increasingly dystopian pronouncements that characterized his work from 1926, and that culminated in the disastrous political positions he adopted in the 1930s.[6]

These initial remarks suggest that there was a tension in Lewis's work between the satirist who inveighed against *homo stultus*, disparaging the majority of humankind as graceless puppets, and the utopian who wrote book after book of cultural criticism intended to enlighten the general reader and who saw art as the means by which escape from mechanism may be effected.[7] Lewis could be contemptuous of the majority, nor can there be much doubt that he considered all significant human achievements to be the work of solitary titans. But was this work, which he saw as the *product* of difference, to be deployed as a segregating agent that upheld hierarchical social distinctions? The evidence is inconclusive. Consider, for example, this account of what he termed 'the politics of the intellect':

> It is my effrontery to claim that men owe everything they can ever hope to have to an 'intellectual' of one sort or another. . . . The intelligence suffers today automatically in consequence of the

attack on all authority, advantage, or privilege. . . . There is nothing 'aristocratic' about the intellect . . . the word 'aristocratic', with its implication of a crowd within the bigger crowd, organized for the exploitation of the latter, is peculiarly inapt for the essentially individual character of the intellect.

The intellect is more removed from the crowd than is anything: but it is not a snobbish withdrawal, but a going aside for the purposes of work, of work not without its utility for the crowd. The artificial barriers that an aristocratic caste are forced to observe are upheld to enhance a *difference* that is not a reality. It is because they are of the same stuff as their servants that they require the disciplines of exclusiveness. (*ABR* 373–4)

For the purposes of work, the individual was to be unhampered. Lewis presented this as a *practical* matter that concerned the conditions required for thought or creativity to flourish; it was not meant to suggest repugnance for those who do not work in these fields.[8] He argued that the language of 'aristocratic' distinctiveness encoded differences that were imaginary. Such language naturalized *social* differences, ratifying relations of power in which, by birth, some were forced to serve while others were enabled to rule. Elsewhere, however, Lewis refused to back away from the discomfiting claim that at any given time there is only a small number of individuals with the ability to think, create, or rule; this led him to derive a caste-based model of society from Sorelian syndicalism and, in the process, to make use of an alternative naturalizing discourse, which focused not on heredity but on aptitude.[9] It was here that Lewis's pessimism came to the fore.

Lewis was from the outset sceptical about humanity's capacity to rise up out of a vegetative torpor. *Blast*, for example, can within a single manifesto oscillate between hope for a nation of transformed individuals and insistence that humanity's unconsciousness was the prerequisite for a creativity that aimed only at artists' perfectibility.[10] Translated into political terms, such contradictory views and aspirations led Lewis to veer from the dream of social transformation to the fear that people are slothful creatures of habit, incapable of change, and that all politics was a 'racket' masking struggles for power. *The Art of Being Ruled*, a jagged and fragmentary text bursting with ideas

79

and bite-sized chunks of polemic, exhibited both tendencies in about equal measure. Lewis argued that the majority, incapable of governing themselves, not only *require* rulers but also *desire* them (see *ABR* 89, 92). The problem of coercion was thus dispelled, for he claimed that the majority voluntarily accede to the authority of governing groups that are better suited to this arduous task. The subsequent division of society into two groups – the rulers and the ruled – he then presented in terms of a naturalizing discourse heavily reliant on biological metaphors. Lewis described this as a caste system based on something akin to a 'deep racial difference' that divides 'mankind into two rigorously separated worlds' (*ABR* 127). This separation was predicated not on class or heredity but on innate aptitudes; it was 'something like a *biological* separating-out of the chaff from the grain', which, Lewis argued, although it ratified social hierarchies, carried no connotations of inferiority or superiority but articulated a distinction between 'kinds' (*ABR* 127). Lewis's view was thus hostile to rights-based political theories, since he held that the concept of rights obscured the differences between human beings, mistakenly treating them as equals.[11] In opposition to this democratic conception, he invoked Goethe's division of people into 'natures' (agents) and 'puppets' (automata), arguing that most people are programmed machines mimicking human life (see *ABR* 125).

The Art of Being Ruled bristles with ambiguities, not least around the explosive question of 'caste'. Despite Lewis's claim that his version of it was value-neutral, his language frequently contradicted him, and the slipperiness of his definitions of caste did little to aid his case. I have criticized this aspect of Lewis's politics elsewhere, so here I shall simply summarize my objections.[12] First, Lewis's views are contradictory, since, despite his protestations that no slight is intended against those who do not belong to the ruling caste, his division of people into two 'species' or 'sexes' carries stigmatizing overtones; furthermore, his vision of Goethe's puppet as a *machine* is a dehumanizing one, which strongly suggests a cartesian body bereft of soul, in short, a blind mechanism devoid of purpose. Second, this dehumanization strips those who are not seen as 'natures' of personhood, and it is personhood, Lewis argued in *Paleface*, that entitles individuals to rights; to be ruled is on this view to risk being denied the kind of consideration accorded those who are granted rights.[13] Third, the puppet/ nature distinction is based on different, and incompatible, arguments, for it is claimed as an *empirical* fact (that people so differ) and as a *psychological* account of their alleged desires (that they wish to forfeit their autonomy and rights). Fourth, the sharp distinction between puppets and natures is in fact unstable in this account, since Lewis portrayed his imagined society as a meritocracy in which social mobility is a distinct feature, and this cannot be squared with notions of groups divided into biological species or sexes. Fifth, the claim that puppets are happy to see themselves as such and to submit to the care of benign rulers is undermined when Lewis describes the use of both force and ideological state apparatuses as the necessary tools of government.[14] Finally, the account leaves one vital question unanswered: *quis custodiet ipsos custodes*?

The political arguments Lewis advanced in *The Art of Being Ruled*, *Time and Western Man*, and *Paleface* are inseparable from his criticisms of democracy and liberalism. His revaluation of all values in the aftermath of the First World War and the Versailles Settlement was rooted in his conviction that Western society had entered into a paralysing transitional state, a 'capitalo-revolutionary society of the interregnum' (*ABR* 136). The war had destroyed the empires that had ruled over Europe; sown the seeds of future conflicts through the terms of the Versailles Treaty; and led to economic depression. Together with the long-term changes brought about by science and industrialization, the world post-1918 seemed to have experienced a transformation of cataclysmic proportions. Yet Lewis's persistent complaint throughout the 1920s and 1930s was that few people grasped how decisive these changes were, since on the surface much of social and political life (especially in its institutional forms) appeared so familiar. For Lewis, this gave an air of unreality to the whole post-war scene. Whereas, in the past, 'the machinery of society worked in public', it would now 'go underground' (*ABR* 146), politics becoming increasingly oligarchical, and power being wielded by plutocrats. The democracy for which the war had supposedly been fought was for him underpinned by a bankrupt liberalism, which could neither resist the *Machtpolitik* of totalitarian ideologies nor offer any alternative to revolutionary fervour.

Lewis argued that liberalism was ineffectual in a period dominated by multinational cartels and bureaucratic rationalization, but he was above all convinced that it must inevitably lead to a Tocquevillean levelling-down and thus to the disintegration of European political power (see *ABR* 110). Liberalism's consequences were political and social: politically, it gave rise to democracy, which weakened Europe because it gave power to parliaments rather than to autocratic minorities; socially, it gave rise to manipulation by the media and political demagogues.[15] For Lewis, the opposition between democracy and dictatorship boiled down to the question 'of the rule of the minority or the majority; rule by a show of hands or rule by the most vigorous and intelligent' (*ABR* 72–3). His critique of democracy, he maintained, was aimed at the cant by which it is sustained: 'I was setting in a clear light a group of trivial and meaningless liberties, which, in the pursuit of their small claims, obstructed freedom – in any sense in which that word is worth using. My criticism of "democracy," again, was of "democracy" as that is understood today; and it was based on the conviction that democracy is neither free, nor permits of freedom' (*TWM* 117).

What, then, are we to make of the specific invocation of fascism in *The Art of Being Ruled*? And what exactly did fascism, in so far as he did support it, mean to him? The answers to these questions are far from obvious, since the key texts from the 1920s – *The Art of Being Ruled*, *Time and Western Man*, *Paleface*, and *The Enemy* – provide conflicting evidence. Consider Lewis's most explicit statement in favour of fascism:

> If today you must be a socialist of some sort, what order of socialist are you going to be? For, evidently, you will say, 'socialist' means very different and indeed opposite things. I have already said that in the abstract I believe the sovietic system to be the best. It has spectacularly broken with all the past of Europe: it looks to the East, which is spiritually so much greater and intellectually so much finer than Europe, for inspiration. It springs ostensibly from a desire to alleviate the lot of the poor and outcast, and not merely to set up a cast-iron, militarist-looking state. And yet for anglo-saxon countries as they are constituted today some modified form

of fascism would probably be best.... The only socialism that differs very much from *fascismo* is reformist socialism, or the early nineteenth-century utopias, or, to a somewhat less extent, Proudhon. All marxian doctrine, all *etatisme* or collectivism, conforms very nearly in practice to the fascist ideal. *Fascismo* is merely a spectacular marinettian flourish put on to the tail, or, if you like, the head of marxism: that is, of course, fascism as interpreted by its founder, Mussolini. And that is the sort of socialism that this essay would indicate as the most suitable for anglo-saxon countries or colonies, with as much of sovietic proletarian sentiment as could be got into it without impairing its discipline, and as little coercion as is compatible with good sense. In short, to get some sort of peace to enable us to work, we should naturally seek the most powerful and stable authority that can be devised.   (*ABR* 320–1)

The argument advanced here suggests that Lewis's terminology needs to be treated with care. To begin with, Lewis suggests that some version of socialism offers the only viable alternative to a decayed liberalism. The soviet model, a form of syndicalism, initially seems attractive, but Lewis distances himself from it on the grounds that, while it has an abstract, theoretical appeal, it would in practice be unsuitable for Europe. He does not explain why this is so, but moves to the cautious claim that a 'modified form of fascism would probably be best'. Fascism as understood by Lewis is then differentiated from socialist gradualism and is linked to Marxian collectivism, presumably as practised in the newly formed Soviet Union.[16] But Lewis argues that this version of Marxism is linked to Mussolinian fascism, in that it is based on centralization, party discipline, a command economy, and the ruthless exercise of power (see *ABR* 319–22). This is the 'socialism' *The Art of Being Ruled* would advocate: a socialism functioning with 'the regularity and smoothness of a machine', cutting through the last vestiges of democratic parliamentary 'humbug', controlling public opinion through the press, and ultimately taking away the need for politics altogether, thereby rescuing 'masses of energy otherwise wasted in politics for more productive ends' (*ABR* 321).

What emerged from *The Art of Being Ruled* was Lewis's conviction, first, that liberal democracies exercised authority no less than fascist or soviet dictatorships but that they *concealed* the workings of power beneath the cloak of parliamentarianism, and, second, that this way of proceeding made for inefficient, disorganized, and fragmented politics. The attraction of both fascism and communism for Lewis lay in their willingness to confront the issue of power openly and to wield it in the service of clearly defined goals.[17] The giveaway sentence in the long quote above is the last one, for it reveals that what was at stake for Lewis was the peace that would allow artists and intellectuals to *work*.[18] The specific *kind* of society that would guarantee the requisite order was, in the long shadow of the First World War, of less importance than the sheer fact of stability itself. And it was this overmastering desire for respite from a post-war chaos in which all values seemed to have been undermined that played such an important part in Lewis's political thought at this time. All 'any true scientist or true artist asks', he plaintively maintained, 'is to be given the opportunity, without interference, indifferent to glory, to *work*' (*ABR* 111).

There are puzzling features in Lewis's tentative espousal of fascism, which was hardly in keeping with the views he expressed elsewhere at around the same time. If fascism is a form of Marxism with 'a spectacular marinettian flourish', then it is hard to see how it could possibly recommend itself to Lewis, who had, from *Blast* onwards, sought to exorcise from his own thought the Italian Futurist's influence. Indeed, Lewis had consistently associated fascism with the philosophies of action he deplored, singling out Futurism as the most notable example of an aesthetic that glorified action at the expense of thought (see *TWM* 20–1, 34, 203). He, in turn, described communism, as democracy's 'doctrinaire and more primitive relative' (*TWM* 26), and, arguing that it appealed to the emotionalism of hyped-up masses, rejected it out of hand. This suggests that what roused Lewis's ire about *all* current political options was what he perceived as their various appeals to sentiment. Democracy would be fine if only the individuals comprising it were autonomous, reflective, informed, and independently thinking citizens; in the alleged absence of the necessary numbers of such people, fascism seemed an attractive alternative because it claimed to base its art of ruling upon a realistic assessment of the nature of the ruled.[19]

The texts of the 1920s suggest that Lewis desired to *escape* out of politics altogether. He sought the establishment of a system that, once in place, would be so all-embracing that political life – rather like Marx's 'state' after the revolution – would just wither away, leaving all individuals free to pursue their self-appointed vocations (*ABR* 128–9, 324–5, 365–8). And this is why he consistently made the otherwise puzzling assertion that he had no real interest in politics, that he was non-partisan, and that his sole aim was to free art from the demands made of it by ideologues of any persuasion. He put this position with typical bluntness: 'I advance the strange claim . . . to act and to think non-politically in everything, in complete detachment from all the intolerant watchwords and formulas by which we are beset. I am an artist and my *mind*, at least, is entirely free: also that is a freedom that I hold from no man and have every intention of retaining' (*E3* 27). Thus he devoted the last part of *The Art of Being Ruled* to a defence of the aesthetic as the most potent source of 'the pure revolution-ary impulse of creative thought' (*ABR* 359) when it is allowed to function unhampered by any extraneous pressures.

By the 1930s, however, Lewis had changed his mind about power. *Left Wings over Europe* (1936), written as a last-ditch attempt to stave off the oncoming war, had no time for the naive support for totalitarian ruthlessness displayed in *The Art of Being Ruled*. The book was 'one long plea against the centralization of power . . . Centralized power – when it is human power – is for me, politically, the greatest evil it is possible to imagine' (*LWE* 16). This is a far cry not just from the books of the 1920s but also from his first book on National Socialism, *Hitler* (1931), and the reasons for the shift in his thinking are instructive. *Left Wings over Europe* has been read as an appeasement tract, but it is more than this. It is a bitter denunciation of British political hypocrisy written by an angry man unable to align himself with any of the available nos-trums. The book was no *apologia* for fascism, but, because it portrayed Hitler as the outcome of the injustices perpetrated by the terms of the Versailles Treaty, and because it argued that Soviet communism was more tyrannous than Italian or German fascism, it resembles a form of far right fellow travelling, despite Lewis's pleas of mitigation: ' "Fascist" thought is outcast thought, in the same way that certain countries are outcast countries. And although I am very far from being anything that could be described as a "fascist", I consider the "fascist" just as worthy of attention as the communist' (*LWE* 331).

Why was this so? Several reasons came into play here: Lewis's contempt for Britain's foreign policy, which was happy to have the Soviet Union as an ally while claiming that opposition to Hitler was motivated by a desire to make the world safe for democracy; his belief that, of two despotisms seeking to centralize power, fascism was the lesser evil; his view of Hitler as a defensive politician with no expansionist aims; and his desire to prevent another war from breaking out.[20] For Lewis, this was a matter not of allegiance to particular ideologies, all of which he scorned, but of *Realpolitik*. Contrasting the 'decentralized government of sovereign states' with 'a centralized, all-powerful, internationalist oligarchy', he wrote: 'This does *not* make us "fascists", or even "national-ists". It does not mean that we are regarding these alternatives in anything but an objective and opportunist frame of mind. Because a thing is not *red*, it does not follow that it must be *buff, black*, or *green*' (*LWE* 274).[21]

In retrospect, it is clear that Lewis was deeply naïve about Hitler (less so about Mussolini), and that his hostility to abstract political theories blinded him to the realities on the ground. He argued that the 1930s political impasse could be traced back to the Enlightenment and the French Revolution, to the substitution of 'the *abstract* values of theoretic idealism' for 'the *concrete* values of common sense' (*LWE* 319).[22] For Lewis, liberal 'democracy' was a sham, whereas German 'dictatorship' was remarkably libertarian.[23] Thus he blamed the impending war on the policies of the Great Powers, thereby exculpating Hitler, depicted as a victim of League of Nations diplomacy and as a leader primarily concerned to defend German sovereignty, and he argued that war spelt political disaster for Britain because it would in practice safeguard communism, and not democracy at all (*LWF* 47–50, 66).[24] What becomes increasingly clear in texts like *Left Wings over Europe* and *Count your Dead: They Are Alive!* is that, despite his avowed hostility to abstract political theories, it was *Lewis* who conceptualized the political scene in highly abstract language, ultimately reducing it to a straight conflict between two overarching, and radically opposed, political *principles*: centralization versus decentralization. For Lewis, this was the deeper and more momentous conflict that lay half-hidden beneath contemporary political rhetorics. The 'merely fascist-communist wrangle obscures the issue' (*LWE* 275), which was between freedom and enslavement, understood by Lewis not in terms of individual rights but in terms of sovereignty – in other words, the key principle to be defended was that of national self-determination, the right to secede from any centre of control located outside the nation state.[25]

Lewis's analysis of the political situation in the 1930s was simply not fine-grained enough. His obsession with what he perceived as the cartelization of western Europe led him to conclude that democracy had disappeared in all but name: 'England is governed . . . by a financial directorate. It is more a huge Corporation than a political State. This irresponsible Power (irresponsible since it has no official or "constitutional" standing) is camouflaged as a democratic parliamentary system' (*CD* 29–30). Although he never espoused Douglas's theories of Social Credit, Lewis was at this time close to Pound in his denunciations of loan capital.[26] But the preoccupation with an international plutocracy led to the unwarranted claim that democracy in England had ceased to exist; although he made calibrated judgements about the differences between the respective losses of freedom in Soviet Russia and Nazi Germany, he seemed unable to apply the same reasoning to Britain. Unwilling to admit that political processes and civil rights were in Britain of a different order altogether from that of Hitlerite Germany, Lewis shifted the debate away from the issue of rights within nation states onto the global question of monopoly versus anti-monopoly. He argued that monopolistic control of a world economy would result in the loss of national sovereignty and consequently of civic freedoms as envisaged by figures such as Franklin and Jefferson.[27] So he contrasted an abstract and mechanical community with a vision of small-scale productivity and relative liberty, insisting that the opposition between these two political models transcended any conflict between 'democracy' and 'fascism'.[28] Fascism was on this view a lesser evil because it could be seen as defending the general principle of national sovereignty and thus 'standing up for *our* rights (since to stand up for the principle of the Sovereign State is to stand up for us) against our country, "Great Britain" ' (*CD* 323).[29]

Lewis's later repudiation of everything for which National Socialism stood needs to be seen in this context, for his acknowledgment that he had misapprehended German fascism entailed the admission that the policies he had urged in the mid-1930s had been mistaken. Describing himself in 1939 as a former 'neutral' and 'appeaser' who had sought to avoid another war by accommodating Germany, Lewis wrote that its expansionism had since then been so rampant that he now felt he had seen 'nothing at all in Berlin in 1930' (*HC* 9). What had seemed to him primarily a problem of national sovereignty versus internationalism (or monopoly versus anti-monopoly) he now saw as an issue of the defence of democracy against a predatory totalitarianism. He rejected his earlier isolationist position in favour of a European federalism that he hoped would destroy nationalism and 'disintegrate' the 'stupid barriers' (*HC* 244) erected between sovereign states.[30]

Hitler had stressed fascism's violence and extremism, its rejection of Versailles (especially the burden of war reparations), its nationalism, its religion of race and blood, its anti-semitism, and its reliance on a disciplined party machine (see *H.* 7, 4, 34–43, 32–3, 85). But Lewis was in 1931 naive about Hitler's ideology and aims. Although he derided fascism's appeals to nationalism and made it clear that he was 'not an advocate of Hitlerism, nor yet of Italian Fascism' (*H.* 98), he saw Hitler as a patriot seeking to safeguard German interests. Nor can one deny that Lewis was attracted to aspects of fascist thought. He saw 'a great deal of political apropos and sagacity' in the German attempt 'to *draw in* and to *concentrate*, rather than to diffuse, disperse and mix' (*H.* 108), and he wrote that, because of his 'sympathy with this great german party', he wanted to see its 'difficulties brought out into the light, and, it is to be hoped, overcome' (*H.* 143).[31] This misguided book suggests that Lewis was above all sympathetic to National Socialism's stress on sovereignty and efficiency: in contrast to the ramshackle disorder of British parliamentary democracy, it held out the promise of a tightly organized, smoothly function-ing, and internally inviolable state machine in which all individuals could fulfil their allotted function.

The Hitler Cult turned all this on its head. By 1939, it was clear what National Socialism meant and intended.The ideo-logical tendencies of fascism that Lewis had already criticized, without really understanding their implications, he now dis-mantled piece by piece, portraying Hitlerism as an anti-rational 'cult' based on an appeal to the worst aspects of nationalism, such as anti-Semitism and military expansionism. Lewis traced an intellectual genealogy for fascism that ran from Hitler to Mussolini to Nietzsche to Darwin: fascism was an ideology extolling action, the survival of the fittest, and above all a doctrine of force. By 1942 Lewis could admit that he had been 'wrong' and that after Munich he saw 'with anger and dismay, that Hitler was that most detestable of things a chronic and unteachable little militarist, who just would have his good old second war, because it is for such hideous childishness that such men live' (L. 324).

But why had he not seen this before? His answer was revealing. He returned to the books of the 1920s, describing them as 'the records of [his] tendency to aspire to a classless society and a world in which barbaric social values have no part' (HC 21). This utopian longing had been expressed in the form of an authoritarian socialism that aligned early Soviet communism with an incipient Mussolinian fascism. Lewis's later disillusionment with the Soviet experiment had, he now claimed, a decisive effect: 'I am recording my disappointment at a certain period of my life, and saying how that tended to put me out of conceit for a long time with theory, and with theorists – to throw me back upon the pis-aller of the traditional Western scene, with its routine half-measures, of which Na-tional Socialism was a spectacular specimen' (HC 22). But this statement conceals as much as it reveals. It is true that by the 1930s Lewis had moved a long way from The Art of Being Ruled; his political touchstones in Left Wings and Count your Dead were Burke and Jefferson rather than Proudhon and Sorel, and in both books he emphasized pragmatic solutions over abstract theories. But it is not the case that Lewis had ever aligned Hitlerism with some kind of last political resort. On the contrary. He was drawn to National Socialism by the same promise of order, efficiency, and concentration of energy that had attracted him to sovietic centralization and to caste-based political theories in the 1920s: he saw them all as *correctives* to the haphazard nature of parliamentary politics. I would suggest that Lewis briefly confused the historically determinate theories that produced abstract accounts of human nature and political systems for theory *tout court*, and that this confusion, coupled with his 1920s predilection for centralized planning and control, resulted in a short-lived willingness to see in National Socialism a possible alternative to democracy.

This was not just a failure of judgement, though it was surely that too. It was a view implicit in Lewis's own theorizing about these issues, for until the late 1930s his hostility to democracy was so marked that almost any appeal to authority was likely to seem congenial to him. By 1939 he had grasped that the language of exclusion could sanction violence and could lead its proponents to become inhumane. There was also a link between Hitler's separation of 'races' and his extremist conception of the 'nation', in which those marked by virtue, courage, and self-sacrifice strive for supremacy with the lowest 'dregs' who are incapable of offering the country anything at all. Lewis dismissed this 'Sunday-school picture' (*HC* 118) as unworthy of serious consideration, mocking the claim that 'a nation consists of a great mass of negative half-wits, about whom no one can get very excited; and an *elite*, "radiantly heroic", full of civic virtues, brave, and prone to disregard their private interests' (*HC* 120).

How mindful was Lewis that he had relied on similar analogies in *The Art of Being Ruled*, to argue in favour of a distinction between the rulers and the ruled? Did he remember that he had described the majority of people as an unthinking mass desirous of nothing more than a bovine half-life and needing to be governed by a more capable elite? Was he addressing his own earlier self when he remarked in Hitler's depiction of society 'an air of unreality – the note of bogusness' (*HC* 118)? Such questions admit of no answer, but it is clear that by the late 1930s Lewis questioned whether social systems could be built up on the basis of natural differences between human beings, that he saw how the language of difference could do physical and psychological violence just as damaging as the class system he had always despised, and that he turned his attention away from utopian political speculations to a concern with the sufferings it all too often caused. *The Revenge for Love* (1937), in which the entire political arena is shrouded in 'an air of unreality', is a crucial text in this regard, for it focuses less on specific political doctrines and more on those who propagate them and those who suffer their consequences.

The Revenge for Love enters into dialogue not just with 1930s politics but with Lewis's own writings. *The Art of Being Ruled* had flirted with the possibility of remaking individuals, coming close here and there to eugenic speculations (*ABR* 52, 125, 364, 368). Noting that revolution 'is in origin a purely technical process', Lewis seemed tempted by the utility of 'a technique that enables men to regard life itself as something *imperfect*, like a machine to be superseded' (*ABR* 23). By the late 1930s he was convinced that to see life as a machine that could be taken apart and built anew was to ignore the constraints placed on the forms life could take by nature itself.[32] The natural was 'real', the revolutionary 'unreal', and these two tropes dominate *The Revenge for Love*, the novel that showed how the dream of social renewal turns into the nightmare of revolutionary politics. In this novel Lewis dramatizes the effect of communist plotting on a naive and unsuspecting couple, Victor and Margot Stamp. Victor, a genial figure from the African veldt, is an aspiring painter who is aware that he lacks the talent to succeed as an artist. His relationship with the protective, intuitive, but insecure Margot is contrasted with that of the Phipps, Gillian and Tristy – the former a free-thinking, and well-born communist fellow-traveller, the latter a skilled painter and Communist Party acolyte. All these figures are in turn contrasted with the professional revolutionaries (most notably Percy Hardcaster), business sharks and profiteers (Abbershaw and Sean O'Hara), and the priapic 'natural man' Jack Cruze. Victor is eventually drawn into a gun-running intrigue from which Margot tries to save him, but both are killed, leaving Hardcaster to mourn their passing and implicitly to question the politicial ethos to which he has devoted his life.

The Revenge for Love is deeply hostile to socialist politics in general and to revolutionary politics in particular. It is in part a protest against the hegemony of left-wing thought in cultural and artistic circles in 1930s Britain, a hegemony discussed in detail by Orwell in 'Inside the Whale'.[33] This hostility is disclosed through *ad hominem* attacks on individuals; the depiction of political activism as fundamentally duplicitous and manipulative; the portrayal of fellow-travellers' gullibility and even stupidity; and the emphasis on the messianic nature of revolutionary ideology and the fanaticism of its adherents. Viewing communist doctrine as irredeemably abstract, the novel concentrates on the consequences such abstraction can have when it is codified as an ideology and turned into a programme of action that is efficiently implemented by a party machine. Thus the key contrast in *The Revenge for Love* is between the ruthless *agents provocateurs* who are willing to sacrifice others in their pursuit of political justice (though some of them, such as O'Hara, Salmon, and Abbershaw, are double agents or profiteers) and the naive figures who try to escape from the lupine world of politics into the shaky haven of romantic love.

In no sense, however, does the novel present romantic love as a viable alternative to the politicization of human life that it deplores; this is the *revenge* for love, after all, and as soon as any weight is placed on the reality of 'love' it collapses, revealing itself as just one more of the novel's recurring 'false bottoms'. Several critics have argued that *The Revenge for Love* shows Lewis for the first time treating human relationships with tenderness and compassion. The novel can be read in part as a dirge for doomed love, a reading surely sanctioned by the closing paragraph's haunting allusion to 2 Sam. 18–19. But Lewis's novels are never that straightforward, and the text cannot be read in terms of an opposition between 'love' and 'politics' or perhaps the 'private' and the 'public'. *The Revenge for Love* traces the logic by which political intriguing may destroy human beings (it shows in microcosm what Lewis knew was happening on a huge scale in Stalin's Soviet Union) but it refuses the easy consolation of portraying love as an untarnished reality able to withstand political corruption. The ideology of love and the rhetorics by which it is sustained are dismantled in exactly the same way as are the discourses and practices of politics. Thus I would suggest that Lewis makes

Margot an ambivalent figure because he sympathizes with her plight but at the same time undermines her faith in personal relations. In this text the 'almost instinct' is not 'almost true': love will not survive these characters' deaths.[34]

The Revenge for Love is centrally concerned with the instability of language. It excoriates those who subordinate human values to the discourse of politics, yes, but it also discloses the discursive nature of *all* values. In doing so, the novel blocks any move to an extra-discursive (supposedly 'pure') realm of value. These concerns are brought to the fore in its opening sentences:

> 'Claro,' said the warder. 'Claro, hombre!' It was the condescension of one caballero to another. His husky voice was modulated upon the principle of an omniscient rationality. When he spoke, he spoke from the bleak socratic peak of his wisdom to another neighbouring peak – equally equipped with the spotless panoply of logic. Deep answered to deep – height hurled back its assent to height! 'Claro, hombre!' he repeated, tightlipped, with the controlled passion of the great logician. 'We are never free to choose – because we are only free once in our lives.'
>
> 'And when is that?' inquired the prisoner.
>
> 'That is when at last we gaze into the bottom of the heart of our beloved and find that it is false – like everything else in the world!' (*RL* 13)

The ironies pile up on one another here, for the novel about to unfold will depict a world where the strategic arts of concealment, subterfuge, and duplicity are so pervasive that little is clear; where rationality and omniscience are the qualities that are lacking in people's actions, while the effects of passion are all too visible; where a logic supposedly discerned in the historical process congeals into ideological dogmas that cannot be questioned; where the lie is utilized to bring about emancipation. The warder sounds the novel's keynote (the precariousness of all beliefs), but the bathos of his conclusion suggests how little we are to take seriously these two pompous debaters. But in the paragraphs that follow, with their subtle dismantling of the terms just/unjust, which are shown to be empty counters in the service of political power, the real consequences (life or death) of the way such counters are deployed are revealed. Expediency, Hardcaster maintains, may replace the law, and one of the novel's trajectories follows the logic of this apothegm to its bitter end; what Orwell, in another context, described as the 'totalitarian idea that there is no such thing as law, there is only power', will be shown to result in the deaths of Margot and Victor.[35]

I suggested earlier that Lewis had by the 1930s developed a strongly naturalist position with regard to utopian thought, that he believed there were insurmountable limits to how far human beings and their societies could be transformed. The opposition between abstract theory and concrete reality is central to *The Revenge for Love*, and it is elaborated primarily around the trope of 'nature' as represented by the figures of Percy Hardcaster, Victor Stamp, and Jack Cruze. For Hardcaster, nature, 'blind to the intellectual beauties of the Social Revolution, and deaf to the voice of Conscience' (*RL* 46), is an obstinate reminder of a material realm indifferent to human speculation; the 'vast and beautiful neutral system, of the objective universe of things' (*RL* 50) is at the opposite pole to the '*subjective* world' (*RL* 47) of the revolutionary. Stamp, in contrast, 'an animal amongst men' (*RL* 236), is portrayed as a simple character and is associated with a benevolent view of the natural world; he sees his relationship with Margot as a 'pact of nature' that is 'founded upon sentiment, not intellect' (*RL* 79), and he defends her with instinctive loyalty. But the violent Cruze is an untamable, elemental force; 'so natural as to be strange' (*RL* 94), he is a sex-crazed 'faun' and an 'agent of Pan' (*RL* 97) who foreshadows the grotesque otherness of the dwarf in the Plaza Cabrinetty. These figures provide three views of nature: as a static and intractable realm; as a system of socially beneficial relationships; as a malevolent source of destructive energy.

Stamp is the bluff, genial male who gently mocks Margot's suspicions about the intriguing going on all around them because he sees her as slightly unbalanced. But Stamp is in fact the naif, and Margot the sophisticate. It is Margot who senses the unreality of the political sphere in which she and Victor are outsiders. Because she lacks the vocabulary to mount the kind of critique that Hardcaster, an insider, will later offer, her uneasiness is expressed in visionary language and focuses primarily on the personal dimension. O'Hara's apartment appears to her as a box with false sides and a false bottom, and the plotting taking place in it threatens extreme danger:

> It seemed to spell, for her private existence, that of Victor and her, nothing but a sort of lunatic menace, of arrogant futility. They were not so much 'human persons', as she described it to herself, as big portentous wax-dolls, mysteriously doped with some impenetrable nonsense, out of a Caligari's drug-cabinet, and wound up with wicked fingers to jerk about in a threatening way – their mouths backfiring every other second, to spit out a manufactured hatred, as their eyeballs moved. (*RL* 153)

Margot's vision conjoins two aspects of communism that Lewis deplored: its insistence on doctrinal uniformity and its subordination of the individual to the group.

But history shows that possessors of salvific truths are inclined to share them, and the battle over hearts and minds is always bestrewn with casualties. Margot senses that competing accounts of what form human life should take are at issue, and, in what is surely an allusion to the recent history of the Soviet Union, that the stakes are high: 'It was *their* reality, that of Victor and herself, that was marked down to be discouraged and abolished, and it was *they* that the others were trying to turn into phantoms and so to suppress. It was a mad notion, but it was just as if they had engaged in a battle of wills, to decide who should possess most *reality* – just as men fought each other for money, or fought each other for food' (*RL* 163). The conflict over which ideas are to prevail (the struggle for ideological hegemony that was for Lenin of such decisive importance) is precisely a conflict over the nature of reality and the means of commanding it. Communism is for Margot couched in 'the jargon of a false science' (*RL* 153), and this was Lewis's view, but its well-documented claims to offer a nomothetic account of the historical process gave its adherents the belief that they were merely assisting the path of destiny. To help bring the revolution about, an unsentimental toughness was mandatory; thus the aptly named Hardcaster, 'an obedient apologist of terrorist revolutionary power', sees humanitarianism 'as taboo *everywhere*' (*RL* 51).[36] Power, Nietzsche observes, '*makes stupid*'; he might have added that the desire to wield power in the name of the general good

makes *ruthless*.[37] By the late 1930s, Lewis, who had himself
been tempted by extremist politics, was a pluralist who
consistently argued that it 'takes all sorts to make a *civilised*
world', for when 'there is only *one* sort we may know
civilisation has ended' (*L*. 516).

The Revenge for Love offers a political critique of communism,
which it expresses in the main through Hardcaster and the
Phipps, but it undermines the pretensions of revolutionary
rhetoric to scientific status by drawing on the gothic and the
grotesque. Margot is the vehicle by which these elements
infiltrate the text. Unlike Hardcaster or Gillian Phipps, who can
analyse the theory and practice of revolutionary politics in
intellectual terms, Margot is able only to sense the threat it
poses to her individual life, and her dark visions destabilize its
claims to rationality at the same time as they disclose her own
precarious hold on reality. The turn to gothic is fitting, since
part of Lewis's purpose is to portray the 1930s political scene
as a shadowy half-world in which fanciful dreams oust
concrete realities. Thus in *The Revenge for Love* the boundary
between the real and the unreal is blurred, and the novel's
deployment of gothic and grotesque modes enables it to mock
the scientific jargon in which Marxist rhetoric is couched.
Margot experiences this sub-world of political activists and
fellow-travellers as an inferno:

> The darkness would have been much preferred by Margot if she
> had not felt uneasy at the bottom of this immense box in the dark,
> with so many lewd shadow-persons at play, who she felt were
> crawling about and might at any moment attack her. She saw
> visions. For supposing all the lights in the world began going out,
> and they all had to live with each other in darkness forever,
> whispering to people one could not see? (*RL* 169)

Margot's visions traverse the liminal space opened up by the
gothic. But she is not an unproblematic locus of value. She is
as much the product of ideological interpellation as Hardcaster, and her Bloomsbury feminism, her Romantic view of a
beneficent nature, and her faith in love are exposed as the
constituent features of her 'sham-culture outfit' (*RL* 336).
Margot is portrayed as a cultural creation made from equal
parts of Woolf, Ruskin, Tennyson, and Wordsworth (see *RL*

213–15). The novel's representation of nature is again important here, for Margot's idealization of the natural world (taken
from Wordsworth) informs her sentimental conception of
heterosexual love (taken from Ruskin). As a structure of
feeling, this process of idealization parallels the revolutionaries' messianic view of the proletariat. As the novel develops,
Lewis shifts from gothic to the grotesque and the sublime; in a
neat twist, he turns the Ruskin of *The Stones of Venice* against
the Ruskin of *Sesame and Lilies* in order to shatter Margot's
reverie of romantic love as decisively as Hardcaster has
destroyed Gillian's dream of political utopia.

The dwarf in the Plaza Cabrinetty is the first symbol of this
awakening. Victor, who is blind to the dangers besetting him,
is the innocent child to Margot's protective mother. The dwarf
is his double; an emblem of deformed bestiality, he is sent as
a punishment for romantic hubris who revenges a sentimental
conception of love: 'This uncanny parasite upon the normal
world, which it took off and insulted to everyone's extreme
delight, had singled her out. There was no escape, she must
play her part. There was no use pretending she did not belong
to this system of roaring and spluttering bestial life of flesh and
blood. And this subhuman creature had been sent there
expressly to humiliate her' (*RL* 267–8). Here the grotesque
flaunts the intractable materiality of embodied human life; its
realism lies in its insistence on our animal nature and in its
refusal to spiritualize this away. This grotesque apparition is a
bearer of repressed truth: speaking of the *unheimlich* that is
normally kept at bay, it invades the 'constructed' space of
ideology and bursts it asunder. In *The Revenge for Love* this
irruption shatters with equal force the opposed ideologies of
privatized personal relations and Marxist political revolution.
It presents both ways of thinking as sharing a structure of
feeling rooted in sentimental ideals. Like Leonardo's sketches
of deformed heads, the grotesque functions in this text as a
guarantee of what Geoffrey Galt Harpham, in another context,
refers to as 'dense actuality', as a 'resistance to idealization or
generalization'.[38]

Love, of course, never functions in the abstract, and Lewis is
careful to show how Margot's invocation of it belongs to a
particularized literary and cultural tradition. Her view of

nature is from Wordsworth's *The Excursion*, and her fantasy of female heroism from Ruskin's 'Of Queens' Gardens'. A combination of the grotesque and the sublime shatters these constructs. Oppressed by the 'towering landscapes' (*RL* 270) of southern France and disturbed by the 'senseless agitation of unfeeling things' (*RL* 275), Margot is repelled by 'the blatant bustle of these liquids and gasses, the chilly festivity of the organic bodies attached to them, propelled upon wing, foot, fin' (*RL* 276). Her Browningesque perception of nature's otherness seems to 'involve everything upon which her personality had been grounded' (*RL* 276). Her fragile identity begins to fissure, and, realizing that she and Victor are 'hemmed in by a chaotic reality, against which "heroism" (book-heroism) would be of little avail' (*RL* 278), she drifts 'into a world dominated by such figures as the dwarf', finding herself moving 'within the orbit of his spells' (*RL* 327). Nature is reduced in her mind to a 'bleak and senseless bustle of objectless matter' (*RL* 330), and this non-teleological view aligns her perceptions with Hardcaster's.

The Revenge for Love draws on two dominant discourses: politics and the grotesque. It assaults communism on intellectual grounds, proffering a critique that exposes its theoretical weaknesses and its practical consequences. This critique tends to see communism through a Leninist and Stalinist lens, which enables Lewis to focus on its worst excesses: centralization of power in the hands of an autocratic elite; creation of a cadre of professional agitators and export of revolution; insistence on doctrinal purity; suppression of political liberties; murder of unnumbered individuals in successive revolutionary waves. This strategy is unfair to British communists and fellow-travellers, since it relies on guilt by association, but Lewis was appalled at the hypocrisy of common front politics that allowed the left to condone Soviet totalitarianism while condemning Fascist despotism. But in its use of gothic and grotesque the novel works in a different way. The target is the naivety of utopian thought, its dependence on fanciful notions of the potential goodness of human beings and its belief in the power of social structures to liberate it. This aspect of communism is mocked through the nightmarish tropes of the gothic and the grotesque. Lewis was fascinated by Don Quixote, a 'demented character' who 'is the most evident testimony to the dependence on *untruth*, in every sense, in which our human nature and human environment put us' (*TLF* 215). Communism is in *The Revenge for Love* figured as quixotism writ large; a sleepwalker's dream translated into the sphere of *Weltpolitik*, its tragedy, to paraphrase Lewis, is that it is involved in *real* action but it originates in and belongs to an *ideal* world (see *LF* 187).

The most obvious parallel to this double-voiced discourse in a political novel is found in Conrad's *Nostromo*, which offers a clear-sighted assessment of revolutionary politics but tries to redouble its force through the unifying image of the silver, which becomes a transcendent symbol of human corruptibility that *exceeds* the language of political critique. For Conrad, revolutionary aspirations were doomed to failure because they focused on the transformation of social structures rather than on the intractable nature of the human psyche. Looked at from this point of view, *The Revenge for Love* is something more than a political novel. It explores, rather, the workings of *desire*, tracing some of the myriad forms it takes, such as Cruze's sexual rapacity, Gillian's fetishization of the Communist Party, Tristram's projective identification with the proletariat, Margot's self-abasement before Victor, and Hardcaster's commitment to a political cause. For all its much-vaunted humaneness, this stark novel depicts just how profoundly desire, whatever form it takes, blinds individuals to the reasons for and the consequences of their actions. Conrad writes in *Nostromo*: 'A man haunted by a fixed idea is insane. He is dangerous even if that idea is an idea of justice; for may he not bring the heavens down upon a loved head?'[39] Like *Nostromo*, *The Revenge for Love* goes behind politics *per se* in order to expose the motive forces that drive desire. This is why Margot, however much authorial empathy is extended her, is not a final source of value: the novel suggests that her cult of romantic love is in its own way as much a phantasm as any dream of communist utopia. In raptures over Tennyson's *Maud*, fittingly a poem about deluded love, she likens the plunge of a dew-drop to 'a falling world' (*RL* 215), an image we may recall when the novel closes on the tear of self-pity that symbolizes the final collapse of political gullibility.[40]

6

History, Identity, and the Role of Art

Wyndham Lewis claimed in *Rude Assignment* that, although he had changed his views on certain issues, there was a continuity to his intellectual development from the time of *Blast* to the 1940s and that his writings revealed 'a pattern of thinking' (*RA* 153) working in the interests of 'the civilised intelligence' (*RA* 154). *Rude Assignment* is an edgy, defensive text; taking Newman's *Apologia pro vita sua* as a model, it was written as a pre-emptive strike against Lewis's traducers in an attempt to justify his artistic and intellectual positions.[1] In what follows I propose to concentrate on those aspects of this 'pattern of thinking' that help to clarify the nature of the issues that most concerned Lewis throughout his life and that disclose in what respects his convictions had altered towards the end of his career.

The two most obvious shifts concern Lewis's attitude to Western culture and to the political fate of Europe. The key books of the 1920s had been written in defence of a cultural tradition perceived to be under threat from a variety of disintegrative philosophical movements and artistic currents; the key books of the 1930s sought to stave off war by explicating the causes of international conflict and arguing that peace could be preserved only if the principle of national sovereignty was upheld against political centralization. By the late 1940s Lewis had moved away from both positions. The culture he continued to value had, he argued, been destroyed by the two world wars and was being superseded by a more universal world culture. Lewis suggested that the Western tradition had served its purpose and was being incorporated into a 'more comprehensive synthesis' (*RA* 208).[2] This view dovetailed with his rejection of arguments in favour of national sovereignty as the basis upon which peace in Europe could be best maintained; arguing that the new world culture would be ill-served by the preservation of state boundaries, he emerged from the Second World War a federalist and decentralizer.

Did this mean that Lewis now repudiated the intellectual analyses he had undertaken in the 1920s and 1930s? By no means. He was explicit in *Rude Assignment*: the convulsions of the previous thirty years had destroyed the *socio-economic* ground of the culture he had defended, but the *philosophical* basis of his opposition to various intellectual tendencies was still fundamentally sound. Lewis differentiated his historical positioning at that time from the substance of the arguments he had then advanced, arguing that, while it had been a mistake to defend a culture that was passing away, it had been right to reassert its core intellectual values against those of intuitionist, vitalist, and subjectivist philosophies.[3] He suggested that he had been wrong 'to care what happened to Western culture' (*RA* 217) or even to suppose 'that it could survive in the new era we were entering upon: of which world war i [*sic*] and the Russian Revolution were the opening blasts and nuclear energy the perfect symbol' (*RA* 218). In other words, Lewis's own analysis of the increasing power of monopoly capital, the progressive rationalization of social existence, the consequences of war, and the politicization of public life, an analysis he had been advancing from the 1920s onwards, should have shown him that the conditions required for the culture he was defending to exist were being transformed in unprecedented ways. But, if he now recognized this, what did he wish to retain from his pre-war convictions? Post-war texts such as *Self Condemned, The Demon of Progress in the Arts, The Writer and the Absolute,* and *Rude Assignment* provide answers to this question, and in this chapter I want to concentrate especially on Lewis's late reflections on the nature of subjectivity, the role of reason, and the function of the artist.

I suggested in an earlier chapter that in the 1920s and 1930s Lewis focused with almost relentless monotony on the extirpation of reason at the hands of various avant-gardes and vitalist philosophies. In doing so, he foregrounded an issue that traverses political battle-lines. The distance between Lewis and any Marxist, say, lay in what was for him the unbridgeable gap between enlightenment and emancipation. For him, critical thought and creative art produced intellectual enlightenment but not political emancipation. His pessimistic anthropology disavowed the Marxist view that political liberation was an attainable goal. He had always argued, moreover, that in order to perform their speculative function the arts of the writer or painter must be unimpeded by internal constraints and unhampered by external pressures.[4] He defended the inviolability of free thought, arguing that any harnessing of the mind to practical politics would corrupt its disinterestedness. His intellectual purism was inseparable from his aesthetic purism, and this conjunction hints at a link with Kant.[5] With his famous 'sapere aude', Kant saw enlightenment as humanity's 'emergence from its self-incurred immaturity', defined as 'the inability to use one's own understanding without the guidance of another'.[6] Lewis had consistently argued that the ability to think for oneself was the sign of maturity, and it would not be stretching a point too far to suggest that the critical books of the inter-war period were written to help readers do this, since in his view the 'life of the intelligence is the very incarnation of freedom' (ABR 374).

Lewis's desire to safeguard art from ideological pressures, and to protect what Ernst Cassirer terms 'the autonomy of the intellect', belongs to a long tradition of thought that antedates the particular concerns of the Enlightenment *philosophes*, but there are parallels between his oft-stated search for a balanced perspective – beyond action and reaction – and Kant's attempts to reconcile opposing positions.[7] In the inter-war years, however, Lewis's stance was undermined by his often dogmatic language. He adopted an adversarial style in part because it served his polemical purposes, but it also seemed to have the function of holding a disturbingly mutable reality at bay. Lewis's concern with aesthetic stability and intellectual clarity was at this time linked, I would suggest, with a will-to-power over this refractory otherness. Consider a self-description: 'To *solidify, to make concrete, to give definition to* – that is my profession: to "despise the fluid" ... "to postulate permanence" ... to crystallize that which (otherwise) flows away, to concentrate the diffuse, to turn to ice that which is liquid and mercurial' (*P*. 254–5). The way in which these opposing terms are framed suggests his awareness that he was expunging what he knew was there by a decisionist *fiat*. The stress on a conceptual freezing of what he admitted – shades of Bergson and James – may be 'liquid and mercurial' discloses the voluntarism of the sceptic. Voluntarism is in fact a feature of a text like *Time and Western Man*.[8] His inter-war aesthetic was based on his opposition to art that might fall within a Bergsonian orbit, but this oppositionality locked his art in an embrace with its detested other, which unexpectedly revealed the other's truth: his concern with art's stabilizing function pointed to the uncontrollable nature of the world that only art could impel into form.

There was a tendency in Lewis's thought in the 1920s and 1930s to overvalue reason and thus to adhere to one pole of a debilitating dualism. Lewis acknowledged this in various ways after the Second World War (see *RA* 43). This did not mean that he had abandoned his belief in the virtues of reason but rather that he was, like so many intellectuals in the wake of the war, rethinking its limits. In *Dialectic of Enlightenment*, Adorno and Horkheimer suggested that a kind of regression occurs when the intellect subjugates 'sensuous experience', for 'the unification of intellectual functions by means of which domination over the senses is achieved . . . means the impoverishment of thought and of experience: the separation of both areas leaves both impaired'.[9] For Adorno and Horkheimer, there was an inescapable link between the role this dominative process plays in subject formation and in the wider social sphere; the pressing task in the aftermath of the war was to connect the rethinking of human psychology with the critique of institutions and the socio-economic processes that uphold them. *Dialectic of Enlightenment* sought to grasp how enlightenment could be radicalized by reflecting on its complicity with domination; it pressed home the connection between the psychological conflict of the rational and non-rational within the individual and the wider social conflicts generated by a dominative instrumental reason.

Self Condemned is the work in which Lewis's reflections on these issues received their most powerful expression. The novel focuses on the fate of an academic, René Harding, who on the eve of war resigns his chair in history and emigrates with his wife Hester to Canada. Ignored by the Canadian academic community, Harding and his wife lead an impoverished, isolated, tormented life, which ends in tragedy when Hester commits suicide in despair at René's unwillingness to consider a return home, and Harding himself is left a benumbed wreck of a human being. The novel has strong autobiographical elements, based as it was on many of Lewis's wartime experiences, so there is always the temptation of reading it primarily in these terms.[10] It *does*, I think, offer a coded auto-critique, and I shall emphasize the ways in which it enters into dialogue with *Tarr* in order to illustrate this, but more importantly it connects its analysis of Harding's dominative character with broader questions of history and politics, in this way traversing the same terrain as that explored by Adorno and Horkheimer.

A sentence from 'The Meaning of the Wild Body' offers a useful starting point for discussion of *Self Condemned*: 'There is nothing that is animal (and we as bodies are animals) that is not absurd. This sense of the absurdity, or, if you like, the madness of our life, is at the root of every true philosophy' (*WB* 244). In that essay, Lewis went on to cite William James's puzzlement over the fact of being, his sense of perplexed wonder not only 'that *anything* should be, but that *this* very thing should be', and noted James's claim that philosophy can bring 'no reasoned solution' to this conundrum because 'from nothing to being there is no logical bridge' (*WB* 244). For Lewis, the chasm between these two seemingly unconnectable poles could be leapt by a laughter that acknowledged the absurdity of human life, but such laughter, he argued, is unproductive, since when we indulge in it we 'land plumb in the centre of Nothing' (*WB* 244). While it is easy to be amused by the ludicrousness of others, a sense of the futile nature of one's own existence is unbearable.

The view of laughter articulated here suggests that it functions in mercifully brief bursts as an outlet for the release of dark fears about the meaninglessness of existence – were its insights sustainable across time, petrifaction of consciousness would ensue. Absolute revelation – like seeing the face of God

– means death. Laughter, the characteristic response of René Harding to whatever puzzles or disturbs him, is then a defence mechanism that wards off fear of the seemingly absurd nature of human life. Harding, moreover, identifies the absurd with the irrational (especially as expressed through the inexplicable demands of the desiring body), and this identification recalls Camus's claim that the absurd arises from 'the confrontation of the irrational and the wild longing for clarity'.[11] For Camus, the absurd was a predicate of the relationship between man and world; it was that which bound them together 'as only hatred can weld two creatures together'.[12] Such hatred, or perhaps more accurately self-hatred, marks the existence within Harding of the two poles of reason and emotion, which he persistently tries to sever from one another. Consciousness of the absurd is not a side issue in *Self Condemned* but the trap from which its narrative energy springs, since the absurd is located both in the psyche and in the world at large.[13] Harding associates the absurd primarily with the materiality of the body, and this is in keeping with Lewis's conviction that the 'root of the Comic is to be sought in the sensations resulting from the observations of a *thing* behaving like a person', a view that makes us all comic since we are all '*things*, or physical bodies, behaving as *persons*' (*WB* 246). Harding is, however, a *tragi*-comic figure because he seeks to deny his own physical predilections in an attempt to reduce life to the logical form of an algorithm, only to find that the repressed returns in the form of a growing consciousness of the absurd.[14]

At the end of *Self Condemned*, having proved himself unable to weld together the disparate aspects of his psyche, Harding is alive, but only as a mechanism that has been deprived of selfhood.[15] His doom is prefigured by an arrogance that borders on dementia; references to his solipsism, egotism, emotional coldness, and delusions of grandeur abound. Furthermore, *Self Condemned* relies on repetition of patterns, motifs, and symbols to illustrate the truths about Harding that he will not acknowledge but that end by destroying him: his inability to recognize the otherness of his wife, Hester, is signalled early on when we are told that he 'seldom saw his wife in full focus, but behind, or through, something else' (*SC* 7), and this myopia will have a direct bearing on her suicide;

the bleak flatlet in which he and Hester live in London is the counterpart to the boxlike room they will inhabit in Canada, and Harding compartmentalizes his life in both instances, in London working in a separate flat and in Canada standing a suitcase between himself and Hester, 'so blotting her out while he wrote or read' (*SC* 169); the house in London, with its absurd cast of characters, is as grotesque and surreal in the madness it contains as the Hotel Blundell in Canada, and in both cases these microcosms of life implicate the Hardings in their farcical life; finally, the burnt-out hotel standing in the snow like 'a hollow iceberg' (*SC* 296) is an emblem of Harding's eventual inner desolation, which leaves him 'a glacial shell of a man' (*SC* 407).

The novel's reliance on metonymic substitutions means that it traverses the boundary between self and collectivity. Whereas in earlier work Lewis had sought to police this boundary now, in an introspective text that returns to many of the issues with which he had been concerned throughout his life, he discloses the tragedy that ensues from the refusal to blur it. The novel suggests that Harding's fetishization of rationalism and the intellectual positions he adopts have their source in an ascetic purism (shades of Tarr) that cannot accept life's imperfections. This purism manifests itself in a contempt for others; for his own physical urges and emotional needs; for his wife, onto whom he projects those aspects of the desiring self that he cannot acknowledge; and ultimately for the irrationality of history. Life itself appears preposterous, and the individual confronting this bitter truth is driven either to indulge in defensive laughter at its absurdity or to admit, with Tarr, that contempt for all others ends in self-degradation (see *T.* 246).

Looked at from this perspective, Harding's reading of history is revealed as an attempted resolution to the conflict within him between the passional and the rational. His rejection of historiography as hitherto conceived centres on what he sees as its inability to discriminate between events that are beneficial to civilization and those that are destructive. Just as he tries to reject the passional side of his own nature, so he seeks to expunge the irrational from the historical process. This is not an argument in favour of falsifying the facts of history but one in favour of a normative theory in which the historian's task is to adjudicate between competing interpretations of the past from the standpoint of an ethically conceived rationality. In contrast to the view that the historian must consider *everything* that has occurred, without prejudice, Harding's view is that 'we should reject entirely anything (notwithstanding the fact that it undoubtedly happened) which is unworthy of any man's attention, or some action which is so revolting that it *should not* have happened, and must not be encouraged to happen again' (*SC* 93).

This is a curious view of historiography. Harding appears to be arguing that the recounting of reprehensible deeds accustoms people to them and thus prevents them from being seen in their proper light, as despicable acts. No evidence is adduced to support such a claim, when it might just as easily be argued that people *are* horrified by much of what occurs, even if they are powerless to intervene. There are also difficulties about how agreement could ever be reached over the criteria to be used in deciding what is positive and what negative about the past, even if it were to be conceded that the making of such judgements is the historian's province. The criteria according to which such cases would be judged themselves depend on antecedent values (political, religious, ethical, and so on), and to imagine that concord with respect to them could be achieved is to consider that the Archimedean standpoint is attainable.[16] It is a utopian view of how the writing of history would take 'to its logical conclusion the humane, the tolerant, the fastidious', pursuing them 'with great rigidity and implacability ... to a point where all that doesn't belong to them or contradicts them is absolutely repudiated' (*SC* 95).

This normative position is in any case undermined by the absurd, which leads Harding to question the rationality he espouses. The flip side of his idealism is a scepticism that leads to a tragic view of history as irredeemable. Lacking belief in the possibility of supernatural grace saving humankind from perdition, he argues for the apotheosis of the historian, a position that he recognizes is unviable because people 'do not turn their lives upside down in response to the summons of a professor of history' (*SC* 95). Yet this is what Harding has in mind, since he argues that if, his version of qualitative history were to be hegemonic, then, 'pari passu', this misleading valuation would have to be rooted out of daily life' (SC 355). So there is a link here between an account of historiography and a projected reform of contemporary life; Harding is a crusader trying to redeem the present by rewriting the past, even though he realizes that this strategy is doomed to failure.

When Harding first elaborates this new account of historiography, his views are moderate. He denies that he has a ruling caste of philosopher-kings in mind and repudiates the suggestion that his political philosophy entails support for Nietzsche's *Ubermensch*. He is a gradualist, appealing to a liberal tradition of thought in which the values of a humane governance are said to prevail. But in Canada his tragic view of history turns a darker shade and his position becomes extreme. He identifies a death instinct at work in history, and this, coupled with his contempt for humanity in the mass, leads to the view that the race is doomed unless it can be transformed.[17] Lewis had argued in similar terms in the years after the First World War, but *Self Condemned* shows how far he now was from such views when the narrator glosses this shift in Harding's thinking as a degeneration caused by an incipient 'mental instability' (SC 356).[18] The terms in which he is criticized are revealing: 'One might ... find in his adoption of the Superman position a weakening; the acceptance of a solution which formerly he would have refused. His life altogether was being mechanized upon a lower level – in everything expediency counted more with him' (SC 356).

The roots of this decline lie deep in Harding's psyche, and this is why the novel's reiteration of motifs is important: it suggests that he is taking to a logical conclusion a pattern of behaviour that has long been established. His personal deterioration is foreshadowed by these motifs and heightened by them, since the novel portrays him as condemned to repeat his life, but on a lower plane: cohabitation with Hester in the Hotel Blundell is a more claustrophobic version of their previous existence in the London flat; the denizens of the hotel are more bizarre and grotesque than the inhabitants of the first house; Harding's relationship with McKenzie is a pale imitation of his friendship with Rotter; his second book is a febrile expression of ideas more carefully articulated in the first. But, if the

Hardings' tragedy is inevitable, then it is so only because of the flaws in René's character, and it is here that *Self Condemned* signals its distance from *Tarr*. The central protagonists of both novels demarcate reason and emotion, treating the latter as a destabilizing force that must be kept in order. Tarr and Harding also associate the affects, the sexual impulses, and the body's needs with the female other, splitting off this feared aspect of themselves and projecting it onto *das Weib*. But *Tarr* is an aporetic text that cannot sublate this dualism; the split within Tarr, and that between Bertha and Anastasya, disclose the fissures across which the novel's misogynistic ideology is articulated. This ideology is questioned but not overturned and the structure of feeling that sanctions it remains intact. In *Self Condemned* a very different structure of feeling is in place, and Harding comes in for an indictment that invites us to reconsider the polarities established in the earlier text.

The nature of Harding's psyche is similar to Tarr's. I have already discussed his commitment to rationalism, but his attitude to heterosexual relations is also that of his fictional precursor. Like Tarr, Harding is disturbed by desire, which he sees as a portal for the absurd. The self-contempt he feels for falling victim to his own urges and betraying his rationalist ideals is then translated into contempt for his wife, a strategy the narrative exposes: 'Being a man of great natural severity, an eroticism which did not live very easily with it was instinctively resented: and the mate who automatically classified under the heading "Erotics" was in danger, from the start, of being regarded as a frivolous interloper by his dominant intellectuality' (*SC* 41). Hester is from the outset designated as the site and sign of a carnal excess that must be kept at bay; Harding typically sees her metonymically, itemizing the features that remind him of her irksome sexuality, such as the 'big baby eyes' (*SC* 41), the 'well-tailored tail' (*SC* 43), and 'the big silly mouth' (*SC* 44).[19] The metonymic perspective does not just *reduce* Hester to her physical attributes, it ratifies a view of her (and the female sex) as less than human: 'He always forgot that Hester was a human being, because she was so terribly much the Woman' (*SC* 147). And, although Harding has brief insights into his own projections, as when he grasps that she is 'the most frightful reflection of himself, the image of his lubricity' (*SC* 147–8), such glimmers of understanding are systematically repressed.

This suggests that Harding's disillusionment is bound up with his self-condemnation, and that his rhetoric masks a fearful contempt for his own desire: Hester symbolizes the irrational forces (figured as desire) that threaten to destabilize both the self and the social order. Harding is committed to the view that the history 'worth recording, is about the passion of men to stop sane', whereas history as it is actually written 'is the bloody catalogue of their backslidings' (*SC* 212). Unable to accept this truth about human life and unwilling to condone a historiography that seems to collude in it, he admits that it is 'history itself [he is] displeased with' (*SC* 37). But what he detests about history is what he detests about himself, played out on a broader canvas. His rejection of history derives from an ascesis that cannot tolerate the impurities of life, but it is these impurities within himself that are the motive springs behind the rejection. The attempt to split off this aspect of the self drives him deeper into it through the projection of self-disgust onto the female other: 'Hester's obscene person must henceforth be his Muse, in succession to History. He was going to Canada in order to fornicate with Hester. What else!' (*SC* 148).

Self Condemned disavows this misogyny in a way *Tarr* was unable to do. Criticisms of Harding are articulated by the text's female characters (notably his mother and his sister), but the key witness for the prosecution is his wife. Hester is clear-sighted about her husband.[20] It is she who tells him, with the conviction that carries authority, that he has 'an uncommon capacity for self-deception' (*SC* 364), and, like his mother, she sees him as a deluded fool. The narrator observes that he has insulated his mind 'from the centre of emotional awareness' (*SC* 140) and explains this psychic disassociation in terms of internal self-division.[21] Harding's inability to harmonize the discordant elements of his psyche mirrors his inability to engage with his wife, since in his fantasy she symbolizes that which he cannot face. This results in the self-alienation described in the passage just quoted and that is so powerfully expressed in the scene on the ship where he observes himself as though he were looking at some bizarre stranger.[22] It is true that the couple's plight in Canada causes them to cleave to one another, but their new-found closeness has little substance. René's assertion that he would sacrifice anything for Hester is shown to be an empty promise when he refuses to give up a chair at Momaco, despite her pleas. The possibility of regeneration through love is shattered by egotism, and when Hester dies he inverts the truth, seeing her pleas as the sign of 'a destructive selfishness' (SC 390). Rationalism is shown not just as a defence mechanism against the split-off affects but as a will to power. By the end of the novel, Harding's desire to extirpate Hester from his psyche has redoubled in intensity:

> On all sides he found himself beset by false sentiment. He congratulated himself upon the good work he had done in reducing in his personal life these mounds of slush to reasonable proportions. Towards the end of this period he felt he had cleansed things to such an extent that he could end this particular activity. He had driven Hester out of his mind, in which she had dangerously intruded.   (SC 395)

Here, Harding sees Hester as *external* to himself, but in expunging her from his mind he destroys a fundamental part of his own self, an act resulting in 'the extinction of his personality' (SC 406).

In portraying Harding's tragedy in this way, *Self Condemned* weaves together the themes that *Tarr* strove to keep apart. It is not just that Tarr's asceticism is shown to be a disaster for the subject, but that it is connected to a wider historical macrocosm. The novel implies that any attempt to achieve enlightenment by suppressing affect and desire, on the grounds that they are irrational, cannot succeed. The unruly forces at work in history are equally present within the unregenerate self: 'Something in him was as severe and mirthless as those uncivilized forces with which he had contended' (SC 145). Internal repression mirrors the utopian desire to exclude the irrational from history, and the text portrays this as insane idealism. It is the mark of the promethean fantasist, as exemplified by the permanently adolescent Romantic hero. Like Byron's Manfred, Harding's fate suggests 'there is no future pang | Can deal that justice on the self-condemned | He deals on his own soul'.[23]

111

Self Condemned works hard to sustain the parallels between Harding's internal conflicts and those it identifies in history. It is in Sartre's sense a *situated* book, which implicates itself in its time. One consequence of this situatedness was the realization that the refusal of emotion results in the petrifaction of the self; another was the recognition that the European culture defended by Lewis prior to the Second World War had been laid to waste and that a new conception of public life was required. In their existentialist reading of the same historical moment, Camus and Sartre focused on the metaphysical dimension of human situatedness, stressing the individual's obligation to create meaning in an indifferent world. But, unlike Camus and Sartre – whom he criticised for their exaltation of action – Lewis focused less on the problem of meaning in the aftermath of the war than on the erosion of the public sphere.

He had been concerned with this issue in the 1920s and 1930s, so it was no surprise that he returned to it in the 1940s, but his views had now altered. Whereas in 'The Credentials of the Painter' he had claimed that art should be 'the monopoly of the intelligent few' and should not allow itself to be dragged 'down to the level of a possible general humanity' (*WLA* 224), he argued in *Rude Assignment* that the writer must repudiate the ivory tower. Lewis had never believed that art should serve politics, so his rejection of Sartre's call for *engagement* was predictable. But he had maintained that the artist's function was to offer new valuations of life, so he perceived any threat to the public sphere as a calamity. He was specifically concerned to overcome the division of the public into two blocs, a division he had earlier seen as necessary. The very idea of a public, as he acknowledged, was the product of the tradition he had sought to defend but which was now disintegrating. The creation of a minority public addressed by intellectuals left them facing 'an unrepresentative fraction of the whole', whereas 'it *is* the whole, in some form or other, that is required by a writer' (*RA* 18).

But *Rude Assignment* is a contradictory text, and, although the arguments just canvassed hint that he had made peace with some of the oppositions that had characterized his earlier work, elsewhere in the text this is less clear. In his most extreme formulations Lewis had dramatized these conflicts in terms of alienation. In *Enemy of the Stars* the tormented Arghol describes life as 'a grotesque degradation, and "souillure" of the original solitude of the soul', arguing that anything or anybody 'but yourself is dirt' (*B1* 70). But this fixation on the self was fraught with perils and difficulties, as *Enemy of the Stars* revealed, for even the gifted individual was divided against himself, split between the desiring body and the rational mind. *Enemy of the Stars* and *Self Condemned* display in different ways the consequences of the failure to integrate the self and to make peace with the outer world. In one respect, however, Lewis had not changed his views, and this refusal to alter undermines the arguments about the public made in *Rude Assignment*. The issue concerns his view of the individual, specifically his contention that distinctions between people could be traced back to natural differences in disposition and ability. *The Art of Being Ruled* had been explicit about this, and other pre-war texts pushed a similar line. Lewis argued in *Paleface* that only 'a *person* can be susceptible of a *right*', maintaining that people could not possess rights by virtue of belonging to the species *homo sapiens,* on the grounds that what is owing to another 'is "due" not because the object of it is "human" … [but] it is "due" because in some way we recognize an entity with superior claims to ours upon our order, kind or system' (*P.* 76). This account lay behind his Goethean division of people into 'puppets' and 'natures', and it informed his belief that social hierarchies were ratified by the natural order, a position that led him to argue that 'puppets' had no desire to be 'natures' but were satisfied with their status, which meant in turn that the democratic emphasis on equality between human beings was both delusional and destructive.

Lewis had by the 1940s moved from the authoritarian politics he had espoused before the war, but *Rude Assignment* suggests that his conception of the self was still largely asocial. He reiterated the thesis of *The Art of Being Ruled*, arguing that a hierarchical social structure was necessitated by the natural differences in aptitude between individuals, and claiming that no disrespect to those of lesser ability was implied. For Lewis, to fix differences between people was to make them happy, since such differences could not be overcome and people had no desire to leave the place to which nature had allotted them.[24] The main difference between people lay in their capacity for independent thought and creative power; this meant that society should have at its apex not a political oligarchy but a small nucleus of those who 'are fundamentally the most complex, conscious, and highly individualized' (*RA* 202). Differences in *kind* between people were not to be imputed to such proposals; they were based, rather, on a consciousness of differences in *degree* (see *RA* 203). What is absent from this discussion is any sense that the differences among people about which Lewis wrote so breezily are bound up with material and social questions. Everything in this account is reduced to innate predispositions, which are themselves seen in pre-social biological terms. And Lewis's homely, idiomatic style compounds the problem.[25] It simplifies the issues and occludes the ways that subjectivity is formed within specific societies, ignoring the political factors that permit some to discover and develop their abilities while others are denied this opportunity. Lewis's blindness to these considerations is puzzling because elsewhere in *Rude Assignment* he emphasized how important it had been to his own development that money and time had been spent on his education, and we are left with the sense that, although he rejected the notion of a minority culture in favour of a vision of cosmic humanity, he could not bring himself to believe in its viability but chose to hold to the ideals of an intellectual aristocracy and to defend 'the frontier between (1) the changeless Many, and (2) the changeable Few: the unfree and the free' (*RA* 202).[26]

Be this as it may, Lewis argued in *Rude Assignment* that, for the writer to be able to address the community, certain conditions were required, and these, he claimed, were being eroded in the post-war world. On the one hand, the freedom to think independently was being undermined by private monied interests, state-sponsored cultural bureaucrats, and calls for the writer to serve particular causes; on the other hand, the ghettoization of painting and writing, its inaccessibility to the majority, ensured that its public significance was rendered nugatory.[27] Lewis held that writers' claim to social relevance should be based on their capacity to be 'a sort of guardian of the public stock of truth, of the purest objectivity' and that for this role to be fulfilled they must be free 'to speculate, to criticize, to create' (*WA* 12) but must also have an 'outlet in the public life of the community' (*RA* 31). For Lewis a vibrant public sphere was the basis of the civilized existence he sought to defend: 'The present is a private age in-the-making. It is all a question of how long we can fool ourselves, or others, that it is a public age: a *public* age, in my way of speaking, being a free age' (*WA* 198).

Lewis's account of the public sphere focused on its social utility, but it also had a bearing on his view of the form art should take. Art critic of the *Listener* from 1946 to 1951, he was fully aware of developments in British painting, and he filtered what he had learned into *The Demon of Progress in the Arts* (1954). In this brief book he warned that the relentless pursuit of innovation too often resulted in vapid art, and he lambasted the 'pundit-prophets' who in his view circumscribed the artist's independence by encouraging conformity to the fashions of the moment. He was exercised by what he saw as the fetishization of extremism, a view at odds with his Vorticist position, but his explanation for the discrepancy was that the salon art he had then assaulted had been routed and that 'experimentalism' had since hardened into a new orthodoxy. He further argued that post-war extremism in the creative arts could not be explained with reference to their internal development alone but needed to be seen in relation to the dissolution of the public sphere. The creation of two publics, those who, in Ortega y Gasset's words, understand modern art and those who do not, encouraged extremism at both ends of the spectrum, since so-called progressive artists sought to distance themselves ever further from an ostensibly philistine public by becoming progressively more abstruse, while those who identified with this public aimed to provide them with readily accessible product (see *RA* 20).[28] The solution would be to bring together these publics, thus enabling the artist to inhabit the terrain that lay between them.

But what did this mean, exactly? Was Lewis advocating a compromise aesthetic here? Nothing could have been further from his mind. There is a continuity in his thought from the time of *Blast* through to his last published books: we should note that even during the most experimental phase of his

115

career he was urging a position beyond action and reaction and arguing that balance was central to true artistic vision (see *B1* 30; *ABR* 359). This he understood in terms not of an insipid mean but of a transfiguring vision that went beyond the familiar insights of profane life and transcended the clash of ideologies. A version of Keats's negative capability, it envisaged the detached artist 'looking back into the evolutionary machine' and exploring 'its pattern . . . quite cold-bloodedly' (*MWA* 96). The artistry Lewis was defending entailed a different kind of extremism, that of the single-minded visionary who refuses the consolations of ideology in favour of fidelity to the creative act – a position virtually impossible to sustain.[29] So in this account one kind of absolutism – ideology – is replaced by another: artistic objectivity.[30] There was a direct connection between this view and the detached aesthetic perspective that he defended. The point of departure for this invocation of an objectivity comparable to that of science lies in the cartesian revolution, and it belongs to a broad Enlightenment tradition of thought. Descartes's procedure of stripping himself 'of all past beliefs' so as to subject philosophical questions to 'the scrutiny of reason' paved the way for the rejection of external constraints on reflection.[31] Arguments in favour of the autonomy of art translated this *modus operandus* into the realm of the aesthetic – here Kant's separation of the faculties played a decisive role – and Lewis's thought is indebted to this tradition.

It seems vulnerable to two obvious charges: that it relies on an abstract view of disembedded individuality and that it hypostasizes 'objectivity', failing to acknowledge the interested nature of cultural work. But a careful reading of Lewis sheds a different light on these issues. In *The Writer and the Absolute*, he restated his conviction that 'there is in all those arts which parallel nature something like a law obliging the artist to a fanatical scrupulosity. . . . The truth of the great novelists is different from and more personal, certainly, than that of the contemporary "scientific" historian. But in each case a meticulous fidelity to life is of its essence' (*WA* 15). This view was not to be confused with an individualism that sanctioned self-expression but was to be seen in terms of the artist's capacity for a self-overcoming that could produce an almost inhuman lucidity.[32] The individual, he argued, was certainly an over-determined organism, but the artist's gift lay in the ability not to be trapped in contingent situatedness. Thus the psychology on which Lewis's aesthetic relied repudiated any dependance on individual identity, an important issue to which I will return in my concluding remarks: 'The value placed upon the individual here is ... not on account of his *identity*, but because of his remarkable capacity for non-identity, or abstraction' (*WA* 20).

Lewis had in the 1920s and 1930s fought against intellectual currents that sought to destroy this way of thinking by construing knowledge in subjectivist terms. He saw that a particular *tradition* was under threat and that its continuance depended as much on social conditions as on debates internal to philosophy.[33] *Rude Assignment* was more pessimistic than the text with which it was most obviously in dialogue but which it all but passed over in silence: *Time and Western Man*. The earlier work had defended a specific *ethos*, which it presented as still serviceable; but the later text gloomily argued that this tradition had passed into desuetude. Despite Lewis's insistence that the 'bleak fortress' still contained 'much loot' (*RA* 209), he had 'no desire to re-enter it' (*RA* 207), a disinclination that suggests how little he thought could be salvaged from the ruins of a culture that had been dismantled. Looking back, he admitted that this culture now existed only in fragments but still emphasized that it had been 'responsible for [his] mind's particular configuration, for its rational bent' (*RA* 184). It was in relation to *this* cultural inheritance that he continued to situate himself, even as he acknowledged that to all intents and purposes it had passed away.[34]

But within this same culture there is also a long lineage of sceptical thought that has explored the limits of the rational. And Lewis's own work is traversed by scepticism. Montaigne's unanswerable question – *que sais-je?* – lurks just beneath the surface of his compelling prose. If support for rationally conceived and publicly verifiable truths marks one aspect of his thought, then a Stoic acceptance of the impossibility of knowledge and the transformation of human life marks the other.[35] The Stoics' *apatheia* informed Lewis's view of artistic autonomy and detachment as much as any Enlightenment emphasis on the separation of faculties.[36] In 'Physics of the

Not-Self', a key essay that I discuss in my concluding chapter, he traced a path from the Stoics to Socrates, a line of thought that sheds light on his own scepticism, since it was Socrates who insisted that he *lacked* knowledge, professing bewilderment at the oracle's claim that he possessed wisdom. Throughout Lewis's *œuvre* a utopian desire to create 'a new race of philosophers, *instead* of "hurried men," speed-cranks, simpletons, or robots' (*TWM*, p. xvi), wars with a pessimistic view of human irredeemability and the hopelessness of looking to politics or psychology for solutions to the intractable problems of communal life (see *MWA* 213–14).

This pessimism finds its clearest expression at those moments in his career when he stresses his non-teleological and conventionalist view of art's significance, as in this key passage from 'Essay on the Objective of Plastic Art in Our Time':

> I hold that there is never an *end*; everything of which our life is composed, pictures and books as much as anything else, is a means only, in the sense that the work of art exists in the body of the movement of life. It may be a strong factor of progress and direction, but we cannot say that it is the end or reason of things, for it is so much implicated with them; and when we are speaking of art we suddenly find that we are talking of life all the time. The end that we set ourselves, again, and that we are able to imagine but not to possess, is so relative, that we are operating in a purely conventional system of our own.   (*WLA* 200)

In that essay Lewis developed his view of art as a game, which may provide the illusion that something is being achieved, whereas in fact the mind 'is marking time as much as the body, it has the movements of marching forward, but does not march, but is energetically drumming one spot all the while' (*WLA* 204). The language used here hollows out human life, presenting it as a repetition of pointless acts that fill the temporal space between birth and death. Art, like life, is 'a game in the sense that no value can attach to it *for itself*, but only in so far as it is well-played or ill-played' (*WLA* 272), a view of it that puts Lewis closer to an aesthete like Pater than he would have been willing to admit.[37]

But Lewis insisted that, although art could not 'point to anything beyond the thresholds of life, or aspire to transcend the well-defined limits of man's animal status' (*MWA* 231), its roots lay deep in the origins of humanity's species being: it was a constitutional feature of our existence as sentient creatures. The 'artistic impulse', he argued, is 'a very fundamental, semi-magical, thing, of deep organic importance in the life of man' (*WLA* 298). Its importance lay above all in its unflagging testimony to the value of consciousness, language, and intellection, the gifts that differentiate humans from insects or cattle and propel them into social life: 'If we cannot get, at the top, a human world, then art, and everything that we have so far identified with the word civilization, must perish. If our values become the values of stones or matter generally, we perish' (*WLA* 225). Art was for Lewis humanity's most potent form of visionary magic, which gifted it with the power to reflect, interpret, value, and transform. So forceful was it, that it seemed able to draw on some supernormal principle (it is here that Lewis came closest to invoking a transcendent realm), which it could then translate. Crucially, however, this principle was conceived in terms absolutely opposed to neo-heraclitean invocations of the flux or dionysian celebrations of an *élan vital*, the inferior magics Lewis had always impugned. Lewis agreed that 'creative art is a spell, a talisman, an incantation – that it is *magic*, in short' (*TWM* 187), but he added an all-important rider when he explained that for him art was 'the civilized *substitute* for magic' and that it should resist all those who 'wish to lead us down and back to the plane of magic, or of mystical, specifically religious, experience' (*TWM* 188). On this view, civilization is in an inexplicable sense in touch with a supernatural realm but can use it neither to transcend human corporeality nor to reintegrate the human and the divine in some fantasy of primal union. Civilization was of value because it cultivated the peculiar attributes with which humans were endowed, lifting them out of blind mechanism and placing them in a region where conscious agency could be a norm. This was a modest (and in some ways bitter) gain, but its limited benefits were not to be spurned lightly. For Lewis, the overriding question confronting modernity, a question he answered in the affirmative, was 'whether man should maintain himself upon a civilized level, or return to lower levels of life' (*RA* 13).

7

Conclusion: 'Beyond Action and Reaction'?

I have not in this book attempted to provide a complete account of Wyndham Lewis's massive *œuvre* but to highlight those aspects of his writing that are most salient to our understanding of his contribution to modernism. This contribution, I have argued, forces us to rethink contemporary construals of modernism for two reasons: first, because Lewis played a key role in its initial formulation, setting the parameters for an influential phase of its avant-garde activity; secondly, because he became its most trenchant internal critic, assaulting all movements that in his view promoted destructive philosophical/artistic traditions and advocating an anti-subjectivist aesthetic in opposition to them. In my concluding reflections I want to summarize the lineaments of Lewis's alternative modernism and then, more speculatively, to consider its implications for his aesthetics and for his wider analysis of the paths available to a reconstructed 'Western' culture.

Lewis's creative effort aimed at the transformation of life. He defended a transfigurative aesthetic directed at renewal of the here and now. This imperative required the critique of outmoded forms of art that had no purchase on reality and their displacement by new forms that took the conditions of the present as the artist's primary datum without valorizing them unthinkingly. The dead hand of the cultural past was to be 'blasted' away so that a conceptual space could be cleared for the creation of an original artistic lexicon. Closely linked with utopian social aspirations (the emergence of new individuals and forms of communal life), Vorticism promoted an aesthetic conceived as the advance guard of the human race. Looking back on this short-lived cultural moment, Lewis explained that its movements, 'which aimed at a renewal of our artistic sensibility, and to provide it with a novel alphabet of shapes and colours with which to express itself, presupposed a new human ethos' (*WLA* 306).

By the 1920s this optimism had disappeared. The war had provided a bitter corrective to utopian idealism, and post-war socio-economic life was so altered that a new creative and critical effort seemed yet again to be required. But the avant-gardes appeared to Lewis to misapprehend the scale of social change and to fetishize iconoclasm, thus producing a doubly compromised art: it failed to confront the new conditions of life and it reified earlier rhetorics of experimentation and revolt. More generally, the avant-gardes had grasped neither the nature and extent of their involvement in capitalist commodity culture nor their indebtedness to socially and psychologically disintegrative philosophical tendencies. Lewis thus embarked on a wide-ranging analysis of post-war society as a whole, criticized the intellectual/artistic movements that in his view capitulated to its most negative features, and articulated an alternative version of modernism, which combined cultural critique with a spatial aesthetic that defended the continuing viability of publicly shared norms. His writing sought to embody canons that resisted the inner-directed, psychologically-minded modernisms, which for him compromised artistic form and surrendered to the temporal flux; his external aesthetic drew on classicist claims about the need for limits, relied on metaphors that emphasized structure and building, and urged the importance of values held in common by the community at large.[1] This aesthetic informed Lewis's satiric modes, which lampooned publicly observable *behaviour* and thus objectified its victims, lending credence to his claim that 'people seem to me to be rather walking notions than "real" entities' (*BB* 8). It could also mutate into censure of human life *tout court*, which was subjected in certain texts to a corrosive metaphysical scepticism. Above all, it conceived of art as cultural intervention, as a practice seeking to destroy present conditions in the search for a ground zero from which a new history could be created and chronicled. Unlike Eliot, Pound, and even Joyce, this is the Lewis who dismissed the creative revisioning of the past (all those modernist attempts to rewrite earlier traditions, genres, and styles) as empty nostalgia, calling instead for an absolutely new start:

> The kind of screen that is being built up between the reality and us, the 'dark night of the soul' into which each individual is relapsing, the intellectual shoddiness of so much of the thought responsible for the artist's reality, or 'nature' today, all these things seem to point to the desirability of a new, and if necessary shattering criticism of 'modernity', as it stands at present. Having got so far, again, we must sustain our revolutionary impulse. (*P.* 106)

But what did Lewis mean by this? Given his acerbic criticisms of his contemporaries' misguided revolutionary fervour, what kind of 'impulse' did he have in mind? In common with other writers and artists, Lewis followed Nietzsche in urging the complete revaluation of European modernity and arguing for a transformative creativity capable of reimagining and reinventing the present. But he systematically rejected all arts and philosophies of a dionysian hue, on the grounds that their search for cultural renewal entailed the collapsing of subject/object distinctions and depended on the mistaken belief that regeneration may be brought about when the intellect is abandoned and the subject achieves union with a mystically conceived *élan vital*.[2] Lewis was attracted by various transcendental responses to the problem of life's apparent futility and meaninglessness, but he ultimately avowed none of them, finding himself only able to canvas them tentatively, almost as thought-experiments.[3] His thought persistently returned to the impossibility of transcendence, to humanity's inescapable entanglement in matter, and to the inevitability of construing value within a naturalistic frame of reference. Thus far he followed Nietzsche (a huge early influence), but he resisted Nietzsche's celebration of instinctual nature as the corrective to consciousness, which the latter conceived in terms of individual sickness and cultural decadence.[4] There was for Lewis no escape from our embodied existence, no possibility of sloughing off an ectodermic casing

to release some non-material and superior entity.[5] Consciousness, however, offered the capacity for self-reflection and the
ability, through a variety of *techne,* to work at the contingently
bestowed conditions of life in an attempt to improve them,
although both critical thought and the human arts were
conceived by Lewis as functions of nature itself.[6]

Entrapment in mindless corporeality was the besetting
anxiety. Consider the conclusion to a key peroration in *The
Caliph's Design*:

> Let us everywhere substitute ourselves for the animal world;
> replace the tiger and the cormorant with some invention of our
> mind, so that we can control this new Creation. The danger, as it
> would appear at present, and in our first flight of substitution and
> remounting, is evidently that we should become overpowered by
> our creation. Our society might become as mechanical as a
> tremendous insect.   (*WLA*, 156)

Mind is opposed to matter here in time-honoured fashion, but
the all too familiar fear is that a perfectly administered order
may take on an existence of its own, turning the humans who
are meant to direct it into functionaries of its now independent
rationale. In Lewis's work, this deterministic nightmare on the
grand scale is simply the *technological* expression of his horror
at the reduction of human life to the *biological* level of mere
matter. This is why Lewis's individualism struggles against
and strives to rise out of the conditions of 'life' as they are
inherited or found.[7] And it explains why for Tarr the artist's
'first creation is the artist himself' (*T.* 20) and why in *The Enemy*
Lewis contrasts 'the independent life of persons' (*E1*, p. x) with
'the sleep of the machine' (*E1*, p. xi).

The independent life predicated of artists requires them to
be able to stand outside the machine. Its hallmarks are
autonomy, detachment, isolation, and impartiality. Crucially,
in keeping with his hostility to subjectivist versions of modernism concerned with explorations of the inner workings of the
mind, Lewis's conception of how the artist goes about the
process of self-creation relies on a notion of self-emptying that
subsequently ratifies his objectivist ideal. Lewis first articulated
this view in 'Physics of the Not-Self', a still baffling essay
published in 1925 and then rewritten and republished in 1932.

The concept of the *not-self* draws on a number of intellectual sources. In a useful commentary, Alan Munton mentions both Matthew Arnold's reference to the non-human power of God in *Literature and Dogma* and Buddhism's concept of the *anatman* (no-self), noting that in Lewis's development of these ideas the *not-self* refers to 'a capacity for internalization, contemplation, and re-expression particularly the artist's; a self within the artist's self that is detached but active' (*CPP* 222). The essay seems to suggest that the *not-self* allows the subject to free itself from the ego's desires and thus facilitates a form of kenosis in which a truer self emerges. The *not-self* is opposed to the *self*, where the latter is principally associated with the truth of the will while the former reflects the truth of the intellect. This opposition is related to the conflict between the subjectivism Lewis had always impugned for its solipsism and the objectivism he valued for its commitment to reason, clarity, and public norms. The search for truths that could transcend historical contingency and the egotistic will offered the possibility, however tentative and finally unachievable it might be, of putting the individual in touch with a knowledge that was potentially universalizable. The *not-self* provided a way of overcoming 'the chemistry of desire' (*CPP* 199) by which the ego seeks to bend the world to its will, for the '*not-self* established in the centre of the intellect betrays at every moment its transient human associate' (*CPP* 196). That the possibility of altruism was also at stake here may be inferred from the anti-Nietzschean connection made between freedom from personal desire and the ideals of public service: 'If "truth" is the word we give to that disintegrated *not-self* principle which every man necessarily must harbour . . . then every altruism can be traced to the activities of this same principle' (*CPP* 197).[8] The paradox, one of several in the essay, is that 'this speculative organ' (*CPP* 198) is able to serve the good because it can abstract itself from those aspects of the self that typically define it (as a self, identity, or personality) and then function in a seemingly *inhuman* way. Yet it is only through this apparent lack of humanity that art's *promesse de bonheur* has any hope of fulfilling itself.

Despite Lewis's criticisms of T. S. Eliot's theory of impersonality, there are links to his thought here, though less to the early Eliot and more to the poet of *Four Quartets*. But Lewis differed from Eliot in two respects: first, he argued that the release from the self enabled by the *not-self* led not to an openness to the past, which by way of tradition could speak through the poet, but to the transfiguration of the present; secondly, he maintained that even when the *not-self* was active in the creative process, thereby allowing an escape from subjective desire, the personality was still in evidence, so the resulting vision was etched with the lineaments of the mind that produced it. Commenting in *Rude Assignment* on Eliot's description of him as a 'detached observer', Lewis claimed he would accept the designation in the limited 'sense of habitually reserving judgement, and not expressing oneself by action, and, in perhaps the most important things, holding to the *deliverances* of reason', but he rejected Eliot's view of imperso-nality on the grounds that the 'virtue of accurate observation is that it is a *person* observing – stereoscopically ... No person, of course, is capable of perfect detachment: the effort to attain to it would damage the observation' (*RA* 76). Lewis never claimed the artist was capable of perfect vision.[9] But the artist's task was not to model reality on desire, through projective identifications of self and world, but to *dis*-integrate the self so that reality could be seen with a revelatory clarity.[10]

There are also important links with Schopenhauer, and it is likely that 'Physics of the Not-Self' is indebted to his work. Schopenhauer wrote of the self-emptying and the forsaking of will required of the individual who seeks insight, arguing that 'a man who, after many bitter struggles with his own nature, has at last completely conquered, is then left only as pure knowing being, as the undimmed mirror of the world.'[11] Once this beatific state is achieved – like the Buddhist nirvana referred to in 'Physics of the Not-Self' – only 'knowledge remains; the will has vanished.'[12] This is close to Lewis's vision of the knowledge that can only be attained by the holding of a balance – between action and reaction – which he connected in turn with the mind's capacity to be truly speculative only when it functioned in a non-human manner or, to put it in another way, when the principle of the *not-self* displaced the ego-driven desires of the willing self. Schopenhauer saw the roots of compassion in the individual's capacity to pierce

125

the veil of illusion (*Maya*) that separates the self from the other; it is when one grasps that separateness and plurality belong to the realm of phenomena, beneath which lies a hidden essential unity, that one can see oneself in the other and on this basis embrace altruism.[13] Lewis did not phrase it like this, but in his conception the *not-self* liberates the individual from a preoccupation with its *identity* (its own willing and desiring ego) and thus opens the path to a mode of perception that is depersonalized and universal.[14]

'Physics of the Not-Self' helps us understand the serious sense in which Lewis saw himself as an outsider. The essay 'is intended to show the human mind in its traditional role of the enemy of life, as an oddity outside the machine' (*CPP* 195). Such a statement dovetails with Lewis's insistence on the artist's autonomy and independence of mind. But it also toys with a fantasy – escape from the coils that bind knowledge and human interests together. Even as he situated his account of the not-self within the traditions that helped him to formulate it, Lewis tantalized himself with the thought that the truly untrammelled, unillusioned eye exists as a real possibility. As 'Physics' argued, apropos the figure able to deploy this 'speculative organ':

> his altruism only results in differentiating him, and in leaving him without as it were a 'class', even without a 'kind'. For this ultra-human activity is really inhuman ... It is regarded as a breaker-down of walls, a dissolvent of nations, factions, and protective freemasonries, a radio-active something in the midst of more conservative aggregations, as naturally it is. It is an enemy principle.   (*CPP* 198)

We might note here that this vision of perfect disinterestedness reflects a desire to transcend the conditions of life Lewis had himself analysed and that it may be read as the *product* of the loss of agency and the dissolution of a public sphere he had identified. If politics is seen as the source of corruption, as a calamitous trespass on the grounds of art, then all praxis must necessarily be suspect and the resolutely apolitical stance – articulated as the ability to be above the fray – must appear as one of the few principled options available.[15]

But Lewis's account of artistic detachment in terms not of *identity* but rather of *non-identification* should not be read solely in relation to political paralysis. It has productive implications for his much misunderstood 'defence' of 'the West', an issue with which my consideration of his brand of modernism will close. The clue lies in his claim that the truth-teller is without 'class' or 'kind' and that his activity sunders the boundaries upholding the differences between groups (for example, nations and factions). Lewis saw the non-personal approach to philosophy and the arts as a peculiarly Western phenomenon, and this heritage he certainly sought to protect, but he also argued that the intellectual stance he defended was not partisan in any nationalistic sense.[16] The disintegration of the unitary self duplicates the same process that takes place on a global level: neither nation nor a supranational abstraction (such as 'the West') can on this view command the kind of allegiance that identification normally takes for granted and about which Lewis had always been sceptical. But, if this is right, how are Lewis's invocations of categories like 'the West' to be regarded and what role do they play in his modernist sensibility?

Within imperialist and orientalist discourses, the mediation of categories such as 'East' and 'West' has been said to be not only comparative but, in being so, to be marked by hierarchies of value that depict the colonial other as inferior so as to maintain the fiction that the colonizing power is superior and thus justified in its expansionist project. In the wake of the First World War such assumptions came under enormous pressure, resulting in a number of texts devoted to a consideration of them.[17] What is immediately apparent from even the briefest glance at such works is how they vary in their conceptions of what they allege is a *shared* cultural heritage. *Difference*, it turns out, is not produced in relation to some racial or geographical other but is inscribed within the discourses that seek to predicate sameness of a mythical entity variously labelled as 'Europe' or the 'Occident' or 'the West'. In order to demarcate any such entity from external threat, such discourses translate heterogeneity into homogeneity through their invocation of topoi (literally: places). Rhetorical counters like 'the West' function by abstracting a spiritual or intellectual 'essence' from a diversity of conflicting traditions and practices in order to map culture onto space so as to safeguard it from incursions.

Lewis is interesting here because the moves he makes are unexpected when they are seen in relation both to a hardening of East/West divisions in much 1920s writing and to subsequent post-colonial critique, which has urged us to see imperialism in terms of orientalist discursive regimes. Lewis *split open* both categories in order to show that they are mythic constructs and to argue that any critique of 'the West' that reverses its racialized hierarchy of values by embracing the other cannot address the rationale that institutionalized this hierarchy of values in the first place, for valorization of the other on the grounds of alterity alone was for him little more than a reflex of cultural guilt.

Lewis was clearly trying to salvage aspects of what he conceived as a 'Western' set of traditions: he was engaged in the defence of a 'graeco-roman highway' and of the 'type of mind' (*RA* 207) produced within its traditions.[18] Certainly, Lewis had a predilection for inverting the hierarchy between 'West' and 'East', as evidenced by his belief that 'all the very finest plastic and pictorial work has come out of the Orient, and that Europeans have never understood the fundamental problems of art in the way the Indian, Persian, or Chinese have done' (*P.* 69). This conviction, in turn, led him to reject graeco-roman conceptions of classicism: 'The hellenic age has no monopoly of those qualities generally catalogued as "classical"; so, according to me, the term "classical" is used in much too restricted, historical a sense; – in a word, too historically. . . . the seeds of the naturalist mistakes are certainly to be found precisely in Greece: and I believe we should use the *Classical* orient . . . to rescue us at length from that far-reaching tradition' (*P.* 255).

In Lewis's usage, the progressist schema familiar in orientalist discourses was turned upon itself so that it could serve as an account of cultural belatedness: the geometrization of modern art found in Vorticism and consistently championed by Lewis was presented as a long overdue recognition of the superiority of non-European aesthetic canons: 'All primitive people have proved themselves a sort of aesthetic engineers . . . a great suspension bridge, or a modern factory building . . . is only reintroducing into our life an element which the most ancient art supremely possessed, but which has been absent in european art' (*P*. 251). The contrast, then, was not a diachronic one that valorized the present over the past and not a geographic/spatial one that favoured 'the West' over 'the East': it was a contrast between two different forms of 'primitivism' neither of which was conceived in historical or racial terms. Lewis objected to a 'primitivism' that sacrificed the arts of the conscious, valuing mind for an unthinking immersion in the life of instinct, drive, and sensation. His shafts were aimed at the movements that invoked the Dionysian as their *raison d'être*, and his main targets were Futurism, Dada, and Surrealism.

Lewis scorned those who valorized the other in racial terms as the possessor of some kind of authentic unmediated purity of being, and he resisted unitary conceptions of 'the West' that defined it against racially conceived others. The first move was a form of romantic exoticism that conceived cultural renewal through a reversal of hierarchies that left their structural relations unquestioned (see *P*. 20, 41).[19] Lawrence was for him the arch exponent of this mode of thought. Lewis read it as a sentimentalism through which a once hegemonic but now decaying culture avoided the hard task of a nuanced internal critique in favour of the far easier wholesale rejection of itself, a purely destructive approach that was the sign of a profound cultural self-contempt.[20] Lewis saw this tendency as belonging to a particular historical moment; it was the result of a crisis of cultural confidence spawned by the First World War (see *P*. 115, 126). The fact that 'the West' was conceived in monolithic terms meant that, when its values were called into question, it was either defended in a reductive way or was jettisoned entire. So Lewis sought to *split open* an abstraction like 'the West' in order to emphasize its irreducibility to race, place, or *Geist*: 'Western Man, as such, is of course the completest myth' (*TWM* 134). In seeking to make this myth serviceable, he was creating what Benedict Anderson describes as an 'imagined community', but in doing so he was trying to imagine it as plural, heterogeneous, and internally fissured.[21]

Lewis was not consistent in this respect, but in the main he resisted the abject fantasy that one can *become* other in favour of a deconstructive strategy that sought to *reinscribe* otherness within the discourses that excluded it, thus mocking spurious conceptions of cultural homogeneity and making 'the West' other to itself. Otherness, of course, is easily reifiable; to shift Lewis's terms, we might say that the other, as such, is of course the completest myth. There is no other; rather there are numerous discourses that posit others for a range of ideological purposes. Lewis found some forms of alterity distinctly more congenial than, dare I say it, others. At his worst, he invoked the idea of 'race' in an exclusionary and defensive way.[22] At his best, he argued against the policing of his imaginary community's borders and, in opening them up, posited a modernity that began not with the interpellation of the other as an inferior but rather as a partner in dialogue. In doing so, Lewis suggested that, whatever it was, 'the West' was far from being an achieved project and that the modernist arts required by its fall into modernity should oppose the rhetorics of cultural apartheid:

> It is just against that separatism as between the different segments of the West that we have most to contend. We should have – should we not? – our local Melting-pot. It is *a new West*, as it were, that we have to envisage: one that, we may hope, has learnt something from its gigantic reverses. For it is only by a fresh effort that the Western World can save itself: it can only become 'the West' at all, in fact . . . by an act of further creation. . . . 'The West' is for almost all . . . a *finished* thing, either over whose decay they gloat, or whose corpse they frantically 'defend'. It never seems to occur to them that the exceedingly novel conditions of life today demand an entirely new conception. (*P*. 256)

Notes

CHAPTER 1. INTRODUCTION: 'THE POLITICS OF STYLE'

1. Fredric Jameson, *Fables of Aggression: Wyndham Lewis, the Modernist as Fascist* (Berkeley and Los Angeles: University of California Press, 1979), 2.
2. A wide range of evidence could be cited here. Three examples: Lewis's support for Eliot's *Criterion*, for which he offered to write *gratis*, since he believed that 'every failure of an exceptional attempt like yours with the Criterion [*sic*] means that the chance of establishing some sort of critical standard here is diminished' (*L.* 137); the letter he wrote to Herbert Read in 1927, in which he stressed the need for organization, arguing that he did not wish for 'a self-seeking isolation' and that with regard to *The Enemy* it was 'essential not to give the impression of a single spy, but of a battalion' (*L.* 172); his claim that, while independence of mind safeguarded intellectual freedom and the position of outsider allowed the writer to criticize society, he did not believe 'that "to stand outside" is a good thing, except for a specific purpose' (*RA* 75) and would be 'sorry to appear an out-and-out partisan of *outsideness*' (*RA* 77).
3. See Lewis's 1949 letter to the *Partisan Review*. Apologizing for his intrusion on its 'private, and partisan, history-making' (*L.* 491), he wrote: 'That *Blast* was my idea, that I was the editor, that in short the whole show was mine, finally that *vorticism* was purely a painters [*sic*] affair (as *imagism* was a purely literary movement, having no relation whatever to *vorticism*, nor anything in common with it) need not worry you. I should be a very fussy person if I expected people to bother about details of this order. Indeed I was rather gratified to see my name at all' (*L.* 492). With respect to Ford, I think here of such claims as the following: '[Conrad] has done an immense deal for the Nuvvle in England – not so

much as I, no doubt ... I learned all I know of Literature from Conrad – and England has learned all it knows from me ...' (Ford Madox Ford, *Critical Writings of Ford Madox Ford*, ed. Frank MacShane (Lincoln, Neb.: University of Nebraska Press, 1967), 99).

4. Alan Munton has written valuably on Lewis's politics and his importance as a cultural critic. See Alan Munton, 'Understanding the Left', *Stand* 21/1 (1979–80), 41–5, and Alan Munton, 'The Politics of Wyndham Lewis', *PN Review*, 1 (Mar. 1976), 34–9.

5. For information on these groups, see Judith Collins, *The Omega Workshops* (London: Secker & Warburg, 1984), and Anna Gruetzner Robins, *Modern Art in Britain: 1910–1914* (London: Merrell Holberton, 1997).

6. Lewis often referred to his frustration at the time wasted on such activity. See *L*. 120.

7. Alan Munton has some very interesting things to say about Lewis's dialogical approach to his contemporaries in Alan Munton and Michael Durman, ' "Changing our Common Life": Wyndham Lewis Interprets Matisse and Picasso', in Paul Edwards (ed.), *The Great London Vortex: Modernist Literature and Art* (Bath: Sulis Press, 2002), 1–9.

8. *The Childermass* has provoked a number of critical debates among scholars. Interested readers should consult the following texts. David Ayers, *Wyndham Lewis and Western Man* (Basingstoke: Macmillan, 1992); Peter Caracciolo, ' "Demavend! Recalling Zendavesta": Ancient Iranian Myths in *The Human Age*', *Enemy News*, 17 (Autumn 1982), 12–15; John Constable, 'Critic or Creator: Wyndham Lewis and *The Childermass*' *Review of English Literature*, 64 (Sept. 1992), 1–19; Alistair Davies, 'Wyndham Lewis's Fiction of Conspiracy: *The Childermass*' *Enemy News*, 16 (Summer 1982), 22–32; Alistair Davies, 'Wyndham Lewis's Fiction of Conspiracy Revisited', *Enemy News*, 18 (Autumn 1983), 26; Paul Edwards, *Wyndham Lewis: Painter and Writer* (New Haven and London: Yale University Press, 2000), 317–40; Alan Munton, 'A Reading of *The Childermass*', in Jeffrey Meyers (ed.), *Wyndham Lewis: A Revaluation* (London: Athlone, 1980), 120–32; Alan Munton, 'Lewis, *The Childermass* and a German Secret Society', *Enemy News*, 17 (Autumn 1982), 7–11.

9. It was, of course, this aspect of Lewis's work that so interested an earlier prophet of a technologized information age: Marshall McLuhan.

10. The full extent of this alienation becomes clear further on: 'I seized her stiffly round the body. All of her still passably lissom

person – on the slight side – gave. It was the human willow, more or less. It fled into the hard argument of my muscular pressures. Her waist broke off and vanished into me as I took her over in waspish segments, an upper and a nether. The bosoms and head settled like a trio of hefty birds upon the upper slopes of my militant trunk: a headless nautilus on the other hand settled upon my middle, and attacked my hams with its horrid tentacles – I could feel the monster of the slimy submarine-bottoms grinding away beneath, headless and ravenous' (*SB* 48).

11. Paul Edwards, drawing here on Jameson, rightly observes that this style, built from quotation and allusion, shows 'the cliché (particularly the cultural cliché) as dictating in advance the shape of experience: experience is never unmediated' (*Wyndham Lewis*, 323).

12. He was himself aware of this danger, as *The Enemy* makes clear: 'But it has been objected that my own critical writing is full of storm and stress: that I am a counter-storm, merely, and that I do not set an example of Olympian calm to my romanticist adversaries' (*E3* 24). He responded to the charge by arguing that his 'incandescent rhetoric' served a necessary polemical purpose, and that it was to be seen as 'a sudden barrage of destructive criticism laid down about a spot where temples, it is hoped, may under its cover be erected' (*E3* 25).

13. Here is the passage in full: 'The sort of First-person-singular that Hemingway invariably invokes is a dull-witted, bovine, monosyllabic simpleton. This lethargic and stuttering dummy he conducts, or pushes from behind, through all the scenes that interest him. This burlesque First-person-singular behaves in them like a moronesque version of his brilliant author. He *Steins* up and down the world, with his big lustreless ruminatory orbs of a Picasso doll-woman (of the semi-classic type Picasso patented, with enormous hands and feet). It is, in short, the very dummy that is required for the literary mannerism of Miss Stein! It is the incarnation of the Stein-stutter – the male incarnation, it is understood.

But this constipated, baffled 'frustrated' – yes, deeply and Freudianly 'frustrated' – this wooden-headed, leaden-witted, heavy-footed, loutish and oafish marionette – peering dully out into the surrounding universe like a great big bloated five-year-old – pointing at this and pointing at that – uttering simply 'CAT!' – 'HAT!' – 'FOOD!' – 'SWEETIE!' – is, as a companion, infectious. His author has perhaps not been quite immune. Seen for ever through his nursery spectacles, the values of life accommodate themselves, even in the mind of his author, to the limitations and peculiar requirements of this highly idiosyncratic puppet' (*MWA* 27–8).

14. See the witty description of Hemingway's apopleptic response to this critique when he first read it in Sylvia Beach's bookshop, as recounted by Paul O'Keeffe, *Some Sort of Genius: A Life of Wyndham Lewis* (London: Jonathan Cape, 2000), 342–3.

15. This is the burden of his critique especially of Pound and Joyce, which he prosecutes above all in *Time and Western Man*. For Lewis, both writers are primarily interested in what he describes as purely technical (formalist) linguistic/literary innovation and thus neglect the wider implications of the styles they respectively urge. This makes them the purveyors of ideologies they barely comprehend. The importance of *Paleface* to this proto-deconstructive aspect of Lewis's thought can scarcely be overemphasized.

16. John Russell writes of this aspect of Lewis's aesthetic: 'Making art is really an arresting process, an abstracting of ultimate reality . . . from a passing "reality" . . . this is done not in a time scheme . . . but by breaking up actions as they unfold, and externalizing their souls – along with the souls of their perpetrators – in a kind of minute-by-minute changing frieze' (John Russell, *Style in Modern British Fiction: Studies in Joyce, Lawrence, Forster, Lewis, and Green* (Baltimore and London: Johns Hopkins University Press, 1978), 124). See also Jameson's emphasis on Lewis's view of reality as 'infinitely divisible' (*Fables of Aggression*, 31).

17. The productive and conventionalist aspect of art was central to Lewis's conception of it: 'art consists among other things in a *mechanizing* of the natural. It bestows its delightful disciplines upon our aimless emotions: it puts its gentle order in the place of natural chaos: it substitutes for the direct image a picture. And, ultimately, and analysed far enough, it substitutes *a thing* for *a person* every time – and this is as true of the book as of the painted picture' (*MWA* 129).

18. I do not mean to imply that Lewis's writing lacks clarity. On the contrary. His critical works deal with an often dauntingly difficult subject matter, but the demands they make on the reader are caused more by their elliptical structures (see especially *ABR* and *TWM*) than by the quality of Lewis's prose, which is vigorous and direct. But his writing is certainly mannered; it is hard to imagine anybody else creating his particular kind of prose. For an account of the 'defects' of this prose, see Jeffrey Meyers, *The Enemy: A Biography of Wyndham Lewis* (London: Routledge & Kegan Paul, 1980), 146–50.

19. Paul Edwards writes of Lewis's 'mature Modernist style' that 'by its excess it opens a gap between signification and the "reality" it refers to' (*Wyndham Lewis*, 15).

20. Jameson sees this in a more localized way as taking place at the level of the sentence, which is in Lewis 'reinvented with all the force of origins, as sculptural gesture and fiat in the void' (Jameson, *Fables of Aggression*, 2).

21. Paul Edwards's recent book, *Wyndham Lewis: Painter and Writer*, is centrally concerned with this conflict in Lewis's writing, which it discusses in detail.

CHAPTER 2. *BLAST*, VORTICISM, AND *TARR*

1. See e.g. Judith Collins, *The Omega Workshops* (London: Secker & Warburg, 1984), 52–68; Jeffrey Meyers, *The Enemy: A Biography of Wyndham Lewis* (London: Routledge & Kegan Paul, 1980), 39–54; Paul O'Keeffe, *Some Sort of Genius: A Life of Wyndham Lewis* (London: Jonathan Cape, 2000), 129–38.

2. There has been a good deal of scholarship on Italian Futurism. See Gunter Berghaus, *Futurism and Politics: Between Anarchist Rebellion and Fascist Reaction* (Oxford: Berghahn, 1996); Caroline Tisdall and Angelo Bozzola, *Futurism* (London: Thames & Hudson, 1977); and John J. White, *Literary Futurism: Aspects of the First Avant-Garde* (Oxford: Clarendon Press, 1990).

3. C. R. W. Nevinson, *Paint and Prejudice* (New York: Harcourt, Brace & Company, 1938), 76.

4. Collins, *The Omega Workshops*, 110–11.

5. The phrase is taken from the title of Richard Cork's book, *Vorticism and Abstract Art in the First Machine Age*, i. *Origins and Development* (London: Gordon Fraser, 1976).

6. See especially *Blast 2*, where the 'Review of Contemporary Art' and the 'History of the Largest Independent Society in England' reveal this tendency. In the former essay, Lewis wrote that his inspection of contemporary art movements 'was undertaken . . . to show the ways in which we DIFFER, and the tendencies we would CORRECT . . . They are definitely a criticism, then, and not an appraisement' (*B2* 41).

7. The overweening, but also tongue-in-cheek, scope of *Blast*'s cultural ambitions may be discerned in its claim that, with subscribers 'in the Khyber Pass' and in 'Santa Fe', the 'first stone in the structure of the world-wide reformation of taste has been securely laid' (*B2* 7).

8. For an analysis of this aspect of modernism, see Laurence Rainey, *Institutions of Modernism: Literary Elites and Public Culture* (New Haven: Yale University Press, 1998).

9. Hugh Kenner, *A Sinking Island: The Modern English Writers* (London: Barrie & Jenkins, 1988), 138.

10. Scorning the 'abasement of the miserable "intellectual" before anything coming from Paris', Lewis claimed that there 'is nothing Chauvinistic or picturesquely patriotic about our contentions' (*B1* 34). For a different reading of *Blast 2*, see Paul Peppis, ' "Surrounded by a Multitude of Other Blasts": Vorticism and the Great War', *Modernism/Modernity* (Wyndham Lewis Number), 4/2 (Apr. 1997), 39–66.

11. John Rothenstein, *Wyndham Lewis and Vorticism* (London: Tate Gallery, 6 July–19 Aug. 1956), 6.

12. Lewis consistently claimed that the artist's task was to deal with the here and now. This did not mean that Vorticism celebrated technology, as Lewis claimed the Futurists did, but that it took it as a point of departure: 'It did not sentimentalise machines, as did the Italians . . . it took them as a matter of course: just as we take trees, hills, rivers, coal deposits, oil-wells, rubber-trees, as a matter of course' (*WLA* 341).

13. After his quarrel with Fry, Lewis tended to deny that Fry had ever influenced him, but there are clear parallels between Vorticism's architectural emphases and Fry's account of Post-Impressionism in terms of structure and architecture. See Collins, *The Omega Workshops*, 45–6, and Paul Edwards, *Wyndham Lewis: Painter and Writer* (New Haven and London: Yale University Press, 2000), 104–8.

14. Rainey, *Institutions of Modernism*, 29, 38.

15. See, for just a few examples, *L.* 41–3; Meyers, *The Enemy*, 60–2; Peter Nicholls, *Modernisms: A Literary Guide* (London: Macmillan, 1995), 173; and Paul Edwards, 'Afterword', in Lewis, *Time and Western Man* (Santa Rosa, Calif.: Black Sparrow Press, 1993), 459.

16. Umbro Apollonio (ed.), *Futurist Manifestoes* (London: Thames & Hudson, 1973), 23.

17. Edwards, *Wyndham Lewis*, 144. Edwards provides a detailed reading of the text, which is attentive both to its formal features and to its philosophical implications. See his fine chapter, 'The Modernism of *Enemy of the Stars*', 139–65.

18. Meyers, *The Enemy*, 66.

19. For a thorough discussion of these issues, to which I am indebted here, see Edwards, *Wyndham Lewis*, 146–8.

20. Ibid. 150.

21. Meyers, *The Enemy*, 62.
22. For a later view about the importance to Lewis of a cultural inheritance and for criticism of Marinetti's destructive programme, see *L*, 367–8.
23. Lewis wrote in 1917: 'The Bee in the Bonnet [*sic*] about Modernity . . . seems to me an imbecility' (*L*. 86).
24. T. E. Hulme, *Speculations: Essays on Humanism and the Philosophy of Art*, ed. Herbert Read (London: Routledge & Kegan Paul, 1960), 76–7, 94.
25. As Lewis put it: 'To synthesize [the] quality of LIFE with the significance or spiritual weight that is the mark of all the greatest art, should be . . . the work of the Vorticists' (*B2* 77).
26. Lewis wrote, for example: 'There is only one thing better than "Life" . . . and that is something very abstruse and splendid, in no way directly dependent on "Life". It is no EQUIVALENT for Life, but ANOTHER Life, as NECESSARY to existence as the former' (*B1* 130).
27. Jose Ortega y Gasset, *The Dehumanization of Art and Other Essays on Art, Culture, and Literature*, trans. Helene Weyl (Princeton: Princeton University Press, 1968), 25.
28. Lewis often emphasized this jokey aspect to the whole avant-garde 'game' in his retrospective accounts of it. See e.g. *BB*, 32–9.
29. For Lisa Tickner, there is nothing surprising about fancy-dress parties and pageants on which aristocrats and advanced artists collaborate, but she argues that what is new here is 'the sense that they have an audience beyond their participants, that they provide copy and photographs for the press and can be restaged for new purposes' ('The Popular Culture of *Kermesse*: Lewis, Painting, and Performance, 1912–13', *Modernism/Modernity* (Wyndham Lewis Number), 4/2 (Apr. 1997), 67–120, at 95). See also O'Keeffe, *Some Sort of Genius*, 139–46.
30. Peter Burger, *Theory of the Avant-Garde*, trans. Michael Shaw (Minneapolis: University of Minnesota Press, 1984).
31. For a brief discussion of this aspect of Vorticism, see Nicholls, *Modernisms*, 166–7.
32. Lewis was explicit about the link himself, as a later essay made clear: 'Mr Wyndham Lewis, the vorticist of 1914–15, was a "sea-green incorruptible" . . . He thought the time had come to shatter the visible world to bits, and build it nearer to the heart's desire: and he really was persuaded that this *absolute* transformation was imminent' (*WLA* 340).
33. Daniel Schenker puts the point well: 'The novel is not *dead* . . . it does traffic with the souls of men and women, and it often

explores an inner landscape that the eye cannot see' ('Homo Ex Machina: Wyndham Lewis on the Definitions of Man', *Blast 3*, ed. Seamus Cooney (Santa Barbara, Calif.: Black Sparrow Press, 1984), 96–108, at 96).

34. For the view that Kreisler is associated with the id and Tarr with the ego, see Fredric Jameson, *Fables of Aggression: Wyndham Lewis, the Modernist as Fascist* (Berkeley and Los Angeles: University of California Press), 98–9. Jameson also sees the importance of the Kreisler–Soltyk couple, but he reads their conflict in terms of national allegory (pp. 91–2).

35. David Trotter has described Lewis's 'subject matter' as a 'fruitless negotiation with the abject', but I shall argue that this negotiation is not fruitless, for, although *Tarr* finds no way to overcome or break out of the firm grip exerted by abjection, it demonstrates its destructive power with uncanny acuity. See David Trotter, *The English Novel in History: 1895–1920* (London: Routledge, 1993), 284–5.

36. For a good discussion of the text's unresolved viewpoints, see Peter Burger, 'Dissolution of the Subject and the Hardened Self: Modernity and the Avant-Garde in Wyndham Lewis's Novel *Tarr*', in Burger, *The Decline of Modernism*, trans. Nicholas Walker (Cambridge: Polity, 1992), 131–2.

37. Friedrich Nietzsche, *On the Genealogy of Morals and Ecce Homo*, trans. Walter Kaufmann (New York: Vintage, 1969), 36–7.

38. Consider the similarities between these two descriptions. Nietzsche writes: 'the man of *ressentiment* is neither upright nor naïve nor honest and straightforward with himself. His soul *squints*; his spirit loves hiding places, secret paths and back doors, everything covert entices him as *his* world, *his* security, *his* refreshment' (*On the Genealogy of Morals*, 38). Julia Kristeva writes: 'Abjection . . . is immoral, sinister, scheming, and shady: a terror that dissembles, a hatred that smiles, a passion that uses the body for barter instead of inflaming it, a debtor who sells you up, a friend who stabs you' (*Powers of Horror: An Essay on Abjection*, trans. Leon S. Roudiez (New York: Columbia University Press, 1982), 4).

39. Melanie Klein writes that 'the projection of a predominantly hostile inner world which is ruled by persecutory fears leads to the introjection – a taking-back – of a hostile external world; and vice versa, the introjection of a distorted and hostile external world reinforces the projection of a hostile inner world' (*Envy and Gratitude and Other Works, 1946–1963* (London: Virago, 1990), 11).

40. Max Scheler, 'Ressentiment', in Robert Solomon (ed.), *Nietzsche: A Collection of Critical Essays* (New York: Anchor, 1973), 244.

41. Nietzsche, *On the Genealogy of Morals*, 230.
42. The passage reads as follows: 'Casting desperately about for means of handling the situation, he remembered she had spoken of getting a dog *to guide* her. What had she meant? However, he grasped at the dog: he could regain possession of himself in romantic stimulus of this figure. He would be her dog! Lie at her feet! He would fill with a merely animal warmth and vivacity the void that must exist in her spirit . . . All he asked was to be her dog! Only wished to impress her as a dog! . . . . The sense of security ensured him by the abjectness of this resolution caused him to regain his self-possession. Only it imposed the condition, naturally, of remaining a dog' (*T*. 103).
43. Kristeva, *Powers of Horror*, 6.
44. For the social issues raised here, see *T*. 261, 262, 269, 271.
45. For Sigmund Freud, 'even where it emerges without any sexual purpose, in the blindest fury of destructiveness, we cannot fail to recognize that the satisfaction of the [death] instinct is accompanied by an extraordinarily high degree of narcissistic enjoyment, owing to its presenting the ego with a fulfilment of the latter's old wishes for omnipotence' (*Civilization and its Discontents*, trans. James Strachey (New York: W. W. Norton, 1962), 68). There is, of course, a highly charged sexual element to the Kreisler–Soltyk doublet.
46. Two further examples are relevant. Consider this meeting with Hobson: 'Taking crudely the subject that was foremost in his existence he imposed it upon their talk' (*T*. 14). Or this account of his attempt to break with Bertha: 'Tarr felt that she too must, naturally, be enjoying his points: he forgot to direct his exposition in such a way as to hurt her least. This trivial and tortured landscape had a beauty for him he was able and eager to explain, where for her there was nothing but a harrowing reality' (*T*. 63).
47. When he gazes at a photograph of himself and Bertha, his thoughts take the following turn: 'How strangely that twist of his, or set angle of the head, fitted in with the corresponding peculiarities of the woman's head and bust. What abysms of all that was most automatic and degrading in human life: rubbishy hours and months formed the atmosphere around these two futile dolls!' (*T*. 49–50).
48. Elizabeth Grosz, *Sexual Subversions: Three French Feminists* (St Leonards: Allen & Unwin, 1989), 74.
49. This view is lent support by Lewis's rejection of essentialism in *The Art of Being Ruled*; he argued that the male 'is not naturally "a man" any more than the woman. He has to be propped up

into that position with some ingenuity, and is always likely to collapse' (*ABR* 247). For Lewis, gender identity was basically a social construct, thus he maintained that the 'position of the male today, and the symbolism of the word MAN, are purely artificial: no more for one sex than for the other are the heroic ardours, "intellectuality", *responsibility*, and so forth, that we associate with the male, *natural* (*ABR* 249).

50. Robert Louis Stevenson, *Dr Jekyll and Mr Hyde and Other Stories* (Harmondsworth: Penguin, 1979), 84. Tarr alludes to *Jekyll and Hyde* in one of his self-descriptions (*T.* 23).

51. Thus René Descartes: 'I ... concluded that I was a substance whose whole essence or nature consists only in thinking, and which, that it may exist, has need of no place, nor is dependent on any material thing; so that "I", that is to say, the mind by which I am what I am, is wholly distinct from the body, and is even more easily known than the latter, and is such, that although the latter were not, it would still continue to be all that it is' (*A Discourse on Method*, trans. John Veitch (London: J. M. Dent, 1975), 27).

52. Jameson, *Fables of Aggression*, 4.

53. Hulme, *Speculations*, 86, 90.

CHAPTER 3. AVANT-GARDE AND MODERNIST POLEMICS

1. The essays I have in mind are 'Prevalent Design', published in *The Athenaeum* 1919 and 1920; *The Caliph's Design*, published under the imprint of Harriet Weaver's *The Egoist* in 1919; 'Essay on the Objective of Plastic Art in our Time', published in *The Tyro* 2; and 'The Credentials of the Painter', published in *The English Review* in 1922.

2. 'The Children of the New Epoch' was explicit: 'We are at the beginning of a new epoch, fresh to it, the first babes of a new, and certainly a better, day. The advocates of the order that we supersede are still in a great majority. The obsequies of the dead period will be protracted, and wastefully expensive. But it is nevertheless nailed down, cold, but with none of the calm and dignity of death. The post-mortem has shown it to be suffering from every conceivable malady' (*WLA* 195).

3. Lewis wrote that 'those *whose interests lie all ahead*, whose credentials are in the future, move ... forward, and away from the sealed and obstructed past' (*WLA* 195).

4. Thus Lewis admits that he traces his own theory back to the eye and that it is 'in the service of the things of vision that my ideas are mobilized' (*TWM* 134). When he later criticizes Alfred North Whitehead, he explains that 'the machinery of the physicist is one thing, and the predilection of the artist for concrete objects is another, and that in my criticism it is *only* that predilection that is at stake' (*TWM* 193).

5. This is potentially confusing, of course, since Berkeley argued that his philosophy safeguarded the 'common-sense' world, whereas most of his critics claimed that he dissolved it altogether.

6. His position has often been misrepresented, as he anticipated it would be. Referring to the philosopher Edward Caird's account of Cynic thought as 'one of those beginnings of progress which take the appearance of reaction' (*TWM* 130), he remarked that, although his critique would be mistaken for conservativism, he was in fact impatient with 'many of the forms that "revolution" takes, in art, sociology, science and life', and would 'hasten the day when "revolution" should become a more rigorous business, humanely and intellectually, if undertaken at all, and no longer be left only in the hands of people who do nothing but degrade and falsify it' (*TWM* 131).

7. Lewis also raised the problem of how he was perceived elsewhere: 'Is it possible to launch and develop this criticism without being accused of bias of an opposite sort – in a word, of being a "reactionary", of the nature of Thomas Carlyle? My answer is that it is impossible. But that does not make the accusation necessarily true' (*E3* 28).

8. He wrote: 'It is everywhere obligatory – just as evening dress has become more or less obligatory, at the same time, in our society. Every one who has money enough is today a "revolutionary"; that and the dress suit are the first requisites of a gentleman' (*ABR* 33).

9. Gerald Graff, *Literature against Itself: Literary Ideas in Modern Society* (Chicago: Chicago University Press, 1979), 119. See also Suzy Gablik, *Has Modernism Failed?* (London: Thames & Hudson, 1984).

10. Graff, *Literature against Itself*, 8. Karl Marx and Friedrich Engels, *The Communist Manifesto* (Harmondsworth: Penguin, 1974), 83.

11. Revolution, Perry Anderson points out, refers to 'the political overthrow from below of one state order, and its replacement by another. Nothing is to be gained by diluting it across time, or extending it over every department of social space ... it is necessary to insist that revolution is a *punctual* and not a

permanent process' ('Modernity and Revolution', *New Left Review*, 144 (Mar.–Apr. 1984), 96–113, at 112.

12. Eugene Jolas, 'Notes', *transition*, 14 (Fall 1928), 180–5, at 180.

13. As one critic points out: 'He was right in perceiving that *transition* was neo-romantic and that it was in revolt against old ways of thought, but he greatly oversimplified and overemphasized the political identity of the magazine' (Dougald McMillan, *transition: The History of a Literary Era, 1927–1938* (London: Calder & Boyars, 1975), 34–5).

14. Henri Bergson, *The Age of Analysis: 20th Century Philosophers*, ed. Morton White (New York: Mentor, 1963), 76; William James, *A Pluralistic Universe*, ed. Fredson Bowers and Ignas K. Skrupskelis (Cambridge, Mass.: Harvard University Press, 1977), 96–7.

15. Louis Aragon, quoted in Robert Sage, 'La Reálité', *transition*, 2 (May 1927), 160–3, at 160.

16. He made this claim in a number of texts, but, for a clear statement, see *ABR* 334. How far the claim about Nietzsche's and Bergson's direct influence on these movements can be substantiated is beyond the scope of this study, but their importance to European culture in the first decades of the century is beyond dispute.

17. For Lewis, the 'act of creation . . . is always an act of the human will' (*WLA* 209).

18. *WLA* 216–25, esp. 224–5, and *ABR* 92, 108–10, 125–9, 373.

19. Lewis was explicit about this in *ABR* 125–9. For French notions of an intellectual aristocracy, see Venita Datta, *Birth of a National Icon: The Literary Avant-Garde and the Origins of the Intellectual in France* (Albany, NY: State University of New York Press, 1999), and Linda L. Clark, *Social Darwinism in France* (Tuscaloosa, Ala: University of Alabama Press, 1984).

20. My thanks to Paul Edwards for clarifying this aspect of Lewis's thought for me. Lewis was perhaps engaging in personal revisionism when, looking back on this period in *Rude Assignment*, he made the link between the Plato of *The Republic* and the eighteenth-century philosopher and statesman Bolingbroke, suggesting that at that time he had been in search of a Patriot-King. For Bolingbroke, see Bernard Coltret (ed). *Bolingbroke's Political Writings: The Conservative Enlightenment* (London: Macmillan, 1997). It was presumably Bolingbroke's emphasis on 'absolute power' (p. 418) coupled with complete integrity that led Lewis to claim that already in 1926 he was attracted to the notion of the Patriot-King, a very different conception of how to wield power from the Leninist one.

21. He wrote, for example: 'Art always has been, and within limits must remain, the monopoly of the intelligent few. . . . Art is either an improvement of the head, of the summit of a society, or it is popular art, which, given primitive conditions, can be admirable, but will not satisfy the civilized man' (*WLA* 224).

22. Lewis's pronouncements on the subject of communism are contradictory, but he did fear that it would lead to a Tocquevillean levelling-down rather than to a levelling-up. See, for example, the remarks in *TWM* 35.

23. Lewis's lampooning of a particularly purple Lawrencian passage on 'woman' is merciless: 'What would the Indian think if he heard his squaw being written about in that strain? – "delicate, marvellous sensitiveness." He would probably say "Chuck it, Archie!" in Hopi. At least he would be considerably surprised, and would probably squint very hard, under his "dark" brows, at Mr Lawrence' (*P*. 185–6).

24. See Dennis Brown, *Intertextual Dynamics within the Literary Group: Joyce, Lewis, Pound and Eliot: The Men of 1914* (London: Macmillan, 1990); Reed Way Dasenbrock, *The Literary Vorticism of Ezra Pound and Wyndham Lewis: Towards the Condition of Painting* (Baltimore: Johns Hopkins University Press, 1985); Timothy Materer, *Vortex: Pound, Eliot, and Lewis* (Ithaca, NY, and London: Cornell University Press, 1979); Timothy Materer, *Pound/Lewis: The Letters of Ezra Pound and Wyndham Lewis* (London: Faber & Faber, 1985); and Vincent Sherry, *Ezra Pound, Wyndham Lewis, and Radical Modernism* (Oxford: Oxford University Press, 1993).

25. There is good warrant for both views. Brown makes a persuasive case in favour of seeing all four writers as part of a complex group dynamic. On the other hand, Lewis and Pound, who were in some ways closer to each other than to Eliot and Joyce, repeatedly emphasized that the image of the group was more of an illusion than a reality. See e.g. Materer, *Pound/Lewis*, 150–2, 247; Materer, *Vortex*, 34–7; *L.* 491–2; and *WLA* 336, 451, 454, 456–7.

26. Materer suggests that Pound and Eliot did not take Lewis's criticism's personally because they regarded the work as more important than the individual. See Materer, *Pound/Lewis*, p. xviii, and Materer, *Vortex*, 36. Joyce's reaction to Lewis's attack has been discussed at length in Brown, *Intertextual Dynamics*, 114, 125–32; Scott W. Klein, *The Fictions of James Joyce and Wyndham Lewis: Monsters of Nature and Design* (Cambridge: Cambridge University Press, 1994); and McMillan, *transition*.

27. Dennis Brown suggests that 'the difference between the two men is less to do with the fact that one was more radical than the other

(as Lewis would have it) than that Lewis's genius was aggressive and monovocal, and Pound's lyrical and polyphonous' (*Intertextual Dynamics*, 78).

28. Materer, *Pound/Lewis*, 248. With regard to Lewis's first book of sociocultural criticism, *The Art of Being Ruled*, Pound wrote to him: 'It wd. be hypocrisy fer me to say that books all erbout everything in general are of any gt. interest to me in partikiler. Have turned out too much generality myself to care a damn whether there is any more done or not' (Materer, *Pound/Lewis*, 166).

29. The most detailed study of the Joyce–Lewis relationship is Klein, *The Fictions of James Joyce and Wyndham Lewis*. Klein argues that 'Lewis cast Joyce as his aesthetic opponent, explicitly in his criticism and implicitly in his own massive fictions, particularly *The Apes of God*' (p. 3), and he argues that 'Lewis's most important fictions . . . are in large part parodic responses to Joyce' (p. 8). See also Brown, *Intertextual Dynamics*, and McMillan, *transition*.

30. Thus Lewis: 'It is such people that the creative intelligence fecundates and uses; and at present that intelligence is political, and its stimuli are masked ideologies. He is only a tool, an instrument, in short. That is why such a sensitive medium as Joyce, working in such a period, requires the attention of the independent critic' (*TWM* 88).

31. T. S. Eliot, *The Complete Poems and Plays of T. S. Eliot* (London: Faber & Faber, 1982), 175.

32. *Time and Western Man*, as I have pointed out, was explicitly partisan, defending a certain kind of aesthetic. Hence Lewis's claim that 'I did not regard what I said as in any way personally offensive to Joyce: nor did I anywhere imply that he was not worthy of the greatest attention and respect – the space I allotted to him is evidence of that; or that his work was other than *of its kind* a masterpiece. It was the *kind* I did not like so much as some other kinds' (*RA* 59).

33. T. S. Eliot, 'Tradition and the Individual Talent', *The Sacred Wood: Essays on Poetry and Criticism* (London: Methuen, 1928), 53.

34. Thus Eliot: 'my meaning is, that the poet has, not a "personality" to express, but a particular medium, which is only a medium and not a personality, in which impressions and experiences combine in peculiar and unexpected ways' (ibid. 56).

35. This is the force of Eliot's claim in 'Tradition and the Individual Talent' that 'not only the best, but the most individual parts of his work may be those in which the dead poets, his ancestors, assert their immortality most vigorously' (ibid. 48).

36. See especially Eliot's approving view of Hulme's uncompromisingly illiberal theology in T. S. Eliot, *Selected Essays* (London: Faber & Faber, 1972), 489–91. See also *After Strange Gods: A Primer of Modern Heresy* (London: Faber & Faber, 1933), which is one long diatribe against liberalism – see especially the remarks on Hopkins (p. 48).

37. Thus he wrote: 'I am not using a "personality" in the *Ballyhoo* sense – I do not mean an individualist abortion, bellowing that it wants at all costs to "express" itself . . . I mean only a constancy and consistency in being, as concretely as possible, *one thing* – at peace with itself' (*MWA* 62).

38. See especially *P*. 74–9 and *TWM* 181, 341–2.

39. Thus in *Time and Western Man* he emphasizes 'all the advantages for man in having a specifically intellectual centre of control, and principle of authority' (*TWM* 298). For the view that Lewis's anti-Nietzschean conception of the self is close to Plato's, see Andrzej Gasiorek, ' "The Cave-Men of the New Mental Wilderness": Wyndham Lewis and the Self in Modernity', *Wyndham Lewis Annual*, 6 (1999), 3–20.

40. Hence Lewis's insistence that: '*You must get Painting, Sculpture, and Design out of the studio and into life somehow or other*, if you are not going to see this new vitality dessicated in a pocket of inorganic experimentation' (*WLA* 131). For the importance to Lewis of *conscious* planning in *The Caliph's Design*, see *WLA* 137, 139. His later remarks on *The Caliph's Design* brought out the originary nature of this impulse, especially when he observed that he 'would have had a city born by fiat, as if out of the brain of a god, or someone with a god-like power' (*RA* 169).

41. Paul de Man, *Blindness and Insight* (Minneapolis: University of Minnesota Press, 1983), 148. De Man's words are strikingly relevant to Lewis's retrospective account of Vorticism in pieces such as 'The Skeleton in the Cupboard Speaks', the 'Introduction' to the 1956 exhibition, and the *Vogue* article on Vorticism. See *WLA* 334–45, 451–3, and 454–8. We must note, however, that after the *Blast* period Lewis rarely spoke of rejecting the past in its entirety. He drew on the past in selective ways but was hostile to any romanticization of it and any attempt to blur the boundaries between it and the different problems and needs of the present. His opposition to Eliot's and Pound's attitude to the past was in this respect the same as his opposition to Spengler: 'The Past as *myth* – as history, that is, in the classical sense – a Past in which events and people stand in an imaginative perspective, a *dead* people we do not interfere with, but whose integrity we respect

– that is a Past that any person who has a care for the principle of individual life will prefer to "history-as-evolution" or "history-as-communism" ' (*TWM* 223). Lewis's orientation to the here and now is later linked to his particular view of classicism: 'I, unfortunately, *live* in this Present; I have not the time-mind. I am what Spengler would call a "Classical" intellect' (*TWM* 288).

42. Lewis returned to this issue twenty years later: 'It is fashionable to speak of consciousness as of something quite unimportant. And certainly without consciousness there would be great uniformity, which currently is a main objective. In surrendering awareness – in a blissful drowning of the ego – substituting reflexes for acts of consciousness and will, one is moving backwards into the primitive' (*RA* 194).

43. Lewis's assault on behaviourism extended across several books. The key objections, especially his scorn for its reductive mechanizing agenda, may be found in *ABR* 339–42; *TWM* 297–8, 318–44, and of course throughout *Snooty Baronet*.

44. Quoted in Paul O'Keeffe, *Some Sort of Genius: A Life of Wyndham Lewis* (London: Jonathan Cape, 2000), 229. Lewis described Kell-Imrie as 'an ill-mannered and lunatic puppet' and as a '*behaviourist* puppet' (*L.* 206) in a letter to Roy Campbell. Although these remarks need to be treated with care, since he was in this letter explaining that Kell-Imrie's sentiments about the character of Rob McPhail (who was based on Campbell) were not his own, I believe they still indicate how Lewis wanted the baronet to be regarded.

45. Kell-Imrie later describes himself as a 'Nature-crank', asserting that 'D. H. Lawrence and Yours Truly . . . are on the same side of the argument' (*SB* 86). Given Lewis's critique of Lawrence in *Paleface*, the critical distance between Kell-Imrie and his author could hardly be more apparent.

46. Realizing that he has been 'badly checkmated' by Humph and Val, Kell-Imrie grasps that they 'desired me to be their automaton!' but thinks to himself that he will '*in the end become their Frankenstein!*' (*SB* 131). Later, after the episode with the hatter's automaton, he sees a billboard advertising a film of the book and is reminded of his earlier thought processes (*SB* 138).

47. The relevant passage reads as follows: 'The fellow was playacting – and what I resented in this comedy was the fact that I knew (or thought I knew) that he was not *real*. There was something abstruse and unfathomable in this automaton. Beside me a new arrival smiled back at the bowing Hatter's doll. I turned towards him in alarm. Was not perhaps this fellow who had come up

beside me a puppet too? I could not swear that he was not! I turned my eyes away from him, back to the smiling phantom in the window, with intense uneasiness. For I thought to myself as I caught sight of him in the glass, smiling away in response to our mechanical friend, *certainly he is a puppet too!* Of course he was, but dogging that was the brother-thought, *but equally so am I!'* (*SB* 135–6).

48. John Addington Symonds, *Essays Speculative and Suggestive* (London: Smith, Elder & Co., 1907), 155.

CHAPTER 4. FROM CLASSICISM TO SATIRE

1. See especially Geoffrey Wagner, *Wyndham Lewis: A Portrait of the Artist as the Enemy* (London: Routledge & Kegan Paul, 1957). Mark Perrino describes Lewis as a 'writer who tirelessly defended "classicism" ', although he notes that Lewis's work often fails to conform to classical precepts. See Mark Perrino, *The Poetics of Mockery: Wyndham Lewis's The Apes of God and The Popularization of Modernism* (Leeds: W. S. Maney, 1995), 44. For a subtle account of Lewis's response to the post-war classical revival in France, see Paul Edwards, *Wyndham Lewis: Painter and Writer* (New Haven and London: Yale University Press, 2000), 261–7.

2. For discussions of these tendencies, especially with regard to painting, see Elizabeth Cowling and Jennifer Mundy (eds.), *On Classic Ground: Picasso, Leger, de Chirico and the New Classicism 1910–1930* (London: Tate Gallery, 1990); Briony Fer, David Batchelor, and Paul Wood (eds.), *Realism, Rationalism, Surrealism: Art between the Wars* (New Haven and London: Yale University Press, 1993); Kenneth E. Silver, *Esprit de Corps: The Art of the Parisian Avant-Garde and the First World War, 1914–1925* (Princeton: Princeton University Press, 1989); Peter Nicholls, *Modernisms: A Literary Guide* (London: Macmillan, 1995), 242–50.

3. Fer et al., *Realism, Rationalism, Surrealism*, 12.

4. Lewis was in texts like *The Art of Being Ruled and Time and Western Man* centrally concerned with elucidating an aesthetic and a philosophy that could be genuinely critical of 'modernity' and not slavishly follow its dictates. As he wrote in *Paleface*: 'Having got so far, again, we must sustain our revolutionary impulse' (*P.* 106). But for him this entailed a hardheaded analysis of the underlying forces at work in the technical, economic, and social innovations brought about within modernity, hence his claim that 'a new revolution is already on foot, making its appearance first under

the aspect of a violent reaction, at last to bring a steady and growing mass of criticism to bear upon those innovations' (*P.* 106).

5. This emphasis is central to *Blast*: 'When I say poetry ... I mean the warm and steaming poetry of the earth, of Van Gogh's rich and hypnotic sunsets, Rembrandt's specialized and golden crowds, or Balzac's brutal imagination. The painter's especial gift is a much more exquisite, and aristocratic affair than this female bed of raw emotionality. The two together, if they can only be reconciled, produce the best genius' (*B1* 44). See also *WLA* 125 for a different statement of the same basic duality.

6. Lewis put it as follows: 'To be impersonal, rather than personal; universal rather than provincial; rational rather than a mere creature of feeling – those, and the rest of the attributes of a so-called "classical" expression, are very fine things indeed: but who possesses more than a tincture of them today? It would be mere effrontery, or buffoonery, in an artist of any power, among us, to lay claim to them – to say, "as an artist I am a classicist". With all of us – and to this there is no exception – there are merely degrees of the opposite tendency, at present labelled "romantic" ' (*MWA* 157).

7. For an interesting discussion of the link between contingency and disenchantment, see T. J. Clark, *Farewell to an Idea: Episodes from a History of Modernism* (New Haven: Yale University Press, 1999), 1–13.

8. See, for example, this description of these two writers: 'They were as simple as a couple of noisy peasants – in a sense: and *art* filled the whole of their minds and bodies. A passion for a concrete realization of all the mysterious energies with which they were wound up like clocks, possessed them night and day' (*MWA* 87).

9. For his humorous account of this 'role', see Lewis's short article 'What it Feels Like to be an Enemy', which first appeared in the *Daily Herald* in 1932. See *WLA* 266–7.

10. There were those who considered Lewis's writing to be under-valued, and comparisons between him and Joyce were common. A. J. Symons, for example, wrote to Lewis to tell him that he thought *Tarr*, which Lewis rewrote and republished in 1928, was 'what *Ulysses* is given the credit for being – the novel of the last 20 years' (*L* 188). Lewis was himself conscious of the rivalry with Joyce, as his letters reveal. See e.g. *L.* 190–1, 273.

11. This issue is hard to disentangle. Lewis was clearly furious about Campbell's treatment by the *New Statesman*, and he was convinced that many influential figures wished to suppress *The Apes*. He

wrote to Augustus John that what 'happened in the offices of the *New Statesman* happened (no doubt) in at least half-a-dozen other editorial offices' (*L.* 194), a claim that might have been true but for which he had no evidence. But he saw a tremendous opportunity for self-publicity in the affair, and he sought to exploit it in every way possible. John thought Lewis's behaviour was misguided, writing to tell him that it was one thing for Campbell to enter the lists on his behalf but another thing altogether for Lewis to do the same: '*He* was right to make a fuss – but *you!* Its [*sic*] a good job you had some disgraceful notices. Unanimity is suspect' (*L.* 195). John seemed to suggest that, contrary to Lewis's view that a cabal was out to get him, *The Apes* had in fact been fairly well received. Lewis would have none of it. In an extraordinary letter to the Catholic writer Shane Leslie, who had claimed that no periodical was interested in a review of the book, Lewis encouraged him to write something, remarking that 'best of all would be to print an article of yours as a sort of rejected review, as in fact it would be. With it a note from you mentioning the fact that you experienced difficulty when you turned to the papers for which you were in the habit of writing. This would so tremendously reinforce the evidence already of what happened to Roy Campbell, that *The Apes of God* had been unjustly treated, for this reason or that' (*L.* 197–8). So convinced was Lewis that a boycott was effectively in place, and so determined was he to get others to believe this, that he was willing to countenance the fiction that a review of Leslie's (which had in fact not yet been written) had been rejected, in order to strengthen his own case.

12. Eliot was at this time editor of the influential *Criterion*, was being published by Faber & Faber, whose poetry editor he became, and was increasingly moving in established Anglican circles; Joyce had the support of people such as Sylvia Beach and Harriet Shaw Weaver, was published in 'little magazines' like the *Little Review* and *transition*, and was gradually developing into something of a cult figure on the avant-garde scene; Woolf, of course, was connected to a wide range of powerful individuals through the Bloomsbury set, wrote regularly for a number of important periodicals, and was published by the Hogarth Press, which she and her husband Leonard set up and ran from 1917.

13. For more on this aspect of Lewis's placement, see his later remarks on the period in *RA*, 210–11.

14. Lewis, 'Introduction', *The Apes of God* (London: Arco, 1955), unpaginated.

15. *Paleface* is an important text in relation to these issues. Lewis stated in it his conviction that a public world was being substituted by a private one. See especially *P.* 99–106. The opening 'Editorial' to *The Enemy 1* is also pertinent. There Lewis wrote: 'No abstract "time" or epoch has ever taken it into its abstract head to deconcretize, as this one has, its children. In its progressive prescission of all that is individual, its rage to extinguish the independent life of persons, this abstraction has assumed, for us, a physiognomy, along with its purpose, not possessed by other mere "times", mere "epochs", coloured and characterized by the individuals within them' (*E1*, p. x).

16. For an extended account of the role played by Edith Sitwell's *Façade* in *The Apes*, see Tyrus Miller, *Late Modernism: Politics, Fiction, and the Arts between the World Wars* (Berkeley and Los Angeles: University of California Press, 1999), 102–6. Lewis's attacks on Bloomsbury as a coterie have often been taken as malicious; in this respect, it is interesting to note that Virginia Woolf wrote to Eleanor Cecil in 1916 that she and Leonard 'wanted to start a printing press "for all our friends [*sic*] stories" '. See Hermione Lee, *Virginia Woolf* (London: Vintage, 1997), 362.

17. John Gawsworth, *Apes, Japes and Hitlerism: A Study and Bibliography of Wyndham Lewis* (London: Unicorn Press, 1932), 63. For the link between Boleyn and Dedalus, see, for example, the description of his progress through London during the General Strike. The use of free indirect discourse here (see *AG* 638 especially) is distinctly reminiscent of Stephen's thought processes when a schoolboy at Clongowes in the first chapter of *Portrait*.

18. The reference is to an article by Montagu Slater, who described Lewis as 'a *personal-appearance* satirist' in the course of a criticism of the latter's methods. Arguing that Slater entirely misunderstood his external approach, Lewis took over the designation and made it his own: 'But that is a compliment. Its author lays great store by that *externality*, in a world that is literally inundated with sexual viscera and the "dark" gushings of the tides of *The Great Within*. Call him a "personal-appearance writer" and he is far from being displeased! You please *him* by that, even if *he* displeases so many people (it would appear) by treating of their *externals* in the way that he does – just by being so *personal-appearance!*' (*MWA* 100–1).

19. He discusses Low in detail in order to explain his own style and objectives. See *RA* 48–9. The phrase 'gargantuan puppet-show' derives from an account of his method offered by Augustus John, which Lewis quotes. See *RA* 215.

20. E. W. F. Tomlin, *Wyndham Lewis* (Norfolk, Conn: New Directions, 1954), 35.

21. T. S. Eliot, 'The Pensées of Pascal', in Eliot, *Selected Essays* (London: Faber & Faber, 1972), 405.

22. See Robert Graves, *The Greek Myths* (Harmondsworth: Penguin, 1992), 118–20.

23. It should not be forgotten that, one year before *The Apes* was published, Lewis had devoted several pages of *Paleface* to the disintegration of the 'law', arguing there that 'there is no law to which we can appeal, upon which we can rely, or that it is worth our while any longer to interpret, even if we could. We, by birth the natural leaders of the White European, are people of no political or public consequence any more, quite naturally. Even, we are repudiated and hated because the law we represent has failed, not being as effective as it should have been or well-thought-out at all' (*P*. 81–2). In the context of such observations, Zagreus's role as lawgiver should be treated with deep scepticism.

24. For useful discussions of the fool and the trickster, see Enid Welsford, *The Fool: His Social and Literary History* (London: Faber & Faber, 1968); Lewis Hyde, *Trickster Makes this World: Mischief, Myth, and Art* (New York: Farrar, Straus & Giroux, 1998); Paul Radin, *The Trickster: A Study in American Indian Mythology* (New York: Schocken, 1973).

25. Thus Zagreus to Dan: ' "I will tell you all about Pierpoint – I am his Plato." And the bronzed albino left his disciple laughing – saying "I am his Plato!" ' (*AG* 331).

26. Zagreus confirms this view of him when he writes to Boleyn that Pierpoint 'is in everything my master – I am nothing, he is everything' (*AG* 125).

27. It is other characters who see Pierpoint as God's analogue and therefore as a source of life, but I take this mistaking of him as just another sign of their failures of judgement. See, for example, Zagreus's view of Klein's attitude to Pierpoint (*AG* 302). Note also that Boleyn resents Pierpoint's primacy in this hierarchy of individuals, since it places *his* mentor, Zagreus, in a subordinate position. See *AG* 253.

28. See especially *AG* 268, 278–81, 414, 469.

29. John Burton Russell, *Satan: The Early Christian Tradition* (Ithaca, NY, and London: Cornell University Press, 1981), 94.

30. Lewis's concern with this issue may be seen in text after text. Consider the unreality of Humph in *Snooty Baronet*, described as a 'walking cartoon by the Newyorker' (*SB* 76), the depiction of

Martin in *The Vulgar Streak* as a 'little imitation Belloc' (*VS* 32), or this account of the 'highly bogus personage' Abbershaw from *The Revenge For Love*: 'He smiled and then went back, with a sudden collapse of the countenance, to his watchful owlishness, in a manner that positively advertised its automatism, and shouted at you that it was *unreal* . . . here was a mask of such transparent *fauxbonhomie* – a presence which displaced so many meaningless square inches of the ether, as to pose the whole problem of *the real* and of its various mixtures and miscegenations with its opposite, right up to the negative pole of absolute imposture' (*RL* 165).

31. For Plato's account of anamnesis, see the *Meno* in *Protagoras and Meno*, trans. W. K. C. Guthrie (Harmondsworth: Penguin, 1981), at 81a–86b. For an excellent account of Augustine, see Denys Turner, *The Darkness of God: Negativity in Christian Mysticism* (Cambridge: Cambridge University Press, 1995).

CHAPTER 5. LITERATURE AND POLITICS

1. The fullest discussions of Lewis's politics may be found in D. G. Bridson, *The Filibuster: A Study of the Political Ideas of Wyndham Lewis* (London: Cassell, 1972), and Tom Normand, *Wyndham Lewis the Artist: Holding the Mirror up to Politics* (Cambridge: Cambridge University Press, 1992).

2. Wyndham Lewis, 'The Code of a Herdsman', in Lewis, *The Essential Wyndham Lewis* ed. Julian Symons (London: Vintage, 1989), 25–30, at 26, 28. The lineaments of the later puppet/nature distinction were already in place here. Members of the herd resemble the herdsmen, of whom they are 'unsatisfactory replicas', yet they are revealed to be *'nothing* but limitations and vulgarities' because they lack the power of intellection: 'Matter that has not sufficient mind to permeate it grows . . . gangrenous and rotten' (p. 28). It is on the basis of this distinction that the herdsmen must keep the herd at bay: *'There are very stringent regulations* about the herd keeping off the sides of the mountain. In fact your chief function is to prevent their encroaching' (p. 29). Compare Friedrich Nietzsche, *Twilight of the Idols/The Anti-Christ*, trans. R. J. Hollingdale (Harmondsworth: Penguin, 1990), 99–103.

3. Lewis, 'The Code of a Herdsman', 30. For similar sentiments, see *T.*, 25–6, 327–8. Tarr, however, talks of burying his face in 'the gases that rise from the dung-heap' in order to transform 'daily ooze' into art (*T.* 17–18). For Lewis's belief that artistic creativity requires processes of this kind, see *B1* 144 and *WLA* 134.

4. *Paleface* provides a good example of the way Lewis's naturalism subserves a hierarchical view of social life: 'the plan is, of course, not mine at all, but nature's . . . Why does not nature produce a dense mass of Shakespeares or Newtons or Pitts? That has been the idea; and means have been considered and plans worked out for assisting nature in this respect. But it is conceivable that nature after all may usually produce as many as are needed of these "persons", and that this ratio may be according to some organic law we are too stupid or conceited to grasp' (*P*. 74).

5. Lewis, 'Long Live the Vortex!', *B1*, unpaginated manifesto.

6. See, for example, statements such as this: 'this Everyman (that is 99 per cent. of mankind), these Everymans are being forced backwards – simply because they have repeatedly demonstrated their inability to improve in any of the arts and sciences of life, and so it would be simply foolish any longer to waste and blunt the brilliant natural gifts of the elect minority over this huge silly baby-mule and brutal dunce – that is to say, the greater part of men' (*OG* 14).

7. These points are worth reiteration. For Lewis's emphasis on the need to lay bare the concealed truths about English social, political, and cultural life, especially for those who have not the time, education, or natural aptitude to do this for themselves, see *ABR* 13; *TWM*, pp. xi–xix, 247–8; *P*. 109. The coda to *The Art of Being Ruled* is from Parmenides: '*I wish to communicate this view of the world to you exactly as it manifests itself: and so no human opinion will ever be able to get the better of you*' (*ABR* 375).

8. The need for stable conditions for creative work was a constant preoccupation. See *WB* 242; *TWM* 155–6; and *ABR* 321.

9. Although he was critical of Sorel, Lewis described him in *The Art of Being Ruled* as 'the key to all contemporary thought' (*ABR* 119) and he linked his account of a caste system to Sorel in *ABR* 29–31.

10. See Lewis, 'Long Live the Vortex!', *B1*, unpaginated manifesto. For Lewis's oft-repeated claim that such a mass was necessary to artistic creativity, see also *B1*, 32–3 and *MMB* 116–18.

11. See his rejection of the general applicability of rights to all people, regardless of some kind of merit, in *P*. 76–9. For his belief in natural differences between individuals, see also *E3* 71.

12. Andrzej Gasiorek, ' "The Cave-Men of the New Mental Wilderness": Wyndham Lewis and the Self in Modernity', *Wyndham Lewis Annual*, 6 (1999), 3–20.

13. For a general discussion of this issue, see Martha C. Nussbaum, 'Human Functioning and Social Justice: In Defense of Aristotelian Essentialism', *Political Theory* 20/2 (May 1992), 202–46.

14. See especially the following statements from *The Art of Being Ruled*. First: 'For the sake of the ruled ... the ruler should be forced to rule by force, ostensibly, responsibly, as does (to the great disgust of our western liberals) the soviet or fascist government' (*ABR* 94). Second: 'Education plays, and will continue to play, a much more important part in government than physical and exterior force. Force is a passing and precarious thing, whereas to get inside a person's mind and change his very personality is the effective way of reducing him and making him yours' (*ABR* 94).

15. For Lewis's hostility to parliamentary democracy, see *ABR* 70, 321–3, and *LWE* 24–5, 94–104.

16. Thus he writes: 'An extreme version of leninist politics ... is fascismo. Or, if you like, it is leninism adapted to an ancient and intelligent population' (*ABR* 71). He differentiates fascism and communism more clearly elsewhere in the text: 'I am not a communist; if anything, I favour some form of *fascism* rather than communism. Nevertheless, when two principles are opposed, and one of these is that of English liberalism, in most cases I should find myself on the other side, I expect' (*ABR* 35).

17. See especially *ABR* 74–5. This is why Lewis found Michael Farbmann's *After Lenin* so persuasive. Farbmann argued that Lenin's great contribution to the Bolshevik cause lay in his organizational abilities and his single-minded focus on the gaining and retaining of power. For an account of Lenin that bears Farbmann out in most particulars, see Leszek Kolakowski, *Main Currents of Marxism 2: The Golden Age*, trans. P. S. Falla (Oxford: Oxford University Press, 1981), 381–98. Kolakowski concludes that under Lenin the party 'was to be a kind of universal machine, uniting social energies from every source into a single current' (p. 412).

18. *The Art of Being Ruled* is concerned all the way through with articulating ways in which radical social change could be effected by peaceful means, Lewis repeatedly emphasizing his hostility to 'catastrophist' political policies. See *ABR* 52–5, 122, 358.

19. Lewis was clear as to the kind of person required for the ideal functioning of democracy, just as he was equally clear that this ideal was the purest utopianism: 'The ideally "free man" would be the man *least* specialized, the *least* stereotyped, the man approximating to the *fewest* classes, the *least* clamped into a system – in a word, the most individual. But a society of "free men", if such a thing could ever come about, which it certainly could not, would immediately collapse' (*ABR* 151).

20. For his view of British hypocrisy vis-à-vis the two forms of dictatorship, see *LWE* 70–1, 129–31, 275, 287; for his reading of Hitler's Germany as a beleagured nation to which there was no reason to be hostile, see *LWE* 14–15, 90–1, 110–11, 280, 298; for his criticisms of Great Power policies towards Germany, see *LWE* 32–3, 86–9, 92–3, 115–16, and 311–13; for his contempt for the terms of Versailles, see *LWE* 168–9, 274–5.

21. Claiming that, in the face of the 'common front' of the 1930s, criticism of democracy was most likely to be made by the extreme right, Lewis noted that in making use of such criticism it 'does not at all follow that our aims are identical with those of the militant "right"-winger' (*LWE* 54). He knew, of course, that he would be pigeon-holed in precisely such terms: 'if you are *not* in favour of an out-and-out internationalism, that does not necessarily mean that you are a "nationalist", in the blackshirted sense. You may be, as you may not. It does not at all follow that you are, although it is quite certain that people will say that you are. Which is of course quite another matter' (*LWE* 274). Lewis was throughout his life preoccupied with the way linguistic 'counters' were used to pin people to univocal 'positions' and thereby to empty their views of nuance and complexity.

22. There is a strange twist here. Lewis claimed that liberal ideology's dependence on abstract theories blinded its advocates to concrete empirical political truths, but his own hostility in *Left Wings over Europe* to virtually any kind of abstract principle in fact blinded *him* to the true nature of Nazi policies and ambitions.

23. He wrote, for example: 'it is an undeniable fact that *democracy* is being practised in Germany at present, with surprising success. It was a pure parliamentary democracy that voted in – as nearly by democratic vote as it is humanly possible to get – and has periodically confirmed in power, the great patriot who is now the "Dictator" of the German Democracy' (*LWE* 298). For his assault on British democracy, see especially *LWE* 25. For the view that fascism and democracy need not be incompatible, see *CD* 276.

24. For Lewis's view that the League of Nations was principally to blame for the onrushing war, see *LWE* 32. Hitler is 'a man . . . who has sacrificed himself, literally, to a principle; that of national freedom. That principle may be ill-conceived or not: that I am not concerned to debate. But this man does not conform to the popular conception of a "tyrant", at least. He is more like one of *the oppressed!*' (*LWE* 280).

25. Thus he writes: '*No* way should be regarded as too unorthodox to obstruct and to prevent this transfer and translation of our

hereditary freedom, from within the frontiers of a recognized and homogeneous state, over into the keeping of some abstract international arcanum' (*LWE* 273).

26. See, for example, the words given to Ned in *Count your Dead*: 'Fascism means business. It really means to get rid of the incubus, which is crushing us all down into the gutter. . . . Fascism is a revolt of the People. A revolt against debt. I am no Fascist. But I love Freedom. Also I hate Usury. If Fascism triumphed the credit-web that has spread itself over the earth would be broken, and the big abstract money-spinner at its centre killed' (*CD* 275–6).

27. For sketchy, but positive, references to Franklin and Jefferson, see *CD*, 284–5, 296, 330–1. For a brief statement of how Lewis believed democracy used to function in England, see *CD* 45.

28. For the view that these political labels are misleading, if 'not plain humbug', see *CD* 296. For the Jeffersonian vision, see *CD* 284.

29. Ned adds: 'A difficult position for a patriot, if ever there was one! For if this war ended in the extinction of all nations, as independent polities, would it not be better for those countries to succeed who could be fighting to retain their *own* independence, and so finally that of other nations?' (*CD* 324). The question of sovereignty, he insists, must supersede any question of political affiliation: 'But it is not a matter of conservatism or of radicalism . . . You can be either conservatively-minded, or radically-minded, it makes no difference, and with equal fervour object to world-uniformity, and cast your vote for world-diversity' (*CD* 298).

30. For a full discussion of the issue, see *HC* 236–44. For Lewis's rejection of isolationism, see *HC* 165. Lewis moved further and further towards a centralizing, federalist position during the war years. He spoke positively of Roosevelt's New Deal, for example, and argued in favour of global centralization. See *L.*, 292, 328–9.

31. Although he did not 'regard many of their dogmas in detail as acceptable' (*H* 108), he looked to the National Socialists 'for a great movement of political *concentration* – to call a halt to the growing stagnation and diffusion elsewhere' (*H*. 143).

32. For Lewis's repeated emphasis on the organic, which surely derives from Burke, see *MMB* 259–65 and *L.* 246, 274.

33. George Orwell, *Inside the Whale and Other Essays* (Harmondsworth: Penguin, 1979), 32–5, 40.

34. 'The stone fidelity | They hardly meant has come to be | Their final blazon, and to prove | Our almost-instinct almost true: | What will survive of us is love' (Philip Larkin, 'An Arundel Tomb', in *The Whitsun Weddings* (London: Faber & Faber, 1990), 45–6).

35. Orwell, *Inside the Whale*, 71.
36. Leon Trotsky offered unequivocal support for terrorism as a technique of revolution in *Terrorism and Communism*: 'The revolution "logically" does not demand terrorism ... But the revolution does require of the revolutionary class that it should attain its end by all methods at its disposal – if necessary, by an armed rising; if required, by terrorism.' The revolution, he chillingly added, 'kills individuals and intimidates thousands' (*The Age of Permanent Revolution: A Trotsky Anthology*, ed. Isaac Deutscher (New York: Bell, 1973), 115–16.
37. Nietzsche, *Twilight of the Idols*, 70.
38. Geoffrey Galt Harpham, *On the Grotesque: Strategies of Contradiction in Art and Literature* (Princeton: Princeton University Press, 1982), 177.
39. Joseph Conrad, *Nostromo: A Tale of the Seaboard* (Harmondsworth: Penguin, 1979), 315.
40. Lewis wrote, for example, that once one realizes (following Burke?) that there are insurmountable *organic* obstacles (human nature and the sediment of the past) to utopian social engineering, one knows 'from that moment that one will never build again, except in one's dreams' (*MMB* 232–3).

CHAPTER 6. HISTORY, IDENTITY, AND THE ROLE OF ART

1. Interestingly, Lewis is concerned in this book not just with his reputation as an author but also as a person. It is written to do him justice 'as citizen rather than as author' (*RA* 13); it aims to show that his 'writings have not been wanting in humanity' (*RA* 153); and it defends 'character and motives', since, as he sardonically points out, 'no one cares about the intellect ... but what the domestic requires in applying for a job – a good character' (*RA* 238).
2. He wrote (with more than a touch of irony) as follows: 'At this time I am perhaps culturally – politically – a little where I was in "The Caliph's Design". I perceive as it were a white and shining city, a preposterous Bagdad, in place of the contemporary ruins, social and architectural, of 1947' (*RA* 208).
3. Thus Lewis: 'If when I wrote my book, or now, the Western spirit were defensible, that would be the way to defend it. The second, or more purely philosophic, part – and the more valuable – attains, I venture to think, a validity distinct from the issues

prompting the construction of this dialectical fortress' (*RA* 209). He continued to see 'time-philosophers' as destructive 'of an ancient culture', but he now acknowledged 'that these disagreeable vultures had their role to play, as agents of change' (*RA* 237).

4. See, for example, the following statement: 'It is absolutely necessary to make an absolute distinction between (1) *political* revolution . . . and (2) on the other hand, all thought and activity that is certainly revolutionary, and so disturbing to the comfortable average, but not committed to any particular *political* doctrine – that is to say to any practical programme of change' (*E3* 74).

5. We should note, however, that in *Time and Western Man* Lewis asks if Kant's awakening from his 'dogmatic slumber' and his subsequent elaboration of 'criticism' have really been so positive. See *TWM* 237–8.

6. Immanuel Kant, 'An Answer to the Question: "What is Enlightenment?" ' in *Kant's Political Writings*, ed. Hans Reiss, trans. H. B. Nisbet (Cambridge: Cambridge University Press, 1971), 54–60, at 54.

7. Ernst Cassirer, *The Philosophy of the Enlightenment* trans. Fritz C. A. Koelln and James P. Pettegrove (Boston: Beacon, 1965). Cassirer suggests that the Enlightenment's 'first important victory' was its marking-off of 'a definite field for rational knowledge within which there was to be no more restraint and authoritative coercion but free movement in all directions' (p. 49).

8. For examples, see Lewis's account of the development of his self in *TWM* 131–4; his bracketing-off of the question of the philosophical truth of time philosophies in *TWM* 110; and his self-confessed zealotry in *TWM* 109.

9. Theodor Adorno and Max Horkheimer, *Dialectic of Enlightenment*, trans. John Cumming (London: Verso, 1979), 36. Lewis remarks in *Rude Assignment* that as well as being 'fascinated and amused' by the social disintegration he saw around him he was also 'depressed'. He goes on to note that his 'sentimental side . . . suffered (I think now) more deeply than it should' (*RA* 184).

10. See, for example, the reading offered by Jeffrey Meyers, *The Enemy: A Biography of Wyndham Lewis* (London: Routledge & Kegan Paul, 1980), 312–20.

11. Albert Camus, *The Myth of Sisyphus*, trans. Justin O'Brien (Harmondsworth: Penguin, 1980), 26, 39.

12. Ibid. 26.

13. See, for example, a passage such as this: 'There was nothing he dreaded so much as the absurd in himself . . . his growing sense

of the absurd in everything was painful and to suspect its presence in himself supremely uncomfortable ... What was the rational, after all? Where was one to look for the norm? The nervous impetuousness of his movements, of which he was perfectly aware, he had once compared with the charlady's. However, he had concluded, with a laugh, if it is a question of the human kind and its essential absurdity, then of course all right, why should I care? In so absurd a place it was hardly likely that he himself could be otherwise than absurd' (*SC* 29–30).

14. His various attempts to plan out strategies for overcoming Hester invariably dissolve as they find themselves heading inexorably for the marital bed: 'Eros was a factor he always left out of his calculations and when he first remarked that the above pressures were resulting in the same warmth on his side as he had intended them to induce on hers, he was traversed by what almost amounted to a shudder. The absurd was happening. He was unable to escape from the absurd; that absurd which was for him an analogous enormity to *l'infame*' (*SC* 44). It should be noted that Harding is a gourmand, and that good food is able to disrupt his rationally conceived plans as effectively as sex. See *SC* 32.

15. 'The man of former days had been replaced by a machine, which was a good imitation of the reality, which had superficially much of the charm, even the vivacity of the living model, but, when it came to one of the acid tests of authenticity, it would be recognized as an imposture' (*SC* 400).

16. Hence Harding's reliance, during the course of an argument, on a naive opposition between subjective emotion and historical truth: 'Upon what plane, sir, are we discussing this? Upon the plane of contemporary political passion, or as History sees these things: not *subjectively*, sir, but subspecie aeternitatis' (*SC* 129). Here, 'History' is envisaged as speaking for itself and thus requiring no biased human mouthpiece.

17. His thoughts take the following turn: 'Having more fiercely than ever derided the monotonous, unvarying mediocrity and criminality which History regales us with; having with more violence than before related this to our own mediocrity, he then proceeded to go over, lock, stock and barrel, into ... the Party of Superman. We obviously would perish ignominiously if we continued as we were at present. We must train and compress ourselves in every way, and breed an animal superior to our present disorderly and untidy selves' (*SC* 356).

18. I have in mind here remarks such as the following: 'Our problem is, no doubt, "to perfect a larva", but not, as that statement

suggests, the larva "Mankind", the whole of that dense abstraction. The system of "breeding horses for speed" is a far better one. That is no doubt the solution. But the slowness, sloth, and commonness of the stock of *Homo stultus* would still be there when the sub-species, or the super-species had been bred' (*ABR* 125).

19. Hester's sexuality is a threatening emblem of the absurd, for Harding, and his responses to it, when he is not indulging his own desire, oscillate between rejecting anger and defensive laughter. After an early quarrel, for instance, he sees her as follows: 'With the best will in the world, he could not refrain from noting the ludicrousness of her expression. She stood lady-likely at bay, exposing reproachfully her "eyeballs" and holding her "big silly mouth" ostentatiously sealed; to laugh was the only rational action, and he came very near to surrendering to the dictates of common sense' (*SC* 43).

20. When he asks himself why he lives with Hester, his reflections take the following turn: 'Nothing would have induced him to live with a man of Essie's disposition and mediocre intellect. For though smart enough, she had not a fraction of Mary's or of his mother's judgement' (*SC* 31).

21. The text reads: 'In order not to be at the mercy of his emotions, he had been obliged to effect a division of his personality into two parts: he had created a kind of artificial "unconscious" of his own, and thus locked away all acuity of realization ... His callous self was so well insulated from the compartment of the imagination that he was able to pass as a somewhat unemotional man. On the other hand, he *did*, as in the present case, experience a certain number of violent surprises' (*SC* 140).

22. The title of the chapter, 'The Passenger who Wore the Ribbon of the Legion of Honour', already hints at the self-alienation it will portray. Shocked by the pleasure he feels at being recognized by 'common' Americans, Harding goes through a period of 'terrifying self-revelation' (*SC* 161) that is nonetheless experienced as it were from the outside: 'Who was this man warming himself at such a fire as this? Could it be the René Harding he had known all his life? Was this foolish creature indeed *himself*, converted, by some witchcraft, into the gentleman he was gazing at across an interval of only twenty-four hours? ... he had this picture incessantly before him – of a degraded self, not known to him before, by some subconscious convulsion thrown up into time, and sitting there for all eternity at that restaurant table, with its ridiculous red boutonniere. He brooded for hours together over

this obscene image of his past self. It had a terrifying fascination for him: at one time he lay back in his chair and howled with derisive laughter at it' (*SC* 161).

23. Byron, *Manfred*, in *The Complete Poetical Works* ed. Jerome J. McGann (Oxford: Clarendon Press, 1986), 90, ll. 76–8.

24. The similarities between *The Art of Being Ruled* and *Rude Assignment* are in this respect striking. In the earlier book, for example, he wrote: 'A beaver does not compare itself with a walrus or an antelope. There is no "upper" and "lower" between a cat and a dog. So it would be with the new species of man' (*ABR* 127). And in the later book we find the following: 'Once again: no hardship or indignity is implied in such proposals. A ratcatcher likes catching rats: he does not want to play the piano. He despises the piano. The ploughboy does not want to think, but to plough' (*RA* 200). So he argues that his view of social differentiation is based on 'a happy recognition of structural unchangeability' (*RA* 202).

25. The tone is chatty and colloquial throughout, but, for a particularly clear example of what I have in mind, consider Lewis's description of his relations with his plumber, Harry (*RA* 203).

26. He wrote, for example: 'I had what is called an "allowance" as a student: and I was a student for a long time. I should, I feel, never have started . . . had much money not been spent to launch me' (*RA* 115).

27. René Harding is in this respect clearly speaking for Lewis when, having described the insistence on abstraction as 'a new academicism in the making', he concludes: 'I read some of their writings. *You must* abstract. It is categorical, it is as if it were a branch of revolutionary politics. Oh, I do not like that *must* of theirs, I hate these twentieth-century *Absolutes!*' (SC 134–5).

28. Ortega y Gasset wrote that the 'new art . . . divides the public into the two classes of those who understand it and those who do not' (*The Dehumanization of Art and Other Essays on Art, Culture, and Literature* trans. Helene Weyl (Princeton: Princeton University Press, 1972), 6).

29. As he readily admitted: 'If a writer desires an easy life, he should be an extremist: if one could be mathematically at the point farthest from both extremes, which is of course impossible, one would be entirely alone. And any position near to this imaginary absolute of objectivity cannot but be an exceedingly uncomfortable one, for there is another extremism of the Middle of a much realer kind than the more usual extremes such as those of Left or Right' (*WA* 195).

30. In a letter of 1948, he stated his fundamental convictions on this topic: 'Upon exactly the same footing as the scientist, the writer should be permitted to investigate and to aim at any objective (not a subjective) truth ... that is the *only* method. Such a position, however, is unpopular. Even if I modified this, substituting: 'That is the kind of truth that *interests me*', it would be no good either. Yet should you impose upon the scientist the kind of truth he *must* find, he would decline so to make the facts fit a preordained solution: that would not be research but concealment. – The *kind* of truth. Such is the issue. One is an adulterated truth, and is not worth having. That is the truth of the *partisan*. Yet the latter gent says *your* truth is *against* him, because it is not *for* him. Truth as I see it lies outside the *for* and the *against*' (*L* 433).

31. René Descartes, *A Discourse on Method*, trans. John Veitch (New York: Dutton, 1975), 13, 12.

32. This was an oft-repeated theme. Lewis claimed, for example, that 'the artist, as much as the scientist, must exclude as far as possible the specifically human from the organization of his intellect. In his way, it is incumbent upon him to be just as cold-blooded as the efficient surgeon or duellist; his eye must be as detached, his hand as firm as theirs' (*WLA* 283).

33. For his own sense of belonging to a tradition of social and cultural criticism that stretched back to the mid-nineteenth century, see *MWA* 213.

34. See, for example, the remarks in *WA* 5–6 and *RA* 194–5 and 207–9.

35. Jürgen Habermas's description of Foucault could have been tailor-made for Lewis: 'in him the stoic attitude of keeping an overly precise distance, the attitude of the observer obsessed with objectivity, was peculiarly entwined with the opposite element of passionate, self-consuming participation in the contemporary relevance of the historical moment ('Taking Aim at the Heart of the Present: On Foucault's Lecture on Kant's *What is Enlightenment?*', *The New Conservatism: Cultural Criticism and the Historians' Debate*, ed. and trans. Sherry Weber Nicholsen (Cambridge: Polity, 1989), 173.

36. I think here of his claim that Vorticism 'was a stoic creed: it was not an *uplift*' (*WLA* 341) as well as his assertion that the 'central doctrine' of *The Art of Being Ruled* was 'something like the *apathy* of the Stoics' (*RA* 183).

37. See Walter Pater's oft-quoted claim in the 'Conclusion' to *The Renaissance* that 'art comes to you proposing frankly to give nothing but the highest quality to your moments as they pass, and simply for those moments' sake' (*The Renaissance: Studies in*

Art and Poetry, ed. Adam Phillips (Oxford: Oxford University Press, 1990), 153.

CHAPTER 7. CONCLUSION: 'BEYOND ACTION AND REACTION'?

1. Lewis consistently emphasized the need for limits (in terms of conceptions of human subjectivity as much as of art). With respect to experimental art he developed this point at length. See e.g. *DPA* 30–5. For two statements on the importance of public norms, see *MWA* 153 and *TWM* 177.
2. Lewis argued for the possibility and indeed necessity of '*a third method, between subject and object*' in 'Essay on the Objective of Plastic Art in our Time'. See *WLA* 210–11.
3. For a fuller discussion of Lewis's struggle with these issues, see Paul Edwards, *Wyndham Lewis: Painter and Writer* (New Haven and London: Yale University Press, 2000), 307–15.
4. For relevant passages, see Friedrich Nietzsche, *Twilight of the Idols/The Anti-Christ*, trans. R. J. Hollingdale (Harmondsworth: Penguin, 1990), 55–6, 134–5.
5. Perhaps the clearest statement of this view is in *MWA* 231–2. But for a different formulation see also *TWM* 110.
6. Thus he writes: '*Freedom* is certainly our human goal, in the sense that all effort is directed to that end: and it is a dictate of nature that we should laugh, and laugh loudly, at those who have fallen into slavery, and still more, those who batten on it. But the artistic sensibility, that is *another* "provision of nature".' The artist steps outside this evolutionary upward march, and looking back into the evolutionary machine, he explores its pattern – or is supposed to – quite cold-bloodedly' (*MWA* 95–6). Lewis's important 'Essay on the Objective of Plastic Art in our Time' is also relevant here. See *WLA* 200–15, esp. 204–5.
7. Lewis reiterates this view tirelessly, but I am particularly reminded of an early statement in *Blast*: 'Nature will give you, then, grass enough for cow or sheep, any fleshly conquest you can compass. One thing she is unable to give, that is peculiar to men. Such stranger stuff men must get out of themselves' (*B*. 129). He goes on later: 'There is only one thing better than "Life" – than using your eyes, nose, ears and muscles – and that something is very abstruse and splendid, in no way directly dependent on "Life". It is no EQUIVALENT for Life, but ANOTHER life, as NECESSARY to existence as the former' (*B*. 130).

8. Thus Friedrich Nietzsche: 'To choose what is harmful to *oneself*, to be *attracted* by "disinterested" motives, almost constitutes the formula for *decadence* ... Man is finished when he becomes altruistic' (*Twilight of the Idols/The Anti-Christ*, trans. R. J. Hollingdale (Harmondsworth: Penguin, 1990), 97).

9. Lewis wrote, for example: 'Perfection ... appears as a platonic ideal, and is a thing with which we have not very much to do on our present road. With perfect snowballs or lightning conductors, we have some commerce; but not with "perfect" works of art or human beings' (*WLA* 208).

10. For Lewis, artists were visionaries whose visions did not drive them deeper into subjectivity but took them out of it: 'A great artist falls into a trance of sorts when he creates, about that there is little doubt. The act of artistic creation is a trance or dream-state, but very different from that experienced by the entranced medium. A world of the most extreme and logically exacting physical definition is built up out of this susceptible condition in the case of the greatest art, in contrast to the cloudy phantasies of the spiritist' (*TWM* 109). Toby Avard Foshay's observation that Socrates was a touchstone for Lewis is pertinent here: he argues that in 'Physics of the Not-Self' Lewis championed 'an Apollonian, logical transvaluation of values in contrast to Nietzsche's Dionysian apotheosis of the self as will to power' (*Wyndham Lewis and the Avant Garde: The Politics of the Intellect* (Montreal: McGill-Queens University Press, 1992), 42).

11. Arthur Schopenhauer, *The World as Will and Representation*, trans. E. F. J. Payne (New York: Dover, 1969), 390.

12. Ibid. 411. Lewis connects the self with egoism in *Time and Western Man* in terms that suggest Schopenhauer's account of the will in terms of desire: 'we apply ["romantic"] to the effects of an egoism that bathes in the self-feeling to the exclusion of contradictory realities, including the Not-self' (*TWM* 10).

13. Arthur Schopenhauer, *On the Basis of Morality* trans. E. F. J. Payne (Providence, RI: Bergahn, 1995), 209–10. There is surely also a link here between Schopenhauer and Lewis's account of Socrates as one who invites you 'to abstract yourself, and, as far as possible, withdraw your mind till it passes momentarily into the cathartic peace of the Eternal' (*CPP* 201).

14. For the latter claim, see *WLA* 20. The nearest parallel to this view of writing may be found in the work of Kundera, whose own attempt to oppose to ideological conformism 'a lucid, unillusioned eye' led him to the novel, the form that ruled out 'identification with any politics, any religion, any ideology, any

moral doctrine, any group; a considered, stubborn, furious *nonidentification*, conceived not as evasion or passivity but as resistance, defiance, rebellion' (Milan Kundera, *Testaments Betrayed*, trans. Linda Asher (London: Faber & Faber, 1995), 157, 158. Lewis wrote in *The Enemy*: 'If I am asked, "What are your Politics?" I can truly answer, I have none ... That does not impose a profession of indifference to the spectacle of political obliquity; just as the other (its "moral" counterpart) does not involve a person so answering in a doctrine of Art-for-Art's-sake, or in an exhibition of diabolics or defiance of some useful code of social conduct' (*E1*, pp. xiv–xv).

15. Hence Lewis's oft-stated desire to establish a position that was *beyond* action and reaction, and his claim that 'Truth has no place in action' (*RA* 138).

16. He wrote in *Time and Western Man*, for example: 'It is in non-personal modes of feeling – that is in *thought*, or in feeling that is so dissociated from the hot, immediate egoism of sensational life that it becomes automatically intellectual – that the non-religious Western Man has always expressed himself, at his profoundest, at his purest. That is ... the heritage that is being repudiated ... We are busy in everything, in the West, substituting the personal for the impersonal, the private for the public' (*TWM* 255). But he clarified the anti-nationalist aspect of the Vorticist aesthetic in 'Super-Nature versus Super-Real'. See *WLA* 304–6.

17. Obvious examples are Oswald Spengler's *Decline of the West* (1918), Henri Massis's *Defence of the Occident* (1926), and Lewis's own *Time and Western Man* (1927).

18. For Lewis, 'the rational disciplines inherited by the European from the classic world' led to a valuable conception of reality: 'For us the world has presented itself to our senses sharp and hard of outline. It is stamped with the objectivity of the rational. This is a privilege' (*RA* 195).

19. Slavoj Zizek, writing of the Mead–Malinowski view of the South Pacific, points out that it 'provides an exemplary case of ... "abstract negation": it merely projects into the spatio-historical Other of "primitive societies" the fantasy of a "free sexuality" rooted in our own historical context. In this way ... it remains caught in the co-ordinates of one's own historical horizon precisely in its attempt to imagine a "radical" Otherness' (*The Ticklish Subject: The Absent Centre of Political Ontology* (London: Verso, 2000).

20. Lewis's fullest critique of Lawrence occurs in *P*. 169–97.

21. Thus Lewis wrote: 'The modern man, our perfect "Western Man", would have to be about six different people, perhaps; taking his science, and the scientific spirit, still from Greece, its home, but taking his art from somewhere else – only to consider these two factors' (*TWM* 236). On the concept of an 'imagined community', see Benedict Anderson, *Imagined Communities: Reflections on the Origin and Spread of Nationalism* (London: Verso, 1991).

22. Most obviously in *H.* 109, 122–3. Two points should be noted here. First, that Lewis tended to emphasize *ideas* rather than spurious *racial* or *national* characteristics (see *P.* 169–73). Secondly, that on this basis he saw invocations of 'race' as either stupid or dangerous. Two examples must suffice: in the course of his anti-Spenglerian diatribe he argues of the attempt to establish cultural-historical 'periods' that: 'The *race* basis is, at all events, a hopeless one on which practically to found anything of this sort at all' (*TWM* 264); and in *The Hitler Cult* he writes: 'By putting others outside the human canon the Germans have, in the sequel, manoeuvred themselves into the same undesirable position. Such a boomerang is race theory, after all. And once you start erecting barriers you are apt to end by finding yourself *outside*, instead of inside, as you had thought' (*HC* 72).

Select Bibliography

WORKS BY WYNDHAM LEWIS

Tarr: The 1918 Version, ed. Paul O'Keeffe (Santa Rosa, Calif.: Black Sparrow Press, 1990).

The Caliph's Design: Architects! Where is your Vortex? (1919), ed. Paul Edwards (Santa Barbara, Calif.: Black Sparrow Press, 1986).

The Art of Being Ruled (1926), ed. Reed Way Dasenbrock (Santa Rosa, Calif.: Black Sparrow Press, 1989).

The Lion and the Fox: The Role of the Hero in the Plays of Shakespeare (London: Grant Richards, 1927).

Time and Western Man (1927), ed. Paul Edwards (Santa Rosa, Calif.: Black Sparrow Press, 1993).

The Wild Body (London: Chatto & Windus, 1927).

The Childermass (London: Chatto & Windus, 1928).

Tarr (rev. edn.) (London: Chatto & Windus, 1928).

Paleface: The Philosophy of the 'Melting-Pot' (London: Chatto & Windus, 1929).

The Apes of God (1930) (Harmondsworth: Penguin, 1965).

The Roaring Queen (1931) (London: Secker & Warburg, 1973).

Hitler (London: Chatto & Windus, 1931).

The Diabolical Principle and the Dithyrambic Spectator (London: Chatto & Windus, 1931).

The Doom of Youth (London: Chatto & Windus, 1932).

Filibusters in Barbary: Record of a Visit to the Souk (London: Grayson & Grayson, 1932).

Enemy of the Stars (rev. edn.) (London: Desmond Harmsworth, 1932).

Snooty Baronet (1932), ed. Bernard Lafourcade (Santa Barbara, Calif.: Black Sparrow Press, 1984).

The Old Gang and the New Gang (London: Desmond Harmsworth, 1933).

Men Without Art (1934), ed. Seamus Cooney (Santa Rosa, Calif.: Black Sparrow Press, 1987).

Left Wings over Europe: Or, How to Make a War about Nothing (London: Jonathan Cape, 1936).

Count your Dead: They are Alive! Or, a New War in the Making (London: Jonathan Cape, 1936).

The Revenge for Love (1937), ed. Reed Way Dasenbrock (Santa Rosa, Calif.: Black Sparrow Press, 1991).

Blasting and Bombardiering (London: Eyre & Spottiswoode, 1937).

The Mysterious Mr Bull (London: Robert Hale, 1938).

The Jews: Are they Human? (London: George Allen & Unwin, 1939).

Wyndham Lewis the Artist: From 'Blast' to Burlington House (London: Laidlaw & Laidlaw, 1939).

The Hitler Cult (London: Dent, 1939).

America, I Presume (New York: Howell, Soskin, 1940).

Anglosaxony: A League that Works (Toronto: Ryerson, 1941).

The Vulgar Streak (1941), ed. Paul Edwards (Santa Barbara, Calif.: Black Sparrow Press, 1985).

America and Cosmic Man (London: Nicholson & Watson, 1948).

Rude Assignment: An Intellectual Autobiography (1950), ed. Toby Foshay (Santa Barbara, Calif.: Black Sparrow Press, 1984).

Rotting Hill (1951), ed. Paul Edwards (Santa Barbara, Calif.: Black Sparrow Press, 1986).

The Writer and the Absolute (London: Methuen, 1952).

Self Condemned (1954), ed. Rowland Smith (Santa Barbara, Calif.: Black Sparrow Press, 1983).

The Demon of Progress in the Arts (London: Methuen, 1954).

The Human Age: Book 2, *Monstre Gai*; Book 3, *Malign Fiesta* (London: Methuen, 1955).

The Red Priest (London: Methuen, 1956).

The Human Age: Book 1, *Childermass* (London: Methuen, 1956).

Wyndham Lewis on Art: Collected Writings, 1913-1956 eds., Walter Michel and C. J. Fox (London: Thames & Hudson, 1969).

A Soldier of Humour and Selected Writings, ed. Raymond Rosenthal (New York and Toronto: New American Library, 1966).

Unlucky for Pringle: Unpublished and Other Stories, ed. C. J. Fox and Robert T. Chapman (London: Vision, 1973).

Collected Poems and Plays, ed. Alan Munton (Manchester: Carcanet, 1979).

Journey into Barbary: Morocco Writings and Drawings, ed. C. J. Fox (Santa Barbara, Calif.: Black Sparrow Press, 1983).

Creatures of Habit and Creatures of Change: Essays on Art, Literature and Society, 1914–1956 ed. Paul Edwards (Santa Rosa, Calif.: Black Sparrow Press, 1989).

Periodicals Edited by Lewis

Blast 1 (June 1914) (Santa Barbara, Calif.: Black Sparrow Press, 1981).
Blast 2 (July 1915) (Santa Barbara, Calif.: Black Sparrow Press, 1981).
The Enemy: A Review of Art and Literature 1 (Jan. 1927), ed. David
     Peters Corbett (Santa Rosa, Calif.: Black Sparrow Press, 1994).
The Enemy: A Review of Art and Literature 2 (Sept. 1927), ed. David
     Peters Corbett (Santa Rosa, Calif.: Black Sparrow Press, 1994).
The Enemy: A Review of Art and Literature 3 (Mar. 1929), ed. David
     Peters Corbett (Santa Rosa, Calif.: Black Sparrow Press, 1994).
Satire and Fiction: Enemy Pamphlets No. 1 (Sept. 1930).
The Tyro 1 (Apr. 1921).
The Tyro 2 (Mar. 1922).

Correspondence

Cassidy, Victor (ed.), 'The Sturge Moore Letters: Wyndham Lewis:
     Letters to Thomas Sturge Moore', *Lewisletter*, 7 (October 1977), 8–23.
—— 'Letters of Wyndham Lewis to Sidney and Violet Schiff', *Enemy
     News*, 21 (Summer 1985), 9–31.
Lewis, Wyndham, *The Letters of Wyndham Lewis*, ed. W. K. Rose
     (London: Methuen, 1963).
Londraville, Richard, and Londraville, Jane (eds.), 'Two Men at War
     with Time: The Unpublished Correspondence of Wyndham Lewis
     and John Quinn' [Part 1], *English*, 39/164 (Summer 1990), 97–145.
—— 'Two Men at War with Time: The Unpublished Correspondence
     of Wyndham Lewis and John Quinn: Concluded', *English*, 39/165
     (Winter 1990), 229–51.
Materer, Timothy, *Pound/Lewis: The Letters of Ezra Pound and Wyndham
     Lewis* (London: Faber & Faber, 1985).
Symons, Julian (ed.), *A. J. A. Symons to Wyndham Lewis: Twenty-Four
     Letters* (Edinburgh: Tragona Press, 1982).

BIBLIOGRAPHY

Gawsworth John, *Apes, Japes and Hitlerism: A Study and Bibliography of
     Wyndham Lewis* (London: Unicorn Press, 1932).
Morrow, Bradford, and Lafourcade, Bernard, *A Bibliography of the
     Writings of Wyndham Lewis* (Santa Barbara, Calif.: Black Sparrow
     Press, 1978).
Pound, Omar S., and Grover, Philip, *Wyndham Lewis: A Descriptive
     Bibliography* (Folkestone: Wm Dawson & Co., 1978).

BIOGRAPHY

Meyers, Jeffrey, *The Enemy: A Biography of Wyndham Lewis* (London: Routledge & Kegan Paul, 1980).
O'Keeffe, Paul, *Some Sort of Genius: A Life of Wyndham Lewis* (London: Jonathan Cape, 2000).

CRITICISM

There has been a good deal published on Lewis, especially in recent years. The following list of works restricts itself to monographs.
Agenda (Wyndham Lewis Special Issue) 7/3 and 8/1 (Autumn–Winter 1969–70).
Ayers, David, *Wyndham Lewis and Western Man* (Basingstoke: Macmillan, 1992).
Bridson, D. G., *The Filibuster: A Study of the Political Ideas of Wyndham Lewis* (London: Cassell, 1972).
Brown, Dennis, *Intertextual Dynamics within the Literary Group: Joyce, Lewis, Pound and Eliot* (London: Macmillan, 1990).
Campbell, SuEllen, *The Enemy Opposite: The Outlaw Criticism of Wyndham Lewis* (Athens, Ga.: Ohio University Press, 1988).
Cianci, Giovanni (ed.), *Wyndham Lewis: Letteratura/Pittura* (Palermo: Sellerio, 1982).
Constable, John, and Watson, S. J. M. (eds.), *Wyndham Lewis and I. A. Richards: A Friendship Documented, 1928–57* (Cambridge: Skate Press, 1989).
Corbett, David Peters, *The Modernity of English Art: 1914–30* (Manchester: Manchester University Press, 1997).
—— (ed.), *Wyndham Lewis and the Art of Modern War* (Cambridge: Cambridge University Press, 1998).
Cork, Richard, *Vorticism and Abstract Art in the First Machine Age*, i. *Origins and Development*; ii. *Synthesis and Decline* (London: Gordon Fraser, 1976).
Currie, Robert, *Genius: An Ideology in Literature* (London: Chatto & Windus, 1974).
Dasenbrock, Reed Way, *The Literary Vorticism of Ezra Pound and Wyndham Lewis: Towards the Condition of Painting* (Baltimore and London: Johns Hopkins University Press, 1985).
Edwards, Paul, *Wyndham Lewis: Art and War* (London: The Wyndham Lewis Memorial Trust in association with Lund Humphries, 1992).
—— *Volcanic Heaven: Essays on Wyndham Lewis's Painting and Writing* (Santa Rosa, Calif.: Black Sparrow Press, 1996).

—— *Wyndham Lewis: Painter and Writer* (New Haven and London: Yale University Press, 2000).

Foshay, Toby Avard, *Wyndham Lewis and the Avant Garde: The Politics of the Intellect* (Montreal: McGill-Queen's University Press, 1992).

Grigson, Geoffrey, *A Master of our Time: A Study of Wyndham Lewis* (London: Methuen, 1951).

Handley-Read, Charles, *The Art of Wyndham Lewis* (London: Faber & Faber, 1951).

Harrison, John, *The Reactionaries: W. B. Yeats, Wyndham Lewis, Ezra Pound, T. S. Eliot, D. H. Lawrence* (London: Victor Gollancz, 1967).

Head, Philip, *Vorticist Antecedents* (Ware: The Wyndham Lewis Society, 1997).

Jameson, Fredric, *Fables of Aggression: Wyndham Lewis, the Modernist as Fascist* (Berkeley and Los Angeles: University of California Press, 1979).

Kenner, Hugh, *Wyndham Lewis* (Norfolk, Conn.: New Directions, 1954).

Klein, Scott W., *The Fictions of James Joyce and Wyndham Lewis: Monsters of Nature and Design* (Cambridge: Cambridge University Press, 1994).

Kush, Thomas, *Wyndham Lewis's Pictorial Integer* (Ann Arbor: UMI Research Press, 1981).

Loewenstein, Andrea Freud, *Loathsome Jews and Engulfing Women: Metaphors of Projection in the Work of Wyndham Lewis, Charles Williams, and Graham Greene* (New York: New York University Press, 1993).

Mao, Douglas, *Solid Objects: Modernism and the Test of Production* (Princeton: Princeton University Press, 1998).

Mastin, Catherine, Stacey, Robert, and Dilworth, Thomas, 'The Talented Intruder': *Wyndham Lewis in Canada, 1939–1945* (Windsor, Ontario: Art Gallery of Windsor, 1992).

Materer, Timothy, *Wyndham Lewis the Novelist* (Detroit: Wayne State University Press, 1976).

—— *Vortex: Pound, Eliot, and Lewis* (Ithaca, NY, and London: Cornell University Press, 1979).

Meyers, Jeffrey (ed.) *Wyndham Lewis: A Revaluation* (London: Athlone Press, 1980).

Michel, Walter, *Wyndham Lewis: Paintings and Drawings* (London: Thames & Hudson, 1971).

Miller, Tyrus, *Late Modernism: Politics, Fiction, and the Arts between the World Wars* (Berkeley and Los Angeles: University of California Press, 1999).

Modernism/Modernity (Wyndham Lewis Number), 4/2 (Apr 1997).

171

Nath, Jogendra, *Wyndham Lewis: A Friend to the Enemies* (New Delhi: Vani Prakashan, 1993).

Nicholls, Peter, *Modernisms: A Literary Guide* (London: Macmillan, 1995).

Normand, Tom, *Wyndham Lewis the Artist: Holding the Mirror up to Politics* (Cambridge: Cambridge University Press, 1992).

Perrino, Mark, *The Poetics of Mockery: Wyndham Lewis's 'The Apes of God' and the Popularization of Modernism* (Leeds: W. S. Maney, 1995).

Porteus, Hugh Gordon, *Wyndham Lewis: A Discursive Exposition* (London: Desmond Harmsworth, 1932).

Pritchard, W. H., *Wyndham Lewis* (New York: Twayne, 1968).

Quema, Anne, *The Agon of Modernism: Wyndham Lewis's Allegories, Aesthetics, and Politics* (Lewisburg, PA: Bucknell University Press, 1999).

Rothenstein, John, *Wyndham Lewis and Vorticism* (London: Tate Gallery, 6 July–19 Aug. 1956).

Russell, John, *Style in Modern British Fiction: Studies in Joyce, Lawrence, Forster, Lewis, and Green* (Baltimore and London: Johns Hopkins University Press, 1978).

Schenker, Daniel, *Wyndham Lewis: Religion and Modernism* (Tuscaloosa, Ala.: University of Alabama Press, 1992).

Sherry, Vincent, *Ezra Pound, Wyndham Lewis, and Radical Modernism* (Oxford: Oxford University Press, 1993).

Tomlin, E. W. F., *Wyndham Lewis* (Norfolk, Conn.: New Directions, 1954).

Wagner, Geoffrey, *Wyndham Lewis: A Portrait of the Artist as the Enemy* (London: Routledge & Kegan Paul, 1957).

Wees, W. C., *Vorticism and the English Avant Garde* (Manchester: Manchester University Press, 1972).

Index